Horseback Riding
Trail Guide
to
North Carolina

Horseback Riding Trail Guide
to
North Carolina

Martha Branon Holden

Winston-Salem, North Carolina

Library of Congress Catalog Card Number 94-73148

ISBN 1-878177-09-5

Bandit Books, Inc.

P.O. Box 11721

Winston-Salem, NC 27116-1721

(336) 785-7417

"Hittin' the Trail Tonight" is reprinted courtesy of Bruce Kiskaddon

All photographs, except as noted, are courtesy of Martha Branon Holden

Cover photograph by Tyler Cox

Original cover design by Gray Erlacher

New edition design by Monica Cox

To Mom and Dad
for the encouragement to dream and reach my highest goals

To Scott, Travis, and Shannon
for making my dreams come true

TABLE OF CONTENTS

ACKNOWLEDGMENTS

This trail book is the culmination of a dream many years old. I have always loved horses, a fact my family can attest to! I have experienced every aspect of owning a horse, from riding on trails and in the show ring to breeding, raising and training my very own foals. Horses require vigilant daily care and I have actually enjoyed and survived this constant schedule of feeding, grooming, veterinary care and yes, even those beloved stall muckings!

For several years I collected articles, clippings and information related to horses, trails, trail rides, shows, etc. Anything I could find I filed away in my father's filing cabinet for future reference. This collection eventually led to me writing this book.

I attribute some of my passion for horses, trails, nature and American history to my ancestry; my grandfather was part Cherokee Indian. I have always had a deep appreciation for the Indians and their way of life. They took great care and pride in the natural resources of this land. The Indians were probably the first people to travel through the mountains and forests of North Carolina.

There were so many people that deserve recognition, including some whose names are unknown to me. The rangers and superintendents of the parks and forests were such a great help. Their enthusiastic support helped keep me inspired. A special "thank you" goes out to all the rangers and clerical staff.

Providing help in the National Forests main office was Linda McWilliams, trail supervisor. From the Nantahala National Forest were Joe Nicholson, Wayah Ranger District and Julie Dumas, Tusquitee Ranger District. Information on the French Broad Ranger District in the Pisgah National Forest was given by Kimberly A. Brandel and Darlene Huntsinger. Thanks to Donn Dyer in the Pisgah Ranger District of the Pisgah National Forest for supplying trail information and Suzan Elderkin for taking the time to review the material on their district. Suzan's help was invaluable.

Thanks to the Backcountry Reservations Office of the Park Communications Center in the Great Smoky Mountains National Park for maps and information on the Great Smokies. The park rangers deserve special thanks for answering so many questions.

Darrell McBane from the North Carolina Division of Parks and Recreation main office offered insight into the state parks. Others were Tommy Wagoner, Hanging Rock State Park superintendent, and Larry Milton and Andy Whitaker, Pilot Mountain State Park superintendents. Assistance with the county parks came from Ben Myers, Cane Creek Park; C. Blaine Gregory, Latta Plantation Park; and Lash Sanford, Tanglewood Park. Thanks to Fred Blackley with the Cleveland County Trails Association and Jane Howell of the Biltmore Saddle and Bridle Club for their help with providing maps and information on their areas.

Appreciation is also extended to Dr. Roger Holt, DVM, for his helpful suggestions and technical review of equine first aid.

Thanks to Beverly Duval and Tim and Thelma McKinney for their help with the Sauratown Trail.

To my riding buddy Debby Jennings, thank you for your companionship.

Thanks go to Barry McGee for his support and belief in this project. I admire his ability to turn a manuscript into a finished product.

A special thank you must go to all the trail riders, horsemen, and readers who have made wonderful comments and suggestions about trails and this guide. You helped make a revised edition possible.

Most of all, my family has provided the major support to make this guidebook a reality. Thanks to my parents, Harold and Frances Jeane, for raising me in an old-fashioned Christian home. Our farm in the foothills of the Blue Ridge Mountains nurtured my interests in animals and nature. My mom and dad taught me the value of life and the lesson of perseverance.

Thanks to my mom for reviewing the manuscript and adding helpful ideas to it. Mary and Phillip deserve my gratitude for all their love and patience throughout the years with their "horse-crazy" sister. My grandparents, Floyd and Carolyn Davis, have had a great influence on my life to follow the straight and narrow and always encouraged my writing. Deserving recognition for providing companionship and friendship during my horse endeavors is my cousin, Stacey Wood.

My trusty mounts, Shawna Leigh and Arie, have my extreme gratitude because they have safely carried me over many miles of trails in all types of terrain. On more than one occasion, Shawna has served as my guide when I became lost in unfamiliar territory.

To my son, Travis, and daughter, Shannon, thanks for being incentives to meet my goals. Books and babies both take a lot of time and patience but are definitely worth the effort. And especially to my husband, Scott, thanks for the encouragement and for tolerating all those maps and files, the many long distance calls that ran up the telephone bills, and my late night pecking on the computer. Without my family and the grace and guidance of God, this trail guide would be in a forgotten drawer somewhere.

INTRODUCTION

Welcome to the revised edition of *Horseback Riding Trail Guide to North Carolina*!

There have been many changes in the trails and their administration since the original version of this book first came out. This revised edition provides updated information. New area codes have been added in North Carolina and across the country. Phone numbers listed here are correct at press time, but be prepared for further changes in the future.

Opportunity awaits you outdoors on North Carolina's riding trails. Within a few hours drive, you can be riding down the trail and enjoying a variety of breathtaking scenery. From the mountains to the sea, adventure rewards those who answer its call. The North Carolina Horse Council Trail Division reports there are more than 65,000 horse owners statewide; trail riding is listed by 75% of these owners as one of their main activities. It is a popular pastime and hobby for horsemen regardless of breed interest, riding style, age or experience.

Trail riding is memorable no matter where you choose to ride when you hear autumn leaves rustle beneath your mount's hooves, see startled white-tailed deer leap across your path, hear the sound of wild turkeys gobble in the nearby forest, or watch the rippling of a river on its way to the sea. Those who have never enjoyed the outdoors on the back of a horse have truly missed one of life's treasures.

How can you describe the feeling of crossing a bald mountain peak, only to discover each view is more beautiful than the last? Or the pride felt when the young filly you bred and trained carries you safely through many miles of rugged terrain? What a thrill it is to ride in the same forest where George Vanderbilt hunted wild game and built his famed castle. What better history lesson is there than to ride the same path as the Indians and settlers did so many years ago? Endurance rider Ruth Waltenspiel once put trail riding in perspective when she stated, "The essence...to me, is you and your horse out there with the leaves and the wind, and the moon rising up through the trees, and the sound of the river and the smell of the trail."

Whether you prefer riding just for the day and returning home to the comforts of modern day life, or camping out in the wilderness beneath the stars, North Carolina's trails have something to suit everyone. It is my hope that this guide will benefit horseback riders since we all share similar interests-the love of horses, nature and the great outdoors. We also love the challenge and thrill of riding in new and exciting places. From climbing the hilly trail in Hanging Rock State Park that overlooks the distant Blue Ridge Mountains, to cantering along the sandy river bottoms on the Biltmore Estate, each trail has its share of unique qualities. May this book help you find these special trails.

PART I - BASIC TRAIL GUIDELINES

"Leave only your hoofprints in the mountains, and return with only your memories."

Back Country Horsemen of Missoula

CHAPTER 1

RULES AND REGULATIONS

Trail riders need to be prepared in order to fully enjoy the pleasures these trails provide. Being well-informed and doing a little pre-ride preparation can reduce the anxieties, stresses, and problems that can transform a good day's ride into a nightmare. Make phone calls, obtain current maps, write checklists and most of all, ask questions.

All national forests, state parks and public trails have general guidelines that should be followed by each rider. Read each individual facility's brochure for specific rules and regulations. It is everyone's responsibility to know and observe these rules.

The no-trace ethic is a major guideline that should always be followed. This ethic states that as we travel and camp in the primitive environment of the wilderness, we should leave "no-trace" of ever passing through it—let it remain untouched and unpolluted. We need to take care of public parks and facilities in the same manner. This will help ensure their continued access to not only horseback riders but to all park users. The following rules are most commonly encouraged or enforced:

ALCOHOL

No public display or use of alcoholic beverages. Do not throw empty beer cans along the trail or leave them lying around the camp. Respect the environment and exhibit responsible behavior.

CAMPING

It is best to select a campsite and confine horses at least 100 feet away from streams and creeks to help reduce trampling of the soft ground, and to prevent the water source from becoming contaminated. Protect the environment by using only biodegradable soap. Do not wash dishes, use soap or bathe in the creeks. Bury human waste a minimum of six inches deep and 100 feet away from streams.

Observe campground quiet hours when camping near others. In most parks this is from 10 p.m. to 6 a.m. One rowdy early-bird or night-owl can spoil everyone else's sleep! After a long day on the trail, a good night's sleep is a must.

Keep horses in designated areas. Some facilities do not allow horses in the sleeping and cooking areas of the campground. Remove horse manure and uneaten hay to a designated area or scatter it in an obscure area when leaving camp. This will speed up decomposition and reduce pesky flies. In some facilities, all feed has to be packed out and stalls are required to be mucked out.

Fill in all pawed holes. Clean up and pack out all garbage at your campsite. Be considerate of others who will use the same area after you. Don't leave a trace of where you have been!

A source of public campground information available in most bookstores and libraries is *Woodall's Campground Directory*. It contains addresses and telephone numbers of family campgrounds in all fifty states and includes information on services and activities. If you are planning a trip into a remote region and will be primitive camping, you can check this directory for the nearest modern campground where drinking water and hot showers are available. Most campgrounds permit use of the bathhouse for a nominal fee. After a day or two on the hot, dusty trail, most horsemen can really appreciate the value of a nice, warm shower.

COGGINS TEST

Several public parks and facilities require horses to have a negative Coggins test for Equine Infectious Anemia (EIA) within the past year. A copy of the negative test must be in your possession, and you must show proof either at the entrance gate or before unloading your horse. This test consists of a blood sample your veterinarian must withdraw and send off to a laboratory. Be sure to schedule this test several days before leaving on your trip to allow ample time to receive the results. An increasing number of public facilities are enforcing the requirement for a negative Coggins test before allowing you to trail ride or stable your horse on their premises. It is best to always keep a copy of the current test results in your truck or trailer, just in case.

FIREARMS

The possession and use of firearms is usually prohibited in most parks and private facilities. An exception is the national forests where firearms are allowed during hunting season.

FIRES

Some public parks and trails prohibit campfires. Do not start campfires without permission. Use only dead, downed wood and the existing fire ring; do not build another fire ring. Be sure fires are *completely* out before leaving the

campsite to prevent forest fires! Pour water on
the fire and stir the coals. Repeat this process to
ensure thorough mixing of the water and coals.
If you do not stir, the fire could continue to
smolder.

If you must smoke, be sure to stop in a safe
area. Don't smoke while riding along the trail
and please do not throw cigarette butts on the
ground! There are too many cases when one
carelessly tossed, smoldering cigarette started a
blazing inferno, one that scarred and destroyed
the land for many years.

Use existing fire rings
when available.

HORSE RESTRAINT

Do not tie horses directly to trees, even for a short period of time. They chew
on the bark and paw around the roots, both of which destroys the trees.
Cross-tying by running a picket line between trees is usually the best and safest
way to restrain horses in the backcountry if hitching racks or stalls are not
available. In some parks and national forests, riders who tie their horses directly
to trees are subject to heavy fines. See the chapter "Horse Restraint" for detailed
information.

PARKING

Park your vehicle and trailer only in a designated area. Do not block gates,
driveways, roads or other vehicles.

PETS

It is best to leave pets at home. Some facilities allow pets but they must be
kept on a leash no more than six feet long. Many riders like to take their dogs
with them on a trail ride or camping trip. Always check ahead with the facility
manager or park ranger to see if pets are allowed before bringing ol' Blue along
with you.

TRAILS

Be courteous to fellow riders, hikers and campers. They are also trying to
enjoy the trails and outdoors. Be aware that some trails may be shared with
mountain bikers and motorcyclists. Observe good etiquette while riding and give
up the right of way if possible. When hikers, backpackers or bikers are encountered on the trail, always guide your horse so it faces them with its hindquarters
turned away. A horse is less likely to be spooked if it can actually see the fellow

trail user.

Stay on the horse trails and off the hiking trails unless they are combined. Obey all posted trail signs. Some of the parks and national forests impose heavy fines if horses are not kept in designated areas. Try to follow the no-trace ethic while on the trail. Travel to avoid impact and keep in mind how damaging horses' hooves can be to the trails. Do not make new trails and don't shortcut switchback trails since they help reduce erosion. Travel in small groups whenever possible to decrease adverse impact. A party of eight riders or less is best.

Help keep our trails clean and free of litter and trash. One of the most annoying sights is garbage cluttering a beautiful natural area. The outdoors is not our trash can. Remember, if you "pack it in, pack it out."

Keep your horse under control at all times. Don't carouse and "cowboy" on the trails. Along with littering, this causes most of the problems parks and forests suffer. The careless actions of a few horsemen give the entire equestrian group a bad reputation. We all suffer when parks, facilities and trails are misused and abused-the end result: horseback riding banned.

Trail users all over America have felt the effect of the decreasing riding areas. Additional reasons for the decline of horseback trails include the lack of funding needed for trail maintenance, and conflict of interests with other trail users such as hikers, bikers and hunters. Some horsemen have formed groups and taken the extra step in working with the park rangers to help build and maintain bridle trails. Let's all work together to preserve our public lands so future generations of riders can enjoy these same trails.

Share the trails.

CHAPTER 2

SAFETY GUIDELINES

BEARS

Bears can occasionally be seen in the Great Smoky Mountains National Park and other mountainous areas of the state. They usually do not cause any problems unless humans attract them with food. Be wary and watchful, observing them only from a distance. Store your food properly while in camp to deter animals. This is a rule in the Great Smokies and violators are subject to a fine.

Keep all food in your pack. Do not store food in your tent or near your sleeping bag or you may awake one morning to find a hungry bear knocking on your tent door. It is best to hang your food pack by a rope at least 10 feet high between two trees that are approximately 10-20 feet apart. Be sure the pack is at least four feet away from the nearest tree limb so the bears cannot reach it even if they climb the tree. Any bear incidents should be reported to the park ranger.

The proper way to protect your pack from bears while in the backcountry.

FIRST AID

Carry a first aid kit and know basic first aid techniques for humans and horses. Enrolling in first aid and wilderness survival courses is a good idea for anyone spending time in the backcountry. Outfitting stores often have information regarding these courses. Be prepared as much as possible for the unexpected. In some of the more remote areas, telephones are nonexistent. A cellular phone kept in your truck for emergency use may save a life. Before embarking on your next adventure into the wilderness, it could be extremely worthwhile to know the location of the nearest medical and veterinary facilities in that particular area.

FOOD

Carry nutritious food and snacks with you. Dehydrated foods can be found in most grocery stores and outdoor specialty stores. Pack high energy snacks such as nuts and jerky in plastic bags to save space and decrease the weight in your saddlebags.

HUNTING

Wear blaze orange during hunting seasons and know when these seasons occur. Hunting is often permitted in the wilderness areas, backcountry and national forests. Be careful you don't become a hunting accident statistic! The state parks and the Great Smoky Mountains National Park are wildlife preserves and hunting is not allowed. Trail riding should be safe within the park boundaries; however *always* be wary. In addition to wearing an orange vest and/or cap, for extra protection you can place fluorescent-colored splint boots or wraps on your horse's legs, and use a brightly colored saddlepad. Check with the North Carolina Wildlife Resources Commission for current information on hunting seasons. The address is 512 N. Salisbury St., Raleigh, NC 27604-1188, or call (919) 733-7191.

INSECTS

The main insects in North Carolina that cause problems are bees, ticks, flies, and biting bugs such as mosquitoes. Wear an insect repellent on yourself and do not forget to apply fly spray on your horse before leaving for your ride. Nothing is more annoying than to fight a swarm of bugs during your entire ride. Carry insect bite or bee sting medication. Benadryl® is a good oral antihistamine for bee stings in people. Check your body and clothing regularly for ticks and remove them carefully. Rocky Mountain Spotted Fever and Lyme Disease are real medical threats carried by these parasites. See "Bites and Stings" in the chapter "First Aid for Humans."

LOST

The first rule of thumb when you are lost is to *stay calm!* Do not leave the trail and go cross-country. Try to orient yourself and keep alert for familiar landmarks such as mountain ridges, creeks, or other trails. If possible, find a high open area where you can get a good overall view of the area. This may be impossible in some of the dense forests. Look for a water source such as a creek or river where fishermen, boaters or canoers can be found. Following along a stream or creek downhill will often take you to a road leading out of the area.

Once you plan your route, stick with it. When you start second guessing yourself and backtracking, you become more confused and often travel only in circles. Universal distress signals are given in a series of three: three whistle blasts, three shouts for help, three bright flashes of light, or three smoky fires.

If darkness or bad weather is approaching, find an appropriate spot near the trail to camp for the night. Stay close to the trail in case a search party attempts to look for you. Try to stay warm, dry and out of the wind. Traveling at night is too risky, especially in unfamiliar territory. Wait until daylight to proceed.

Remember–prevention is the key! Always carry a trail map and compass and know how to use them. Travel only on marked trails and stay together as a group. Traveling with at least one companion is safer than traveling alone. Inform a family member, friend, or park ranger of your proposed routes and approximate arrival times. This could save your life!

PARKING

Always lock your vehicle and horse trailer tack compartment whenever parking and leaving camp. Be sure to store any valuables under lock and key and out of sight. Thefts are not uncommon in public parks.

RABIES

Avoid encounters with wild animals, especially one that acts strange or unusually friendly. Observe them only at a distance. An animal that appears completely normal can still carry Rabies. If you or your horse are bitten, seek medical or veterinary help quickly. In North Carolina, Rabies has been documented in some of the wild animal population. Do not think it cannot happen to you.

RIDING GEAR

Comfortable clothing and sturdy shoes with a heel should always be worn while riding. Cowboys wear boots for a good reason–to keep their foot from becoming accidentally caught in the stirrup. Think about it! A shoe without a heel could easily slide through the stirrup. Boots also provide support for the ankles. Tennis shoes are fine for some sports but not for riding. A new type of shoe on the market made especially for trail riding is a hightop tennis shoe with a heel. It incorporates the best aspects of a boot and tennis shoe into comfortable riding footwear that is currently worn by many competitive trail riders.

Long pants or jeans are usually worn while trail riding. Shorts fail to protect your legs, and excessive chafing often results. The sports of competitive and endurance trail riding have helped to improve the quality of riding gear and equipment, especially in the areas of comfort and durability. Check equine catalogs or your local tack shop for accessories specializing in trail riding.

Wear an ASTM/SEI Certified helmet while riding. These approved helmets afford protection should an accident occur. For the die-hard western rider, a riding helmet shaped and styled similar to a western hat is now available. Statistics have shown that 20% of all horse-related accidents involve a head injury and 66% of deaths from equestrian accidents are from head injuries. Be safe! Wear a helmet.

Wear proper clothing when horseback riding.
Courtesy of Scott Holden

SNAKES

Snakes will usually go about their own business if left alone. Problems often occur when a horse accidentally steps near a snake and startles it. If you or your horse are bitten, try to identify the snake if at all possible. You need to know if it is poisonous. See the section on "First Aid" for information on snakebites.

SUN

Wear sunscreen when out in the sun for prolonged periods of time to prevent sunburn. A hat, cap or riding helmet with a visor should be worn to shade your face. A long sleeve shirt will help to protect your arms from the sun.

TRAILERING

Keep your towing vehicle and trailer in good condition so you can reach your destination without becoming stranded somewhere alongside a deserted highway. Make regular checkups and routine maintenance inspections. Always carry at least one and preferably two spare tires that are properly inflated and in good condition. Knowing the location of auto repair and tire centers along your proposed route is also a good safety precaution.

In North Carolina, it is required by law that all trucks and horse trailers must be inspected annually by a qualified person. Make sure you are properly licensed for the amount of weight you are towing. Heavy fines have been levied against drivers not in compliance with the current laws regarding horse trailers. For more information call the DMV Enforcement District Office in Raleigh at (919) 733-2426 or (919) 733-7872; or write to: Enforcement Section, NC Division of Motor Vehicles, 1100 New Bern Ave., Raleigh, NC 27697.

WATER

Safe drinking water for people is not always readily available in some of the more primitive parks and wilderness areas. Drinking water should be carried in from home or from another acceptable source. Small, boxed juices are convenient and easy to carry with you.

Springs and streams are often contaminated with a protozoan called Giardia that can make people sick. Giardiasis causes symptoms of diarrhea, nausea, cramps and lack of appetite, but they may not show up for several days. Water from sources that might not be pure should be treated either by chemicals, filtering, or preferably, by boiling for at least five minutes before drinking. Think before you drink!

WEATHER

Always carry rain gear and a jacket. Dress in layers for warmth and be prepared for drastic weather changes, especially in the high elevations. Remember it is usually several degrees cooler in the mountains, even in the summertime. Sleet, snow and high winds often occur in winter, spring and fall. Fog, cold, and thunderstorms are also potential weather problems. Be wary and seek appropriate shelter. Flash floods are common in the mountains and low lying areas. Camp on high ground during rainy times.

Don't stand out in the open or near a lone tree during thunderstorms. Lightning is more apt to strike a lone tree. Find a ditch, valley, or as a last resort, a grove of trees. Sit or lie down if you are in open country. Dismount your horse to wait out the storm. Listen to updated weather forecasts prior to your trip and always be prepared for the worst.

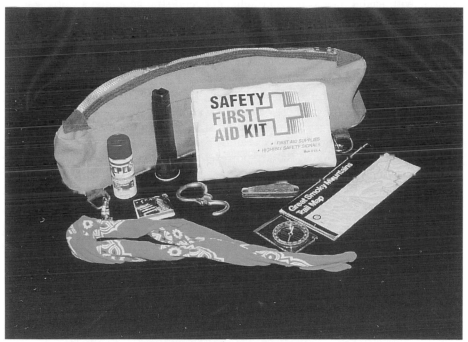

A few essential items for the trail.

CHAPTER 3

HORSE RESTRAINT

There are various methods for restraining horses when camping overnight, such as using stalls, hitching racks, temporary corrals, trailer tie, hobbles or a high picket line. A method that is better for one particular horse may not work for another. Knowing your own horse and its individual tendencies will help to ensure a successful overnight adventure. Three important keys to remember when restraining horses are: do not tie horses directly to trees, only secure compatible horses near each other, and always use a quick release knot.

Some facilities have stalls or hitching racks for horses, and pasture board may even be offered. When these options are not available a suitable alternative must be found. A temporary corral may be set up, but should only contain horses familiar with each other to prevent fights between strange animals. Box stalls, pasture board and temporary corrals have a distinct advantage over other types of restraint since the horse is able to relax and move around more freely. This also helps reduce any muscular stiffness and soreness the horse may have after a prolonged trailer haul or a long day on the trail.

The temporary corral can be made of several different materials including pipe, steel tubing, rope or electric fencing. Tubing panels are commercially available for this specific purpose. The corral should be located well away from any natural water sources to prevent possible contamination with manure. Horses accustomed to electric fences can be restrained overnight in a small area by a portable electric fence. Battery-powered fence chargers are available that eliminate the need for electricity. The fence should be well-marked for better visibility. See "Appendix III-Sources of Trail and Camping Supplies" for more information on manufacturers and distributors of specialized fencing equipment.

Some horsemen prefer to tie the horse to the trailer overnight near the campsite, an acceptable procedure in many areas. Be sure to inspect the outside of the trailer for sharp, jagged edges. Fenders or a license plate that extends beyond the trailer are prime suspects to cause an injury, especially if the horse tends to paw the ground. You may want to wrap its front legs for protection.

Horses that paw while restrained can also be hobbled to protect the ground. Hobbles may be successfully used as the only restraint method on some horses, however others can still move quite well with hobbles on. Pawing usually results from loneliness or boredom, so tying another horse nearby often helps.

Tying horses directly to trees, even temporarily, should be avoided. Horses are notorious for munching on the bark and can do a great deal of damage in a short amount of time. When tied to trees for longer periods of time, horses tend to trample and paw the roots. Help protect the environment and leave no trace by keeping tree damage to a minimum.

A high picket line between trees is probably the best and most accepted way to tie horses in the backcountry when other options are not available. This is also called cross-tying or tethering. A rope should be run between two trees and placed above the horse's head, approximately seven feet high. Always use tree-saver straps to protect the bark. Old automobile seat belts work great as a strap and can be easily acquired from a junkyard. Another method is to wrap an old girth or tire tube around each tree.

A "picket line kit" is now commercially available that includes two tree savers, four Knot Eliminators and rope for establishing a high line to restrain horses. Contact Rollin Beauchane, 29600 S. Dryland Road, Canby, Oregon 97013 or call 1-800-772-6282 or (503) 651-3690 for more information.

Securely attach a two-inch O-ring or swivel snap to the line, making sure the ring or snap cannot slide and is placed well away from each tree. If there is enough distance between the trees, two rings may be used so horses that tie together well can be on one picket line.

Tie the horse's lead rope to the O-ring or swivel snap, leaving enough length in the rope so it reaches approximately two feet above the ground. This will allow the horse to lie down. Do not leave so much slack that the horse can touch the ground with its nose or it may easily get its leg or head caught in the rope.

During feeding times, slightly lengthen the lead rope so the horse can reach its bucket. When the horse is finished, immediately shorten the rope to prevent mishaps. Hay bags may be tied directly to the picket line. Promptly remove them when empty so the horse will not accidentally trap its foot in the bag.

Above all else use common sense, experience and techniques that work for you and your horse when camping overnight. There is no substitute for good, old-fashioned "horse sense." Always follow the no-trace ethic when restraining horses by taking proper care of the trees and campsites. Enjoy a peaceful night under the stars knowing your mount is safely secured and ready to hit the trail come daylight.

A picket line

CHAPTER 4

IMPORTANT POINTS TO REMEMBER FOR YOUR HORSE AND ON THE TRAIL

Be sure to have a copy of your horse's current negative Coggins test in your possession when planning to ride and/or camp within areas that require proof. In North Carolina, most facilities insist on a negative Coggins within the past twelve months. This requirement may vary in other states.

Horses should be well-shod, healthy and sound. Check your horse's shoes regularly and schedule farrier visits well in advance of your trip. Rocky, mountainous terrain takes a toll on horseshoes. Farrier equipment should be carried along on your trip if you know how to reset a shoe. It is also a good idea to carry on the trail some type of temporary hoof protection, such as an Easyboot®, in case of a lost shoe.

Each horse should be currently vaccinated for influenza, rhinopneumonitis, eastern and western encephalomyelitis, and tetanus. This is not a requirement

Carrying an Easyboot® is a wise idea in case of a lost shoe.

14

but it protects your horse and helps to prevent diseases from spreading. In some areas, immunization for rabies or other viral diseases may be necessary. Consult your veterinarian for advice and recommendations.

Good health includes properly deworming your horse. This also contributes to more stamina on the trail. Most veterinarians recommend deworming every six weeks and rotating between different chemical types of dewormers.

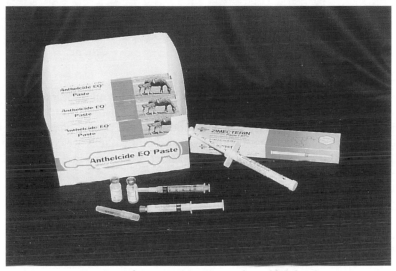

Don't neglect your horse's regular schedule of
deworming and vaccinations.

Train your horse at home to stand still while properly tied, picketed or hobbled. This will eliminate a major headache. The wilderness is not the place to teach your horse proper restraint. Murphy's Law applies to horses: "If something can go wrong, it will go wrong." If your horse fights being tied and breaks away at home, you don't have quite as many miles to walk as you would in the backcountry. Do your homework!

When camping overnight in early spring, fall and winter when frost is possible, blanket your horse. In the high elevations, heavy dews are common and snow may even be seen. A shed-out horse can stand the weather better if it is blanketed for warmth and protection.

Use of a breastcollar and crupper is recommended while riding in some of the more mountainous terrain. Be sure that tack, including the saddle, fits the horse properly. Keep all leather well-oiled and inspect your tack regularly for worn areas. Carry a few spare pieces of leather on the trail. They might come in handy!

Breastcollar   Crupper

Pack an equal amount of weight on either side of your saddlebags. Do not overload one side since this can create a strain on your horse. Reduce the amount of weight you have to carry by packing food in small plastic bags, rather than leaving it in much heavier cans. Cantle bags and fanny packs are convenient and versatile to use and have the capability to pack several items in a small area.

Take along plenty of your own hay and grain. Some stabling facilities do provide feed but check on this prior to your trip. Be sure to pack grain or pellets for your horse if camping overnight in the wilderness. All feeds, including hay, must be packed in and out of the backcountry. There are not always adequate areas to graze and it is not allowed in some facilities, including the Great Smoky

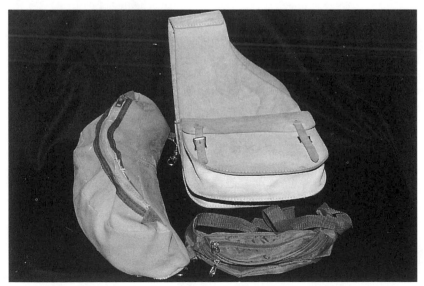

Clockwise, starting from left: cantle bag, saddlebag, fanny pack

Mountains National Park. Use of the pelleted feeds that contain a great deal of roughage is a good idea. It eliminates the need to pack in a lot of hay and reduces the amount of weight you have to carry. Ask your local feed dealer for more information on pelleted feeds containing forage.

A collapsible, vinyl water bucket can be found at most outfitter stores and is a handy item to carry with you. Some creek banks may be too steep for easy access by the horses. A bucket will allow you to reach the water supply and reduce the amount of trampling around the creek banks. Offer your horse water often along the trail. However, don't allow an overheated horse to eat or drink its fill. Offer small amounts of water periodically, and walk the horse to cool it out properly.

Know your horse's and your own limits while riding. Don't take unnecessary chances—especially out in the wilderness. It might be several hours before help could arrive should an accident occur.

Use good riding skills as you travel the trails. Equitation is not just for the show ring. You help your horse and reduce its muscular weariness by being balanced. In addition to being safer, riding properly also lessens your fatigue. Sit deep in the center of the saddle. Keep your head up, hands low and quiet, and heels down. Your legs should also be quiet. Shift your weight in motion with the horse. When climbing up hills, lean your body forward over the horse's withers where it can carry weight more easily. Going downhill, you should try to stay perpendicular in the saddle without leaning back too far. Do not be just a passenger and dead weight in the saddle. Work together in unison for the least stress on horse and rider.

Use common sense in building up yourself and your horse's strength and stamina gradually. After a winter layoff, begin conditioning slowly in the spring. Shorter trail rides should precede longer, more difficult rides. In hot weather, pay particular attention to your horse. Take frequent breaks and allow your horse adequate time to rest, especially if it begins to sweat profusely or its respiration becomes irregular and jerky. Remember traveling up and down hills is more difficult than on the flat. A horse in show ring shape is not necessarily in shape for trail riding in the mountains. Exhaustion and heat stroke can affect horses, sometimes fatally. See "Exhaustion" in the chapter "First Aid for Horses" for more information.

There are several common courtesies horsemen should follow while on the trail. Do not tailgate or crowd the horse in front of or around you. Be sure to let the rider in front of you know when you are attempting to pass. When crossing a creek or attempting a steep uphill or downhill grade, allow the horse and rider in front of you to safely complete passage before you attempt the obstacle.

Likewise, always be sure the riders behind you have safely maneuvered past all obstacles before moving on down the trail. Never leave a dismounted rider behind alone. At least one other rider should wait until he is mounted.

Whenever riding in a group, decide ahead of time which rider is to be in front of the group and who is to be in the rear. The leader should inform the riders behind him of his intentions, especially when increasing or decreasing the pace. The last rider should help ensure all riders safely proceed down the trail and through all obstacles. Other duties of the first and last riders include informing the group of any approaching objects like cars, bikes, hikers or other horsemen. Trail rides should be planned with the weakest member of the group kept in mind.

Accustom your horse at home to as many different trail obstacles as possible. It is not uncommon to encounter dogs, llamas and other pack animals, ATVs, mountain bikers, motorbikers, hikers and backpackers along trails, especially in some of the more popular parks and national forests.

An excellent source of information on trail riding and camping with horses in the backcountry is the *Back Country Horsemen Guidebook.* Copies can be obtained by writing: Back Country Horsemen of America, P.O. Box 597, Columbia Falls, Montana 59912. Single copies for individuals are free upon request while multiple copies for horse groups are fifty cents each. This is a true bargain for a handy, much needed booklet with chapters on trail horse selection, handling, restraint, trail equipment, trip preparation, etc. Diagrams depict proper techniques of restraint and knot tying. This organization encourages horsemen in the United States to unite and preserve trails on public property. Several western states have already formed a BCH club. Contact the above address for more information on the BCH.

CHAPTER 5

TRAIL AND CAMPING CHECKLIST

CAMPING:
- tent
- tarp (ground cover)
- sleeping bag
- pillow
- blankets
- foam pad, air mattress or folding cot
- hammer (for driving tent stakes)
- lantern and fuel
- folding chairs
- small table
- flashlight and batteries
- alarm clock
- small shovel, rake, hatchet
- firewood/kindling
- matches
- plastic trash bags
- portable solar shower bag
- towels and wash cloths
- personal items (shampoo, soap, toothbrush, toothpaste, hair brush, hair dryer, any medications, etc.)
- extra coat or jacket, clothes, boots, shoes
- first aid kit for humans
- road map

COOKING:
- portable stove and fuel
- skillet/frying pan
- saucepans
- coffeepot
- cooking utensils (spatula, slotted spoon, paring knife)

- measuring cup
- eating utensils (plastic forks and spoons)
- plates
- drinking cups
- plastic bowls with lids
- hot pads
- can opener
- aluminum foil
- paper towels
- dishwashing soap
- dish cloths, towels, scouring pad
- coolers
- ice
- drinking water (5 gallon water can)
- salt and pepper
- coffee and drinks
- food and fixings

FOR YOUR HORSE:
- halter and lead rope
- blanket
- leg wraps
- feed and water buckets
- extra rope and snaps
- trailer ties or rope to tie up feed and water buckets
- picket line or hobbles
- hay net
- water
- hay
- grain or pellets
- small salt/mineral block
- saddle
- saddle pad
- bridle and bit
- breastcollar
- crupper (if needed)
- saddlebags and/or cantle bag
- grooming equipment (currycomb, brushes, hoofpick, sweat scraper)

- hoof ointment
- fly spray
- farrier equipment (extra shoes and nails, Easyboot®)
- manure scoop and tub
- equine first aid kit
- copy of current negative Coggins test
- copies of any other required health certificates or papers

ON THE TRAIL:
- halter and lead rope
- picket line and/or hobbles
- fanny pack, saddlebags and/or cantle bag
- rain gear
- riding helmet
- drinking water and any other drinks
- snacks
- sunglasses
- insect repellent
- flashlight
- waterproof matches
- trail map and compass
- small first aid kit
- tissues/handkerchief/bandanna
- whistle (distress signal; 3 blasts signals for help)
- hoofpick
- Easyboot®
- pocketknife
- plastic trash bag
- collapsible, vinyl water bucket
- feed (if backcountry camping overnight)
- camera and film

Courtesy of Tyler Cox

PART II - TRAIL LISTINGS

"You can ride to the skies like Pegasus. It's a wonderful feeling to be on a horse."
Sigrid Heep
California riding instructor

DIRECTIONS FOR USING THIS TRAIL GUIDE

This revised guidebook has been written to assist you in discovering new places to ride and help you plan your trip. It contains the most accurate information currently available. Try to obtain regional or park maps before leaving on your trip. You may call the park or facility and request a map be mailed to you. State park maps are free while maps of the national forests are usually available for a fee of around $4.00. National forest maps can be obtained either by contacting the ranger district you are interested in or through the Cradle of Forestry in America Interpretive Association (CFAIA) at 100 S. Broad St, Brevard, NC 28712; telephone (828) 884-4734. You can call the Cradle of Forestry for an order form or order by telephone. Also, outfitters and other sporting goods stores that carry camping and hiking supplies often sell maps of the national forests and parks.

This trail guide does not attempt to list each individual horse trail located within North Carolina. Instead its purpose is to provide general information on a particular area. A few parks and facilities currently allowing horseback riding may not be found in this trail book for reasons which include extreme overuse of the area, the equine facilities and bridle trails may not be fully operational as of yet, or horses may possibly be banned from these trails in the future. Honoring their requests, these trails are not listed.

The North Carolina trails in this book are divided into six major sections: National Forests, National Parks, National Seashores, State Parks and Forests, Game Lands, and Regional Trails. Regional Trails includes county parks, private clubs, resorts, and camps. Each facility or trail is listed in alphabetical order within its section to make it easier to find your area of interest. The national forests are divided according to their ranger districts, and further divided into alphabetical listings in each respective district. The various areas within the Great Smoky Mountains National Park are also grouped together alphabetically.

All trails in this book are located in North Carolina with the exception of some in the Great Smoky Mountains National Park, and the listings in the chapter "Local Trails Outside North Carolina." The Great Smoky Mountains National Park lies within both North Carolina and Tennessee. Some of the bridle trails in our state connect to trails and backcountry campsites just across the Tennessee state line. Only the trails on the North Carolina side of the park are listed in this book unless they are in close proximity to a backcountry campsite in Tennessee.

The chapter "Local Trails Outside North Carolina" includes listings of popular trails and facilities within a few hours' drive of the state. Mount Rogers National Recreation Area in Virginia has a detailed listing in this chapter due to its great popularity and close proximity to North Carolina. Every year, large numbers of horseback riders from surrounding states routinely use the horse camps in the Virginia highland country.

Each listing has an address and phone number to contact before you make your trip in case there are any changes in the information given in this book. The addresses and phone numbers of the ranger stations in the national forests and parks are included in the first area listed for that district. During peak season and weekends, it is wise to call ahead and possibly make reservations in some of the more popular parks and facilities. This is especially true in the Great Smoky Mountains National Park where some of the backcountry campsites and shelters are rationed. With all the recent additions of area codes, don't be surprised at new ones being added regularly in the future. If your call isn't going through, check the area code first.

Location and accesses are given for each facility or trail, usually beginning from the nearest city or major highway. Parking areas for horse trailers are also included when possible. In some cases, the bridle trails are not accessed from the main park entrance, but from some other area of the park. Please pay particular attention to this because some parks do not permit horses at their main entrance. Daily hours and season are given but should be checked prior to traveling long distances as these tend to change frequently.

The Facility Review section contains information regarding camping, stabling, fees, etc. The facility is listed "day use only" if the use of horses in this area is limited to daytime hours and overnight camping with your horse is not allowed. Horse Camping Facilities refers to overnight horse camping (not regular family camping) and is usually listed as either primitive, modern or backcountry. Primitive camping includes tent or horse trailer camping with no water or electrical hookups. Modern camping usually includes water and/or electrical hookups. Backcountry camping means you pack into an area away from your truck and trailer and all modern conveniences. Fees for the use of the area are noted if applicable, however, be aware prices are subject to change without warning. The availability of hot showers and the type of restroom facilities are also indicated.

Several parks and locations offer stable facilities. The type of stabling available is usually box stalls, tie stalls, hitching racks and/or pasture board. Some facilities do allow horses to be tied securely to the horse trailer overnight near your campsite. This is listed in the guide as "trailer tie." Picketing between trees is also permitted in some areas when camping.

The Trail Review section lists pertinent information for each particular park and/or trail. The name of the trail is given if known, however, not all trails are specifically named. In some of the state parks, they are simply called "Bridle Trail." If several trails are listed for one area, a brief description of length, difficulty and any connecting trails follows each one. In the Great Smoky Mountains National Park section, backcountry campsites and shelters are listed under the appropriate trail. Check a current park map for more information.

Type of trail refers to whether it is a marked, mapped or unmarked trail. Remember wilderness areas and the backcountry are not always well-marked with trail signs. If rental horses and guided trail rides are available within the area, it is also indicated here. Terrain is usually listed as flat, sandy, rolling hills, hilly, mountainous/rocky, or rugged. Difficulty is listed as easy, moderate or difficult depending on the level of skill and amount of exertion needed to travel the trail. Length of trails is given in approximate mileage and is usually based on park maps. Notice some trail lengths are based on the distance one-way. Allow adequate time if planning to return to the starting point.

The availability of water is listed for each area. Unless indicated otherwise, an affirmative answer means water is present for livestock. Most trails have adequate access to water for your horse via streams and creeks. However a few do not and they are marked accordingly. In some of the national forests, wilderness areas and parks, drinking water for people is not always readily available. Water must be treated first before drinking or you may need to pack in your own supply. If in doubt, bring it from home!

The availability and name of a trail map is also indicated. Most of the trails listed in this guidebook are mapped on either a handheld map or a display board near the trailhead. A few areas may not have maps currently available. However, the trails are usually fairly easy to follow if you use some common sense and a compass. Call the contact that is listed in this guide for additional information.

Trail Notes is a brief descriptive section containing information about width and composition of trails in addition to any other important notes. If applicable, it includes whether it is a loop or backtracking trail. Some facilities have their own set of guidelines for use of the trails and stables. These are listed in Rules/Requirements. Please read and follow them! Highlights points out distinctive characteristics and impressive scenic areas. General and/or Historical Notes describes brief and interesting bits of information on the trail or area.

Other Activities includes special events or opportunities these facilities offer in addition to trail riding. Family members and friends who do not horseback ride can enjoy these other activities and be included in the camping trip. Nearest City/Facilities lists the city or cities closest to the park or trail. Any special facilities such as local campgrounds, stables or stores are also included.

This guidebook offers current trail information in an easy-to-use format. However, be aware trail information tends to change frequently. It is wise to call ahead and confirm any questions you may have. Happy trail hunting and have fun ridin'!

ABBREVIATIONS

Abbreviations may be used in some trail descriptions to reduce repetition. The following common abbreviations can be found in this book:

AT	Appalachian Trail
BCC	backcountry campsite
BRP	Blue Ridge Parkway
CCC	Civilian Conservation Corps
elev	elevation
FR	forest road
ft	feet
GSMNP	Great Smoky Mountains National Park
Mt	mount
NC	state primary road
NPS	National Park Service
Rd	roads
SR	state secondary road
TN	Tennessee
US	federal highway
USFS	United States Forest Service

Pisgah
National Forest

Blue Ridge
Parkway

Winston-Salem

Durham

Rocky
Mount

Asheville

Statesville

Greensboro

Raleigh

Charlotte

Uwharrie
National Forest

New
Bern

Pisgah
National Forest

Nantahala
National Forest

Fayetteville

Croatan
National Forest

Wilmington

CHAPTER 6

NATIONAL FORESTS

"Your code to protect the forest: Where I go, I leave without a trace."

The National Forest Service, an agency of the United States Department of Agriculture, manages the national forests within North Carolina. These recreational areas provide numerous opportunities for enjoyment of our natural resources on federally maintained land. All guidelines and rules in "Basic Trail Guidelines" of this book pertain to these national lands. The Forest Service also has a free brochure available entitled "Horse Trails - National Forests in North Carolina" that includes trail and camping tips in addition to general information about horse trails within the forests. Contact your local district ranger's office for a copy.

The Supervisor's Office of the national forests in North Carolina is located at 160A Zillicoa St., P.O. Box 2750, Asheville, N.C. 28802-2750; telephone: (828) 257-4200. For more information on a specific area, it is best to contact the district ranger of that particular national forest. Forest Watch is a Forest Service program created to help protect our natural resources. Call 1-800-222-1155 to report wildfires, vandalism and crime within the national forests. Game law violations should be reported by calling 1-800-662-7137. Please do your part in protecting these national lands.

There are four national forests located in North Carolina covering 1.2 million acres of land. They are named Croatan, Nantahala, Pisgah and Uwharrie. Horseback riding is allowed in designated areas of each forest. Overnight horse camping areas are available within each forest with the exception of Croatan National Forest. Most of these camping areas are primitive, have little or no facilities, and charge no fee. However a few of the ranger districts have begun charging fees to camp on national forest land, or will charge a fee in the future. The national forests are also designated as state game lands, therefore, be aware hunting is also permitted. Please check with the ranger district of that particular area if unsure of the hunting seasons or camping fees.

The National Forest Service trail policy states all trails are hiking trails unless marked for horse use. At most trailheads and intersections within the national forests, signs will bear the horseback riding symbol if horses are allowed on the trail. An unsigned trail is for hikers only. Open and closed roads within the forests can also be used for horseback riding unless signs are posted indicating otherwise.

Croatan National Forest is located on the coastal plains of North Carolina between the cities of New Bern and Morehead City. Currently, horseback riding is allowed on the forest service roads and four-wheel driveways. There are no facilities for overnight horse camping.

Nantahala National Forest is located in the southwest mountains. Near the area of Cherokee and south of the Great Smoky Mountains National Park, it is the most western of the national forests. Four ranger districts can be found here: Cheoah, Highlands, Tusquitee and Wayah. Currently, Highlands is the only district that has no horseback trails. Horses are permitted on designated trails and horse camping is allowed in the other three ranger districts. This area was once home to the Cherokee Indian nation. They named it Nantahala, or "land of the noon day sun," because of the several deep gorges in the region that only have sunlight at midday.

In western North Carolina near Asheville is the Pisgah National Forest. It also consists of four ranger districts: French Broad, Grandfather, Pisgah and Toecane. Trail riding and overnight horse camping are allowed in certain areas of this mountainous region.

One of the most prominent peaks in the Pisgah National Forest is called Mt. Pisgah. A minister named James Hall is credited with naming it. He took the name from the Bible story where Moses saw the promised land from Mount Pisgah after wandering in the wilderness for forty years. Hall traveled through this area in the 1700s and was impressed with the beautiful mountains and river basin. Indeed, the Pisgah National Forest is an incredibly scenic area of vast forests, mile-high mountain peaks, and numerous mountain streams and waterfalls.

The Pisgah Ranger District is a prime example of the Pisgah National Forest. In addition to its scenic areas, the district boasts over 400 miles of well-marked and maintained trails in North Carolina, more than any other national forest in the state. Many of these trails are designated for horseback riding. Overnight camping with your horses is also permitted. The Pisgah District is truly a paradise where many types of recreation can be enjoyed.

Uwharrie National Forest is located east of Albemarle, N.C. in the Piedmont, or "foothills" region of the state. The Uwharrie Mountains are estimated to be one of the most ancient ranges in North America. More than 46,000 acres of government land offer numerous opportunities for horseback riding. A primitive horse camp is located within the wildlife management area of the national forest.

North Carolina is unique because of its varied terrain—crystalline seashores along the coast, beautiful rolling hills and valleys of the Piedmont, and spectacular views from the mountaintops in the western part of the state. These national forests reflect and represent this variety, offering several hundred miles of trails through remote wilderness areas and more developed regions of our state. They are a true legacy for everyone to enjoy and preserve.

CROATAN NATIONAL FOREST

Counties: Craven, Jones and Carteret

ADDRESS: District Ranger, CNF
141 E. Fisher Ave. New Bern, NC 28560
TELEPHONE: (252) 638-5628

LOCATION: From New Bern, go east on US-70. Go 6 miles (the ranger station is on the left after approximately 4 miles) to Catfish Lake Rd (FR-1100) and turn right. Horse trailer parking is allowed along the side of this road.

SEASON: open daily year round

FACILITY REVIEW
TYPE: day use only
HORSE CAMPING FACILITIES: none
RESTROOMS: flush toilets in recreation areas
DAY RIDERS FEE: none

TRAIL REVIEW
TYPE: mapped
TERRAIN: flat
DIFFICULTY: easy
LENGTH: 100+ miles
WATER: yes
TRAIL MAP: Croatan National Forest
TRAIL NOTES: Horseback riding is permitted on the forest roads and four-wheel driveways. Be aware that motorcycles, all-terrain vehicles and four-wheel drive vehicles may be encountered on these roads. No specific trails or campgrounds are designed for horses at this time. Insect repellent is recommended in the warm months due to the prevalence of mosquitoes and insects.

RULES/REQUIREMENTS: Horseback riders must stay on the roads and four-wheel driveways. Horses are not allowed in any other areas.

HIGHLIGHTS: coastal environment, nice forests, wildlife

GENERAL/HISTORICAL NOTES: Croatan is an Indian word meaning "council town." The forest contains many acres of pocosin, or wet, raised boggy areas. Pocosin means "swamp on a hill." Near the Atlantic Ocean, Croatan National Forest is the most coastal national forest in the United States.

OTHER ACTIVITIES: hunting, fishing, boating, swimming, family camping, hiking

NEAREST CITY/FACILITIES: New Bern
    Recreation areas within the Croatan National Forest providing drinking water and sanitary facilities are Cedar Point, Fishers Landing, Neuse River and Pine Cliff.

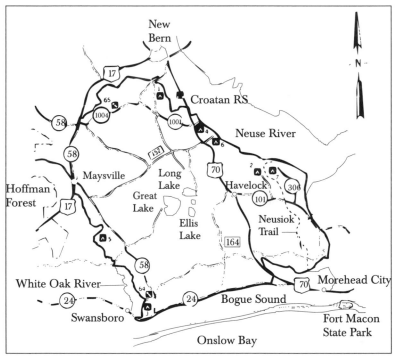

Croatan National Forest
Reprinted courtesy of The National Forest Service

NANTAHALA NATIONAL FOREST

Cheoah Ranger District
Address: Cheoah District Ranger, USFS
Rt. 1, Box 16-A Robbinsville, NC 28771
Telephone: (828) 479-6431

TSALI RECREATION AREA AND CAMPGROUND

Counties: Graham and Swain

LOCATION: Go south on US-19 from Bryson City for 9 miles. Go west on NC-28 for 5.5 miles. Turn right on FR-521 and go 1.5 miles to the Tsali Campground. Horse trailers can be parked in the upper parking lot.

SEASON: open daily year round

FACILITY REVIEW
TYPE: day use and/or overnight horse camping
HORSE CAMPING FACILITIES: 41 primitive campsites (no hookups)
CAMPING FEE: $15.00/night (no reservations are required)
HOT SHOWERS: yes
RESTROOMS: flush toilets
STABLE FACILITIES: hitching racks and water (located about 500 feet from Tsali Campground along a spur trail)
STABLING FEE: none
DAY RIDERS FEE: none

TRAIL REVIEW
TRAIL NAMES and DESCRIPTIONS:
1. Tsali Trail - Left Loop: 11.9 miles
2. Tsali Trail - Right Loop: 11 miles
3. Mouse Branch Loop: 6.5 miles
4. Thompson Loop: 7.7 miles

TYPE: marked (blazed blue)
TERRAIN: hilly-mountainous
DIFFICULTY: moderate-difficult
LENGTH: 38 miles

WATER: yes

TRAIL MAP: Tsali Recreation Area: mecca for mountain bikers, horseback riders

TRAIL NOTES: These trails, also a mountain bike route, follow the peninsulas of Fontana Lake with a system of four loops. To help alleviate problems with the bikes spooking the horses, different trails are used on alternating days by bikers and horsemen. The horse and bike schedule is posted on a signboard along FR-521 near the campground and at all trailheads. Center Road, also called County Line Road, runs from north to south and intersects the Tsali Trail, dividing the right and left loops.

Left Loop: several creek crossings, hilly with rocks and roots. There is a good view from a cliff above Lake Fontana at 8.2 miles.

Right Loop: less creek crossings, fewer hills and a smoother path than Left Loop (can be ridden quicker), shorter 4 and 8-mile loops are possible.

Mouse Branch Loop: consists of singletrack and old logging roads, old homesites, forest wildlife openings.

Thompson Loop: consists of singletrack and old logging roads, creek crossings, old homesites, overlooks.

RULES/REQUIREMENTS: Horses are not allowed in the campground area. No motorized vehicles are allowed on the trails.

HIGHLIGHTS: Fontana Lake, views of Great Smoky Mountains, wildlife

GENERAL/HISTORICAL NOTES: Tsali Trail is named for a Cherokee Indian chief who fled with his family and hid in the Great Smoky Mountains when the U.S. government forced the Indians to move to Oklahoma during the "Trail of Tears" in 1838. Tsali eventually surrendered when the government promised to establish a reservation for his tribe. He was executed upon surrender to serve as an example for the Indians. The Cherokee Indian Reservation, called "Qualla Boundary," was established anyway through the efforts of William Thomas, a white man raised by the Cherokees. The reservation is located northeast of the Tsali Recreation Area.

Tsali was rated one of the top ten singletrack mountain biking trails in the U.S. by *Bicycling* magazine due to its beautiful scenery and excellent trails.

OTHER ACTIVITIES: mountain biking, fishing and swimming in Fontana Lake, boating, water skiing, camping, hiking, picnicking

NEAREST CITY/FACILITIES: Bryson City

Contact Appalachian Packing and Riding at (828) 479-3820 for guided trips on horseback.

Double Eagle Farm in Bryson City offers overnight boarding and several other services (see section on "North Carolina Private Stables and Outfitters.") Contact Greg or Karen Crisp at (828) 488-9787 for information and reservations.

Tusquitee Ranger District
Address: Tusquitee District Ranger, USFS
201 Woodland Drive Murphy, NC 28906
Telephone: (828) 837-5152

FIRES CREEK AREA

County: Clay

LOCATION: From Hayesville, go west on US-64 for 5 miles to Lower Sweetwater Rd (SR-1302) near Bethesda Church. Turn right, cross the Hiwassee River and go 3.7 miles. Turn left onto Fires Creek Rd (SR-1344). Go 1.7 miles to forest boundary (road becomes FR-340) and pass the Fires Creek Picnic Area on the left. Go 4 miles on FR-340 to the horse camping area on the right (same as Bristol Fields Hunter Camp). Horse trailer parking is also available at roadside pulloffs along FR-340.

SEASON: open daily year round

FACILITY REVIEW
TYPE: day use and/or overnight horse camping
HORSE CAMPING FACILITIES: primitive
CAMPING FEE: none
HOT SHOWERS: none
RESTROOMS: pit toilet
STABLE FACILITIES: hitching racks
DAY RIDERS FEE: none

TRAIL REVIEW
TRAIL NAMES and DESCRIPTIONS:
1. Rim Trail: 25 miles (13.7 miles open to horses)/moderate-difficult (USFS #70)
2. Huskins Branch: 1.5 miles/moderate
3. Little Fires Creek: 1.3 miles/moderate-difficult
4. Rockhouse Creek: 2.3 miles/moderate-difficult

5. Phillips Ridge: 4.4 miles/moderate
6. Far Bald Springs: 1.9 miles/moderate-difficult

TYPE: marked
TERRAIN: mountainous
DIFFICULTY: moderate-difficult
LENGTH: 70+ miles
WATER: yes
TRAIL MAP: Forest Service quads–Andrews, Topton, Peachtree, and Hayesville
TRAIL NOTES: Trails consist of old roadbeds and logging roads. Riding is permitted on some of the forest service roads that can combine with trails to form various loops. Fires Creek flows through the basin of this area.

The Rim Trail is a popular one of this area. It follows the ridges of several high elevation bald mountains, including Tusquitee Bald, for incredible views. This trail has few water sources. However, other trails branch off it and lead down to the basin where an adequate water supply can be found for livestock.

RULES/REQUIREMENTS: Stay on designated horse trails and roads.

HIGHLIGHTS: scenic views from mountain balds, nice combination of trails and roads that form loops, wildlife (bears)

GENERAL/HISTORICAL NOTES: Fires Creek is a wildlife management area within the Tusquitee Ranger District consisting of 16,000 acres. Tusquitee Bald Mountain is the highest point in the area at 5,249 feet. The word "Tusquitee" means "where the water dogs laughed" and comes from an old Cherokee Indian legend. The Nantahala National Forest was once home to several tribes of the Cherokee nation and this area was often used by the Indians for hunting and as a travel route between tribes.

A nearby site to the Bristol Fields Hunter Camp is being developed by the Forest Service for use as a horse campground. It will include graveled campsites, tables, and fire rings.

OTHER ACTIVITIES: hunting, fishing, backpacking, hiking, camping, picnicking

NEAREST CITIES/FACILITIES: Murphy, Hayesville
Fires Creek Picnic Area (no horses allowed) is located near the horse camp on FR-340. Three recreation and modern camping areas (no horse camping) are located in this ranger district. Call the ranger station for more information.

1. Jack Rabbit Campground on Lake Chatuge offers showers, flush toilets and drinking water

2. Hanging Dog Campground on Lake Hiwassee offers drinking water and sanitary facilities

3. Cherokee Lake Picnic Area off NC-294 in Cherokee County

Eagle Fork Stables offers guided mountain trail rides within the Tusquitee Ranger District. It is owned by Newell Hogsed and located at Rt. 3, Box 295, Hayesville, NC 28904; telephone (828) 389-9663 (days) or (828) 389-6655 (nights and holidays). Call for more information.

Wayah Ranger District
Address: Wayah District Ranger, USFS
90 Sloan Rd. Franklin, NC 28734
Telephone: (828) 524-6441

STANDING INDIAN BASIN AREA
(Southern Nantahala Wilderness)
CAMP: Hurricane Creek Horse Camp

County: Macon

LOCATION: Go 10 miles west of Franklin on US-64. Turn left on Wallace Gap Rd (Old 64) and go 2 miles. Turn right on FR-67 and go 4 miles (Standing Indian Campground and Back Country Information Center is 2 miles along this road). The horse camp is on the left next to the gravel road, just beyond a low water concrete bridge.

SEASON: open daily year round

FACILITY REVIEW
TYPE: day use and/or overnight horse camping
HORSE CAMPING FACILITIES: primitive (open field camping; capacity of 20 units)
CAMPING FEE: none
HOT SHOWERS: none
RESTROOMS: pit toilets
STABLE FACILITIES: 25 stalls
STABLING FEE: none
DAY RIDERS FEE: none

TRAIL REVIEW
TRAIL NAMES and DESCRIPTIONS:
1. Big Indian Loop Trail: 8 miles/moderate-difficult (USFS #34)
2. Blackwell Gap Trail: 4.2 miles/moderate (USFS #366)
3. Hurricane Creek Loop Trail: 4 miles/moderate (USFS #36)
4. Thomas Branch Loop: 3.5 miles/moderate (USFS #375)
TYPE: marked (blazed orange)
TERRAIN: hilly-mountainous
DIFFICULTY: moderate-difficult
LENGTH: 20+ miles combined
WATER: yes; water trough
TRAIL MAP: Southern Nantahala Wilderness and Standing Indian Basin
TRAIL NOTES: Trails consist of old roads and logging roads that follow and cross several mountain creeks. Trailheads are near the horse camp.

Big Indian Loop Trail (#1) begins on Standing Indian Rd (FR-67). It crosses the Nantahala River at a shallow section and follows Big Indian Creek, Indian Ridge and the eastern side of Blue Ridge. The trail returns to FR-67 that can be utilized to complete a loop.

The same trailhead accesses Blackwell Gap Trail (#2) and Hurricane Creek Loop Trail (#3). It is on FR-67, 1.5 miles past the Back Country Information Center and just north of the horse camp. Go approximately one-half mile from the trailhead on an old woods road. Blackwell Gap Trail (#2) is to the left and follows a woods road beyond Blackwell Gap. The trail changes to old gravel and grassy logging roads that follow Long Branch. It ends on FR-67 but this road can be ridden south to form a loop back to camp.

Hurricane Creek Loop Trail (#3) is a loop with an extension. It begins from the same trailhead as the Blackwell Gap Trail. Travel east beyond the junction with the Blackwell Gap Trail. Hurricane Creek Loop Trail runs along Hurricane Creek following grassy roads and closed roads to form a loop.

Thomas Branch Loop Trail (#4) is a wooded trail along a grassy road.

RULES/REQUIREMENTS: All horses must be stabled in hitching racks overnight. Horse stalls must be cleaned out after use. If no hitching racks are available, horses must be cross-tied between trees where they cannot damage them and at least 100 feet away from creeks. Do not drive nails into or damage trees. No horses are allowed within 100 feet of the cooking and sleeping areas of campsite. Horses must be kept under physical control at all times. Riding is only permitted on designated bridle trails. Horses are not permitted on hiking trails or in Standing Indian Campground.

Campground quiet hours are from 10:00 p.m.-6:00 a.m. Maximum stay is 14 days from Memorial Day to Labor Day and 30 days other times of the year. Dead, downed wood may be used for firewood. Do not cut standing trees. A permit is required for cutting firewood.

HIGHLIGHTS: views of Big Indian Creek, Nantahala River, wilderness, wild-life

GENERAL/HISTORICAL NOTES: The Standing Indian Area was once a logging camp. Locomotives were used in the logging process and old railroad grades still exist today. Standing Indian Mountain is the highest point in the region at an elevation of 5,499 feet and is the source of an old Cherokee Indian legend.

This legend tells of an Indian warrior staked out on a cliff near the mountain-top. He was to serve as a lookout to guard the tribe from a winged monster. This monster had taken a child away from the tribe to a cave on the mountain. The Cherokee tribe prayed to the Great Spirit for help in killing the evil monster. Legend says the Great Spirit sent a powerful lightning bolt destroying the mountaintop and the monster. The Indian warrior was turned to a pillar of stone and all that appeared to be left was a "standing Indian." Even today, the mountaintop is treeless and bald.

OTHER ACTIVITIES: hiking, backpacking, fishing, hunting, camping

NEAREST CITY/FACILITIES: Franklin

Standing Indian Campground (family camping only; no horses) is located 2 miles north of Hurricane Creek Camp on FR-67 and provides hot showers, flush toilets and drinking water. Call the ranger station for more information. A Backcountry Information Center is near this campground on FR-67B.

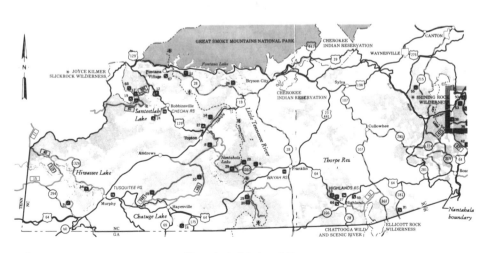

Nantahala National Forest
Reprinted courtesy of The National Forest Service

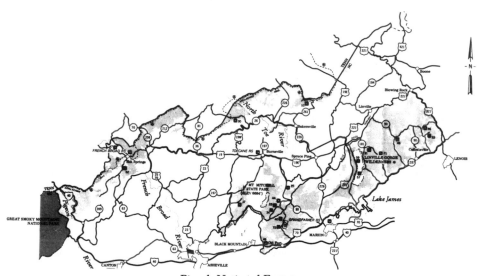

Pisgah National Forest
(French Broad and Toecane Ranger Districts)
Reprinted courtesy of The National Forest Service

PISGAH NATIONAL FOREST

French Broad Ranger District
Address: French Broad District Ranger, USFS
P.O. Box 128 Hot Springs, NC 28743
Telephone: (828) 622-3202

HARMON DEN AREA

County: Haywood

LOCATION: From Interstate-40, five miles east of the NC-TN state lines, take the Harmon Den exit. Follow FR-148 (Cold Springs Rd) up the mountain. Various trailheads and accesses are described below in more detail. On FR-148, an improved parking area with hitching racks and trail bulletin board is located on the left (day use only).

SEASON: open daily year round

FACILITY REVIEW
TYPE: day use and/or overnight horse camping
HORSE CAMPING FACILITIES: primitive camping in dispersed graveled areas along Forest Rd-148
CAMPING FEE: none
HOT SHOWERS: none
RESTROOMS: none
STABLE FACILITIES: none
DAY RIDERS FEE: none

TRAIL REVIEW
TRAIL NAMES and DESCRIPTIONS:
1. Robert Gap: 2.5 miles/difficult
2. Cherry Ridge: 1.1 miles/difficult
3. Buckeye Ridge: 5.4 miles/moderate
4. Cold Springs: 3.6 miles/difficult
5. Cherry Creek: 1.6 miles/difficult

TYPE: marked (blazed with yellow diamonds)
TERRAIN: mountainous-rugged
DIFFICULTY: moderate-difficult

LENGTH: 14+ miles; not including several miles of forest roads
WATER: yes
TRAIL MAP: Harmon Den Trail Map
TRAIL NOTES: These five trails follow mostly old roadbeds and logging roads through forests, wildlife fields and across several creeks and mountain balds. They can be combined with either SR-1182 and/or FR-148 to form various combinations of loops. Robert Gap Trail (#1) and Buckeye Ridge Trail (#3) provide great views of distant mountain ridges and the Great Smoky Mountains National Park.

TRAIL ACCESSES:
1. Robert Gap: From the Harmon Den exit at I-40, take FR-148 for 5.2 miles to the trailhead and parking area at Robert Gap. This is at the intersection of FR-148 and SR-1182.

2. Cherry Ridge: From the Harmon Den exit, take FR-148 for 4.4 miles to the parking area and trailhead.

3. Buckeye Ridge: From the Harmon Den exit, take FR-148 for 4.7 miles to the intersection with SR-1182. Turn left on SR-1182 and go 1.2 miles to trailhead, leaving SR-1182 one hundred yards south of the intersection with FR-3533.

4. Cold Springs: From Harmon Den exit, take FR-148 for 3.4 miles to the trailhead and parking area on the right near Cold Springs Creek.

5. Cherry Creek: Can be accessed from either SR-1182 or FR-148.

RULES/REQUIREMENTS: Stay on the designated trails. Do not ride on Max Patch Mountain or the Appalachian Trail (hikers only). Be sure to pack in and out all garbage as there are no trash receptacles available at the dispersed camping sites. Use the existing fire rings at these sites.

HIGHLIGHTS: spectacular views of distant mountains in Great Smoky Mountains National Park and Tennessee from open balds, excellent system of trails, wildlife

GENERAL/HISTORICAL NOTES: The 80,000 acres of this ranger district contains some of the most remote and rugged terrain in the Appalachian Mountains. It is located near the NC-TN state lines and north of the Great Smoky Mountains National Park. The terrain includes rocky cliffs, gorges, valleys and the beautiful French Broad River. This area is not as developed or populated as the other ranger districts. Camp Creek Bald in Madison County is the highest point in the district at 4,844 feet. Other major mountain peaks are Max Patch,

Rich Mountain, Big Butt, Snowbird, Bluff Mountain and Walnut Mountain. Future plans include the development of an overnight horse camping area.

OTHER ACTIVITIES: hunting, fishing, hiking, boating, camping

NEAREST CITIES/FACILITIES: Waterville, Canton, Hot Springs

The Great Smoky Mountains National Park adjoins the French Broad Ranger District near Waterville. It has a primitive horse camping area named Big Creek Campground. See the section "Great Smoky Mountains National Park" for more information.

Rocky Bluff Campground (family camping only; no horse camping) is located on NC-209, three miles south of Hot Springs. It is the district's main family campground and offers drinking water, flush toilets and picnicking; no showers. Currently, none of the recreation areas in this ranger district have shower facilities or hookups.

French Broad Ranger District

MURRAY BRANCH DAY USE AREA

County: Madison

LOCATION: From Hot Springs, go south on US-25/70. Go over the French Broad River bridge and turn left. Take NC-1304 for 4 miles to the parking area. Additional parking areas are also available in Hot Springs.

SEASON: open daily year round

FACILITY REVIEW
TYPE: day use only
HORSE CAMPING FACILITIES: none
RESTROOMS: chemical flush toilets
OTHER SERVICES: picnic tables, grills, one group picnic shelter
DAY RIDERS FEE: none

TRAIL REVIEW
TRAIL NAME: French Broad River Bike Route
TYPE: marked (blazed blue)
TERRAIN: flat
DIFFICULTY: easy
LENGTH: 6 miles
WATER: yes
TRAIL MAP: Your Guide to Hiking, Biking and Horseback Riding in the Hot Springs Area
TRAIL NOTES: This mountain bike route is also open to horseback riding. It follows the paved and graveled Paint Rock Road along the French Broad River. The road goes from Hot Springs to Paint Rock on the NC-TN border. Riders must backtrack. Murray Branch is located about halfway along the trail.

HIGHLIGHTS: French Broad River, wildlife, forestry

GENERAL/HISTORICAL NOTES: Paint Rock is a rock formation with a scenic overlook located on the North Carolina-Tennessee border. It was used in the past as an Indian outpost and a pioneer fort.

OTHER ACTIVITIES: mountain biking, picnicking, canoeing, rafting, fishing

NEAREST CITY/FACILITIES: Hot Springs

Grandfather Ranger District
Address: Grandfather Ranger District, USFS
Rt. 1, Box 110-A Nebo, NC 28761-9707
Telephone: (828) 652-2144

GRANDFATHER RANGER DISTRICT
(includes Wilson Creek Area, Brown Mountain, Edgemont)

Counties: Caldwell, Burke, McDowell, Avery

LOCATION: This area is located northwest of Lenoir and north of Marion and Morganton off NC-90. There are no designated parking areas for trucks and horse trailers. Park in pulloffs well off the forest service roads. Horse camping is allowed at Boone Fork Recreation Area (see Nearest Cities/Facilities).

SEASON: open daily year round

FACILITY REVIEW
TYPE: day use and/or overnight horse camping
HORSE CAMPING FACILITIES: primitive camping at dispersed sites (see Nearest Cities/Facilities)
CAMPING FEE: none
HOT SHOWERS: none
RESTROOMS: none
STABLE FACILITIES: none
DAY RIDERS FEE: none

TRAIL REVIEW
TYPE: marked and unmarked; most trails are signed at trailheads but many are not well-marked or blazed along the way
TERRAIN: mountainous and rugged
DIFFICULTY: easy-difficult
LENGTH: 100+ miles; connects to several miles of forest service roads
WATER: yes
TRAIL MAP: Wilson Creek Area Trail Map. Pisgah National Forest, includes Grandfather, French Broad and Toecane Districts
TRAIL NOTES: Horseback riding is allowed on any U.S. Forest Service road or trail that is not posted otherwise. Dirt roads can be combined with primitive roads and trails to create loops. These are multi-use trails. Be aware that Brown Mountain is an ORV area and has approximately 40 miles of trails for use by motorcycles, ATVs, jeeps, and 4x4s.

RULES/REQUIREMENTS: Stay on trails and roads designated for horses. When parking horse trailers in pulloffs, do not block the main road.

HIGHLIGHTS: mountainous trails and forest roads, Wilson Creek, wildlife

GENERAL/HISTORICAL NOTES: The Grandfather Ranger District, comprised of 187,000 acres, is the most eastern section of Pisgah National Forest. Located south and southwest of Grandfather Mountain, contained within its boundaries are the Wilson Creek Area, Brown Mountain, and Linville Gorge Wilderness Area. These are popular areas for all types of outdoor recreation.

Wilson Creek runs northeast of a long ridge known as Brown Mountain, the location of the famous and mysterious Brown Mountain Lights. The flickering lights are the source of numerous, conflicting accounts that date back to Indian legends and pre-Civil War time. Even today no one knows the true cause of the lights, but the fact remains that they do exist.

The community of Edgemont, located along SR-1328, was once a resort-type area for tourists traveling to and from Linville and Blowing Rock. Located near Edgemont are the wilderness study areas of Harper Creek and Lost Cove.

The 7,600-acre Linville Gorge Wilderness Area is considered to be one of the most scenic and rugged gorges in America. The Linville River, located within the gorge for twelve miles, begins on Grandfather Mountain before descending into the Catawba Valley. This area derives its name from the explorer, William Linville. In 1766 Linville and his son were scalped by Indians in the Gorge.

OTHER ACTIVITIES: hiking, backpacking, rock climbing, mountain biking, camping, fishing, hunting, motorcycling, four-wheeling (ORV area)

NEAREST CITIES/FACILITIES: Lenoir, Morganton, Marion

Boone Fork Recreation Area allows horse camping and has campsites, vault toilets, picnic tables, and drinking water. Reservations must be made at least 14 days in advance. The maximum number of people per campsite is five. This area may charge a camping fee in the future. Check with the ranger station for additional information and to make reservations. To reach Boone Fork Recreation Area from Lenoir, take NC-90 North for 7 miles. Turn north on NC-1368 and go 3 miles. Turn right onto gravel FR-2055 and go 2 miles.

Pisgah Ranger District
Address: Pisgah District Ranger, USFS
1001 Pisgah Hwy Pisgah Forest, NC 28768
Telephone: (828) 877-3550

COURTHOUSE CREEK AREA

County: Transylvania

LOCATION: From the Pisgah Ranger Station, go north on US-276 for 3.5 miles. Turn left onto Davidson River Rd (FR-475). Go 8 miles to SR-1327; go straight at intersection. Turn right onto NC-215 and go 4 miles to a bridge at Bee Tree Fork crossing and parking area.

SEASON: open daily year round

FACILITY REVIEW
TYPE: day use and/or overnight horse camping
HORSE CAMPING FACILITIES: primitive camping at dispersed sites
(see the Davidson River Area for more information on camping within this ranger district)
CAMPING FEE: no fee for dispersed sites
HOT SHOWERS: none
RESTROOMS: none
STABLE FACILITIES: none
DAY RIDERS FEE: none

TRAIL REVIEW
TRAIL NAME: Summey Cove (USFS #129)
TYPE: marked (blazed blue)
TERRAIN: hilly-mountainous
DIFFICULTY: moderate
LENGTH: 2.0 miles; connects to several miles of forest roads
WATER: yes
TRAIL MAP: Pisgah District Trail Map
TRAIL NOTES: This backtracking trail follows old roadbeds and railroad grades through a hardwood forest up to a large gap at Big Fork Ridge. It steeply descends to Summey Cove and then crosses over Mills Station Branch. Courthouse Falls is a 60-foot waterfall located on the right near the end of Summey Cove Trail. It is accessible by a short footpath (hikers only). Summey Cove Trail continues on and crosses Courthouse Creek before ending on FR-140.

Horseback riding is also allowed on several miles of forest service roads within this area. FR-140, FR-140A, FR-140B and Kiesee Creek Rd (FR-229A) are located near Summey Cove Trail and can be utilized to form loops and one-way trips within Pisgah National Forest.

HIGHLIGHTS: Courthouse Falls, good views near Summey Cove of Devil's Courthouse and Pilot Mountain

OTHER ACTIVITIES: hiking, mountain biking, camping

NEAREST CITIES/FACILITIES: Brevard, Asheville

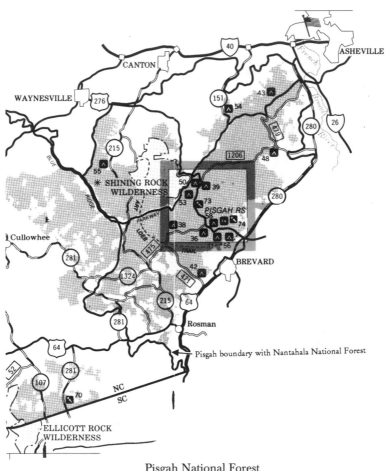

Pisgah National Forest
(Pisgah Ranger District)
Reprinted courtesy of The National Forest Service

Pisgah Ranger District

DAVIDSON RIVER AREA

County: Transylvania

LOCATION: From the Pisgah Ranger Station and Visitor Center, go west on US-276 for 0.4 mile to Avery Creek Rd (FR-477). Turn right and go 1.7 miles to the parking area on the right near Pisgah Forest Stables. Ask the stable operator for the best place to park your vehicle and trailer.

SEASON: open daily year round

FACILITY REVIEW
TYPE: day use and/or overnight horse camping
HORSE CAMPING FACILITIES: primitive camping at campgrounds and dispersed sites (see Nearest Cities/Facilities below)
CAMPING FEE: no fee for dispersed sites; fee for campgrounds
HOT SHOWERS: none
RESTROOMS: none
STABLE FACILITIES: none
DAY RIDERS FEE: none

TRAIL REVIEW
TRAIL NAMES and DESCRIPTIONS:
1. Avery Creek: 1.0 mile/moderate/blazed blue (USFS #327)

2. Buckhorn Gap: 5.2 miles/moderate/blazed orange (USFS #103)

TYPE: marked
TERRAIN: mountainous
DIFFICULTY: moderate-strenuous
LENGTH: 6.2+ miles combined; connects to several miles of forest roads and trails in other areas of this ranger district, including the South Mills River Area
WATER: yes
TRAIL MAP: Pisgah District Trail Map
TRAIL NOTES: These trails follow old roadbeds and railroad grades through the mountainous forest. A gated logging road named Clawhammer Road can be used in conjunction with the trails to create a loop back to the Pisgah Forest Stables and parking area. Its southern trailhead is just east of the riding stable where the road climbs steadily for 4.4 miles to end at Buckhorn Gap.

Maxwell Cove Road is a gated forest road that leads to Pressley Gap. It begins on the right after traveling north on Clawhammer Road for 1.1 miles from the riding stable. Go 2.5 miles on Maxwell Cove Road to Pressley Gap (the road becomes grassy) and a five-way trail junction. The road continues east to a dead end.

From the stable parking area, ride north on FR-477 0.5 mile to access the Upper Avery Creek Trail (#1). This trail follows an old dirt roadbed and descends gradually to Avery Creek. It intersects with Buckhorn Gap Trail (#2) at a wildlife field. Avery Creek Trail continues northwest but horses are not allowed beyond this portion of the trail. Horseback riders must take Buckhorn Gap Trail.

Buckhorn Gap Trail goes north along an old railroad grade as it climbs its way towards Buckhorn Gap. Here it junctions with Black Mountain Trail (hikers only) and then continues downhill to join with the South Mills River Trail (see South Mills River Area). Upon reaching Buckhorn Gap, you may option to create a loop. Backtrack for 1.8 miles on Buckhorn Gap Trail to the logging road, Clawhammer Road. Go straight on this road for 2.6 miles to its end at the stables and horse trailer parking area.

RULES/REQUIREMENTS: Dispersed primitive camping is allowed within the ranger district at least 1000 feet from an open road.

HIGHLIGHTS: scenic views, waterfalls near Buckhorn Gap Trail, nice hardwood forests, forestry management, wildlife

GENERAL/HISTORICAL NOTES: This portion of the Pisgah National Forest was once part of George Vanderbilt's original Biltmore Estate that included over 125,000 acres of beautiful mountain land. The practice of forestry principles were begun here by Gifford Pinchot and Carl Schenck under Vanderbilt's direction. The Cradle of Forestry Visitor Center is located near here on US-276. This is the reconstructed site of the first school of forestry in America.

OTHER ACTIVITIES: guided trail rides at Pisgah Forest Stables from April to October, hiking, mountain biking, family and group camping, fishing, Cradle of Forestry Visitor Center, Fish Hatchery

NEAREST CITIES/FACILITIES: Brevard, Asheville
For additional information on the campgrounds call the ranger station at (828) 877-3550. North and South White Pines are group camping areas located along FR-477 near the Pisgah Ranger Station. They offer primitive tent campsites, drinking water, vault toilets, picnic tables and fire rings. No vehicles are allowed in the group camping areas with the exception of horse trailers with sleepers. Eight hitching rails for horses are available at each camp. Call the ranger station for more information and to make arrangements for access through the locked gate. Reservations are made through Biospherics, Inc. at 1-800-280-CAMP (2267) or TDD (800) 879-4496. There is a $15.00 service charge with each

reservation, so be sure of your plans before making definite reservations. North and South White Pines are open year round and can each accommodate groups of up to 25 people. Group area reservations may be made a minimum of 10 days and a maximum of 360 days in advance. No reservations are taken during hunting season (November and December). Camping fee is $20.00.

Davidson River Campground (no horse camping) is located on US-276 near the Pisgah Ranger Station. Services include primitive campsites, hot showers, drinking water, public telephones and dump station. Call (828) 877-4910 for more information. Reservations may be made for the campground up to two weeks in advance by contacting Biospherics, Inc. at 1-800-280-2267. One-half of the campground is on a first-come, first-served basis.

Horses may also be stabled overnight at the Davis Equestrian Center in Etowah near Hendersonville. Call (828) 891-7396 for information.

Pisgah Forest Stables is located on FR-477 near the ranger station. It is privately operated and offers guided trail rides on rental horses within Pisgah National Forest. Operational hours are from 10:00 a.m. until 5:00 p.m. During the months of June, July and August, guided trips leave on the hour seven days a week. During the months of April, May, September and October, the stable is only open on weekends from Friday through Monday. Reservations are suggested. Contact at (828) 883-8258 for more information.

Pisgah Forest Stables

Pisgah Ranger District

NORTH MILLS RIVER AREA

County: Henderson

LOCATION: From the Pisgah Ranger Station, go north on NC-280 for 10 miles to Mills River. From Mills River Community, go north on NC-280/191 for one mile. Turn west onto North Mills River Rd (SR-1345; becomes FR-1206). Go 5 miles to the North Mills River Recreation Area. Parking for horse trailers is permitted along the side of FR-1206 beyond the campground.

Additional horse trailer parking is available at the Trace Ridge parking area. From FR-1206 just before the North Mills River campground, turn right onto the gravel Wash Creek Road (FR-5000). Go 2.2 miles on FR-5000 to a fork in the gravel road. Turn left on FR-142 and cross a small concrete bridge. Trace Ridge parking area is 0.5 mile beyond the bridge. Numerous trailheads span out from this area.

SEASON: open daily year round

FACILITY REVIEW
TYPE: day use and/or overnight horse camping
HORSE CAMPING FACILITIES: primitive camping at dispersed sites (see the Davidson River Area for more information on camping within this ranger district); two primitive campsites on Wash Creek Rd (FR-5000) can accommodate trucks and horse trailers
CAMPING FEE: no fee for dispersed sites
HOT SHOWERS: none
RESTROOMS: none
STABLE FACILITIES: none
DAY RIDERS FEE: none

TRAIL REVIEW
TRAIL NAMES and DESCRIPTIONS:
1. North Mills River: 2.0 miles/difficult/blazed blue; connects to #2

2. Trace Ridge: 3.1 miles/moderate/blazed orange (USFS #354); connects to #1, 6

3. Fletcher Creek: 2.4 miles/easy/blazed blue; connects to #4, 6

4. Middle Fork: 1.8 miles/easy/blazed orange; connects to #3, 6

5. Big Creek: 4.9 miles/difficult/blazed yellow (USFS #102)

6. Spencer Branch: 2.5 miles/more difficult/blazed orange (USFS #140); connects to #2, 3, 4

TYPE: marked
TERRAIN: mountainous
DIFFICULTY: easy-difficult
LENGTH: 14.8+ miles combined; connects to several miles of forest service roads and trails in other areas of this ranger district, including South Mills River Area
WATER: adequate except for Trace Ridge Trail (#1)
TRAIL MAP: Pisgah District Trail Map
TRAIL NOTES: These trails mainly consist of old roads and railroad grades that are shared with hikers and mountain bikers. Trace Ridge parking area is a source of the trailheads for Trace Ridge Trail (#2), the gated Fletcher Creek Road (also known as the Never Ending Road) and the gated Hendersonville Reservoir Road (FR-142).

Trace Ridge Trail (#2) is a dry ridge trail through the forest that follows an old roadbed. It begins near the gated Fletcher Creek Road. The trail maintains a steady climb to dead end at the Blue Ridge Parkway near Ferrin Knob Tunnels. Horseback riding is not allowed on the Blue Ridge Parkway. Backtrack a short distance and turn onto Spencer Branch Trail (#6) to form a loop.

Access the trailhead of Fletcher Creek Trail (#3) from the Trace Ridge parking area by following the Hendersonville Reservoir Road for 1.2 miles. The trail begins one-quarter mile before reaching the North Fork Reservoir. It mostly follows an old railroad grade that crosses Fletcher Creek several times on its way to a dead end. Fletcher Creek Road can be taken from here to form a loop back to Trace Ridge parking area.

After one mile on Fletcher Creek Trail, Middle Fork Trail (#4) branches off to the left where Fletcher Creek and Middle Fork Creek join. Middle Fork Trail follows an old railroad grade that crosses Middle Fork Creek several times before it dead ends in Middle Fork Cove.

Spencer Branch Trail (#6) branches off to the right of Fletcher Creek Trail (#3) after traveling one mile from the reservoir. Loop pathways can be made by using the logging road, Fletcher Creek Rd, and Spencer Branch Trail. Spencer Branch Trail can also be utilized to form a connector between Trace Ridge and Fletcher Creek Trails.

Big Creek Trail (#5) can be accessed by following the Hendersonville Reservoir Road for 1.5 miles from the Trace Ridge parking area. Go north around the Hendersonville Reservoir and follow the old railroad grade through the forest. Upon reaching Bee Branch, horseback riders must backtrack since horses are not allowed past Bee Branch.

The trailhead of North Mills River Trail (#1) can be accessed from FR-1206 (Yellow Gap Road), west of the North Mills River Campground. It crosses North Mills River and can be used as a connector to the lower Trace Ridge Trail (#2) as it climbs to Trace Ridge parking area.

RULES/REQUIREMENTS: Horses are not allowed along the Blue Ridge Parkway or on any of the Parkway's adjoining property. Dispersed primitive camping is allowed within the ranger district at least 1000 feet from an open road.

HIGHLIGHTS: excellent opportunities for various combinations of loop trails, nice forests, logging history, wildlife

OTHER ACTIVITIES: hiking, mountain biking, fishing, family camping

NEAREST CITIES/FACILITIES: Mills River, Brevard, Asheville

North Mills River Recreation Area Campground (no horse camping) is located on FR-1206 near the junction of FR-5000 and SR-1345. Facilities include primitive campsites, flush and vault toilets, drinking water and dump station. Call the ranger station at (828) 877-3550 for more information on campgrounds.

Davis Equestrian Center in Etowah provides overnight stabling and can be contacted at (828) 891-7396 for more information.

Looking Glass Rock in Pisgah National Forest

Pisgah Ranger District

SOUTH MILLS RIVER AREA

Counties: Henderson and Transylvania

LOCATION: From the intersections of NC-280, US-276 and US-64 near Brevard and the Pisgah Ranger Station, go north 4.6 miles on NC-280. Turn left on Turkey Pen Rd (FR-297). Go 1.1 miles along the gravel road to a parking area at Turkey Pen Gap. This is a popular and often crowded trailhead on the weekends. Be aware that limited turn-around space exists for trucks and horse trailers. Trails can also be accessed from near the Pink Beds Area. From US-276, turn on Yellow Gap Rd (FR-1206) near the Pink Beds Picnic Area. Turn right on FR-476 and go 0.7 mile. Parking is available in the roadside campsite on the right.

SEASON: open daily year round

FACILITY REVIEW
TYPE: day use and/or overnight horse camping
HORSE CAMPING FACILITIES: primitive camping at dispersed sites along FR-1206 and FR-476 (see the Davidson River Area for more camping information)
CAMPING FEE: none
HOT SHOWERS: none
RESTROOMS: none
STABLE FACILITIES: none
DAY RIDERS FEE: none

TRAIL REVIEW
TRAIL NAMES and DESCRIPTIONS:
1. South Mills River Trail: 12 miles/moderate-difficult/blazed white; connects to #4,5,6 and Buckhorn Gap Trail in Davidson River Area (USFS #133)

2. Bradley Creek: 5.1 miles/moderate/blazed orange; connects to #3 (USFS #351)

3. Laurel Creek: 1.8 miles/moderate/blazed yellow; connects to #2,4

4. Squirrel Gap: 7.5 miles/moderate/blazed blue; connects to #1,3,5,6 (USFS #147)

5. Mullinax: 1.2 miles/moderate/blazed yellow; connects to #1,4 (USFS #326)

6. Cantrell Creek: 1.9 miles/moderate/blazed white; connects to #1,4 (USFS #148)

7. Horse Cove: 0.8 mile/moderate/blazed orange; connects to #4,6

TYPE: marked
TERRAIN: hilly-mountainous
DIFFICULTY: moderate-difficult
LENGTH: 30+ miles combined; connects to several miles of trails and forest service roads in other areas of this ranger district, including North Mills River Area and Davidson River Area
WATER: yes
TRAIL MAP: Pisgah District Trail Map
TRAIL NOTES: These trails consist of old roadbeds, logging roads and railroad grades through the forest that are also used by mountain bikers, hikers and fishermen. Turkey Pen Gap parking area is the source for the trailheads of South Mills River Trail (#1) and Bradley Creek Trail (#2). Trails #3, #4, #5 and #6 connect to #1 or #2 and provide various options to form loop trails back to Turkey Pen Gap. During rainy weather, be careful when attempting the numerous creek and river crossings along these trails due to high water and boggy areas. The crossings can be very difficult.

South Mills River Trail (#1) begins along a narrow pathway on the left side of the gated road. This trail follows the South Mills River and is mainly an old railroad grade through the forest. It crosses the river thirteen times in waters varying from one-half foot to three feet high.

Bradley Creek Trail (#2) can be accessed by traveling the gated road that is to the right of the South Mills River trailhead (#1). Go 0.8 mile to a four-way trail junction. Bradley Creek Trail follows an old roadbed as it climbs its way to the top of Pea Gap (elev. 2600 ft). It crosses South Mills River once and Bradley Creek several times. There are good areas for campsites at the wildlife fields on the northern side of Pea Gap. Avoid use of this trail after heavy rainfall.

Laurel Creek Trail (#3) is a remote path along Laurel Creek. It is a connector trail between Bradley Creek Trail and Squirrel Gap Trail (#4) that is heavily traveled by horseback riders. Horse travel is permitted on Squirrel Gap Trail only from Pea Gap to Laurel Creek Trail. It provides access and loop possibilities to several trails (#1,3,5,6).

Mullinax Trail (#5) branches off South Mills River Trail (#1). It begins as an old logging road and then becomes a ridge climb. Beyond the ridge top, it intersects with Squirrel Gap Trail (#4). Beware of washed-out areas due to erosion.

Cantrell Creek Trail (#6) connects to South Mills River Trail on its southern end and to Squirrel Gap Trail on the northern end. It follows an old railroad grade that crosses Cantrell Creek several times. Around the end of May the mountain laurel along this trail are usually in bloom and provide a beautiful sight.

Horse Cove Gap Trail (#7) connects to Squirrel Gap Trail (#4) on its western end and Cantrell Creek Trail (#6) on its eastern terminus. This creates a loop option between Cantrell Creek Trail, Squirrel Gap Trail and South Mills River Trail (#1) at Wolf Ford. As a result, the only section of Squirrel Gap Trail (#4) closed to horse travel is between Cantrell Creek Trail and Horse Cove Gap. This stretch is not open to horses due to its extremely rugged and dangerous terrain.

RULES/REQUIREMENTS: Dispersed primitive camping is allowed within the ranger district at least 1000 feet from an open road.

HIGHLIGHTS: nice forests, logging history, South Mills River, wildlife

GENERAL/HISTORICAL NOTES: At the southern trailhead of Cantrell Creek Trail (#6) is the Cantrell Creek Lodge Site. This is the site of a forest lodge once used by Dr. Carl Schenck, the founder of the first school of forestry in America. The lodge has been restored and moved to the Cradle of Forestry. Remnants of the lodge chimney can still be seen at the original site.

OTHER ACTIVITIES: hiking, fishing, mountain biking

NEAREST CITIES/FACILITIES: Mills River, Asheville, Brevard

Davis Equestrian Center is located in the community of Etowah near Hendersonville and offers overnight stabling. Call (828) 891-7396 for information.

Toecane Ranger District
Address: Toecane District Ranger, USFS
P.O. Box 128 Burnsville, NC 28714
Telephone: (828) 682-6146

COLEMAN BOUNDARY AREA
"Big Ivy"

County: Buncombe

LOCATION: From Burnsville, go east on US-19 for 13 miles. Turn left onto Beech Glen Rd. Go 2 miles to Holcombe Rd and turn right. Go 3 miles to NC-197 and turn left. At Barnardsville, turn right on Dillingham Rd (NC-2173) and go 5 miles to the Forest Service boundary. Horse trailer parking and camping is available in pulloffs along FR-74.

SEASON: open daily year round

FACILITY REVIEW
TYPE: day use and/or overnight horse camping
HORSE CAMPING FACILITIES: primitive
CAMPING FEE: none
HOT SHOWERS: none
RESTROOMS: none
STABLE FACILITIES: none
DAY RIDERS FEE: none

TRAIL REVIEW
TRAIL NAMES and DESCRIPTIONS:
1. Bear Pen: 1.4 miles/moderate

2. Corner Rock: 1.4 miles/moderate

3. Elk Pen: 1.9 miles/moderate

4. Hensley Fields: 1.9 miles/moderate

5. Perkins: 1.1 miles/moderate

6. Stair Creek: 1.1 miles/moderate

7. Walker Creek: 1.6 miles/moderate

TYPE: marked
TERRAIN: hilly-mountainous
DIFFICULTY: easy-difficult
LENGTH: 35+ miles; connects to several miles of forest roads
WATER: yes
TRAIL MAP: Pisgah National Forest, includes Grandfather, Toecane, and French Broad Districts. Forest Service quads–Barnardsville, Mt. Mitchell, and Montreat.
TRAIL NOTES: Horseback riding is allowed on open and closed roads and on designated trails within this area of the Pisgah National Forest. Coleman Boundary Area is located near the Craggy Mountain Scenic Area along the Blue Ridge Parkway and includes several nice vistas and mountain streams.

RULES/REQUIREMENTS: Horses should not be tied directly to trees. Use a picket line between trees or hobble. Horses are not allowed in developed campground or picnic areas.

HIGHLIGHTS: scenic views, waterfalls, several mountain streams

OTHER ACTIVITIES: hiking, picnicking

NEAREST CITIES/FACILITIES: Barnardsville, Burnsville, Asheville
Misty Mountain Riding Center, Inc. offers guided trail rides and horseback holidays within this ranger district. Contact at (828) 626-3644 or 1265 Dillingham Rd, Barnardsville, NC 28709 for information.

Toecane Ranger District

FLATTOP AREA
(Spivey Gap Recreation Area)

County: Yancey

LOCATION: From Burnsville, take US-19E and go west 6 miles to US-19W. Turn right and go 15 miles. Turn right onto gravel FR-1415 and go to camping areas. Additional camping areas are available: on US-19W at Spivey Gap above the junction of US-19 and FR-1415; on FR-5506 across the road from the Spivey Gap Campground.

SEASON: open daily year round

FACILITY REVIEW
TYPE: day use and/or overnight horse camping
HORSE CAMPING FACILITIES: primitive
CAMPING FEE: none
HOT SHOWERS: none
RESTROOMS: pit toilets
STABLE FACILITIES: none
DAY RIDERS FEE: none

TRAIL REVIEW
TYPE: marked
TERRAIN: hilly-mountainous
DIFFICULTY: easy-difficult
LENGTH: 10 miles
WATER: yes
TRAIL MAP: Pisgah National Forest, includes Grandfather, Toecane, and French Broad Districts. Forest Service quads—Chestoa and Huntdale.
TRAIL NOTES: Riding is permitted on FR-278 that follows along the main ridge of this area. Some scenic views are possible at openings along the road. This area is near the NC-TN state lines and Cherokee National Forest in Tennessee.

RULES/REQUIREMENTS: Horses should not be tied directly to trees. Use a picket line between trees or hobble. Horses are not permitted in developed campground or picnic areas, nor on the Appalachian Trail and other trails in the area.

HIGHLIGHTS: Flattop Mountain, nice forests

OTHER ACTIVITIES: hiking, picnicking

NEAREST CITY/FACILITIES: Burnsville

Spivey Gap Recreation Area (no horses permitted) is located on the crest of the Bald Mountains off US-19W. It is for day use only and offers pit toilets, drinking water and picnicking. No camping is allowed.

Toecane Ranger District

PIGEON ROOST AREA

County: Mitchell

LOCATION: From Burnsville, go north on NC-197 for 18 miles. Turn right onto SR-1349 under a railroad trestle and go 4 miles. Turn left on gravel FR-235 and follow to camping areas.

SEASON: open daily year round

FACILITY REVIEW
TYPE: day use and/or overnight horse camping
HORSE CAMPING FACILITIES: primitive
CAMPING FEE: none
HOT SHOWERS: none
RESTROOMS: none
STABLE FACILITIES: none
DAY RIDERS FEE: none

TRAIL REVIEW
TYPE: marked
TERRAIN: hilly-mountainous
DIFFICULTY: moderate
LENGTH: 2-3 miles
WATER: yes
TRAIL MAP: none
TRAIL NOTES: Horseback riding is permitted on open and closed forest roads. This area is located near the NC-TN border and Cherokee National Forest in Tennessee.

RULES/REQUIREMENTS: Horses should not be tied directly to trees. Use a picket line between trees or hobble. Horses are not permitted in developed campground or picnic areas.

OTHER ACTIVITIES: hiking, family camping

NEAREST CITIES/FACILITIES: Burnsville, Bakersville

Toecane Ranger District

SOUTH TOE RIVER AREA

County: Yancey

LOCATION: From Burnsville, go east on US-19 for 4 miles to Micaville. Turn right (south) onto NC-80 and go 14 miles. Turn right onto South Toe River Rd (FR-472). Take FR-472 and go 4 miles past the Black Mountain Campground. Parking area and the southern trailhead for Buncombe Horse Trail is on the right.

Alternate access route is from the Blue Ridge Parkway: at BRP milepost 351.9 near Buck Creek Gap, go north on NC-80. Go 2 miles and turn left onto FR-472.

SEASON: open daily year round

FACILITY REVIEW
TYPE: day use and/or overnight horse camping
HORSE CAMPING FACILITIES: primitive and backcountry
Numerous primitive campsites are available along FR-472 (will accommodate vehicles with horse trailers). A primitive camping area is located 8 miles along the Buncombe Horse Range bridle trail at the former site of the Camp Alice Trail Shelter.
CAMPING FEE: none
HOT SHOWERS: none
RESTROOMS: pit toilet
STABLE FACILITIES: trailer tie, picket line
STABLING FEE: none
DAY RIDERS FEE: none

TRAIL REVIEW
TRAIL NAMES and DESCRIPTIONS:
1. Buncombe Horse Range Trail: 17.5 miles/rugged terrain/difficult/blazed white; (USFS #191)

2. Camp Alice: 2.0 miles/easy-moderate

TYPE: marked
TERRAIN: mountainous-rugged
DIFFICULTY: easy-difficult
LENGTH: 30 miles (combined with forest roads)
WATER: yes
TRAIL MAP: South Toe River Trail Map

TRAIL NOTES: From the southern access, the rocky Buncombe Horse Trail follows old logging roads and railroad grades. It passes through open fields and woods in the Mt. Mitchell Wildlife Management Area, which borders the eastern slopes of Mt. Mitchell State Park. At 7 miles along the trail, it junctions with a road on the left leading to NC-128 and Mt. Mitchell State Park. Turn right to stay on the bridle trail. The area where Camp Alice Shelter was formerly located is at 8.0 miles.

The trail continues along the railroad tramway to 11.0 miles. Beyond this point are mountain balds with nice views of the Black Mountain Research Natural Area. The Buncombe Horse Trail reaches an old logging road at 13.0 miles that leads to its end on Colberts Creek Rd (NC-1159). Riding is also permitted on gated forest roads within the Toecane area (10 miles/easy-moderate) along FR-472.

RULES/REQUIREMENTS: Horses should not be tied directly to trees. Use a picket line between trees or hobble. Horses are not allowed in developed campground, picnic areas, or in Mt. Mitchell State Park.

HIGHLIGHTS: good vistas from mountain balds, wildlife, Camp Alice, located near Mt. Mitchell

GENERAL/HISTORICAL NOTES: The South Toe River Area is located near the Black Mountain Range, the highest mountain range in the eastern United States. Mt. Mitchell is the highest point east of the Mississippi River at 6,684 feet.

The South River Toe Area is the main horse trail and camping area in the Toecane Ranger District. This area contains the only modern family campgrounds in the district (see Nearest Cities/Facilities below). Future plans include the development of a horse camp near the junction of South Toe River Rd and Neals Creek Rd. There are four other dispersed areas for riding and primitive camping within the Toecane Ranger District: Coleman Boundary, Flattop (Spivey Gap Recreation Area), Pigeon Roost and Victor Fields (Victor Tract Camp).

The Toecane Ranger District consists of 82,000 acres of Forest Service land within four counties: Mitchell, Buncombe, Yancey and Avery. It is named for the Toe and Cane Rivers, the two major rivers in its area. The South Toe River received its name from an old Indian legend. Estatoe was an Indian squaw who fell in love with a brave from a rival tribe. He was murdered by her tribe when he came to claim her hand in marriage. Estatoe was so filled with grief that she drowned herself in the river. The Indians named the river Estatoe in her honor, and the name was eventually reduced to Toe by the white settlers.

The stone foundations of Camp Alice are visible today near the site of Camp Alice Shelter. Camp Alice has a history as a logging camp used back in the 1920s. People visiting Mt. Mitchell eventually used the camp as a lodge.

OTHER ACTIVITIES: hiking, cross-country skiing, camping, backpacking, fishing

NEAREST CITIES/FACILITIES: Micaville, Burnsville

Black Mountain Campground is located 2.9 miles from the south trailhead of Buncombe Horse Trail on FR-472. Carolina Hemlocks Recreation Area is located north on NC-80, 5.3 miles from the Blue Ridge Parkway at Buck Creek Gap. Both are modern campgrounds offering showers, flush toilets, and drinking water (no horse camping allowed). Recreational activities available at both campgrounds include swimming, hiking, fishing and tubing. Black Mountain also offers bicycle trails.

At the junction of South Toe River Rd and Neals Creek Rd and one mile east of Black Mountain Campground is the Neals Creek Information Station. It is open daily and offers trail maps and books about the surrounding areas. The Toecane Ranger District Office has an excellent *Recreation Information Guide* on this area of the Pisgah National Forest. Contact the ranger station for more information.

Toecane Ranger District

VICTOR FIELDS AREA
CAMP: Victor Tract

County: Yancey

Location: From the Blue Ridge Parkway in Yancey County, take FR-5511, a gravel road two miles north of NC-80. Victor Tract Horse Camping area is on Seven-Mile Ridge. Horse trailer parking and camping is available in pulloffs along FR-5511.

SEASON: open daily year round

FACILITY REVIEW
TYPE: day use and/or overnight horse camping
HORSE CAMPING FACILITIES: primitive
CAMPING FEE: none
HOT SHOWERS: none
RESTROOMS: none
STABLE FACILITIES: none
DAY RIDERS FEE: none

TRAIL REVIEW
TYPE: marked
TERRAIN: hilly-mountainous
DIFFICULTY: easy-moderate
LENGTH: 12 miles
WATER: yes
TRAIL MAP: Pisgah National Forest, includes Grandfather, Toecane, and French Broad Districts. Forest Service quad–Celo.
TRAIL NOTES: Horseback riding is permitted on open and closed or gated roads. Some roads pass through hardwood forests.

RULES/REQUIREMENTS: Do not tie horses directly to trees; use a picket line or hobble. Horses are not permitted in developed campground or picnic areas.

HIGHLIGHTS: good views of the distant Black Mountain Range

OTHER ACTIVITIES: hiking, cross-country skiing, family camping

NEAREST CITIES/FACILITIES: Burnsville, Spruce Pine
    Carolina Hemlocks Recreation Area and Campground (no horse camping) is nearby in the South Toe River Area.

UWHARRIE NATIONAL FOREST

CAMP: Badin Lake Horse Camp

County: Montgomery

Address: Uwharrie District Ranger, USFS
Rt. 3, Box 470 Troy, NC 27371
Telephone: (910) 576-6391

LOCATION: The horse camp is accessed from NC-109, 1 mile south of Eldorado and 3 miles north of Uwharrie. Turn west from NC-109 onto SR-1154 (later becomes FR-544) at the "Wildlife Area" sign. Go 1.2 miles and the horse camp is in a grassy field on the right on top of a hill. NOTE: After one mile on this road, it becomes a gravel road. Cross a small bridge. The "Blue Hole," a livestock water source, is located on the right after the bridge.

SEASON: open daily year round

FACILITY REVIEW
TYPE: day use and/or overnight horse camping
HORSE CAMPING FACILITIES: primitive (open field camping); also 4B Farm (see Nearest Cities/Facilities)
CAMPING FEE: $5.00/day
HOT SHOWERS: none
RESTROOMS: pit toilet
STABLE FACILITIES: hitching posts, trailer tie
STABLING FEE: none
DAY RIDERS FEE: none; $3.00/day or $30.00/season per horse and rider if using the Badin ORV trails

TRAIL REVIEW
TYPE: marked
TERRAIN: rolling hills-mountainous
DIFFICULTY: easy-difficult
LENGTH: 20+ miles of ORV trails; several additional miles of other trails and forest roads
WATER: yes; water for livestock is available at the "Blue Hole," a creek approximately four feet deep in the center. It is located 0.2 miles northeast of the horse camp on FR-544 near the bridge.
TRAIL MAP: Uwharrie National Forest. Forest Service quad–Badin. Detailed trail map also available at 4B Farm (see Nearest Cities/Facilities).

TRAIL NOTES: The section of Uwharrie National Forest near the horse camp has approximately 4,000 acres and contains a vast network of jeep, motorbiking, and horse trails that crisscross over a variety of terrain. Wooded trails wind through hills and to mountaintops for excellent views of the surrounding ridges. Some trails are narrow paths due to overgrowth of the vegetation. The dense forests along some trails obscure scenic views during the summer. Early spring, fall and winter provide the best panoramas. There are several creek crossings along most trails. The higher elevations tend to be rockier.

Horseback riding is also allowed on several miles of open, gravel forest service roads and off-road vehicle trails. Be aware that some trails share use with motorcycles, all-terrain vehicles, and mountain bikes. Show common courtesy by giving up the right of way to bikers.

Use caution when riding during hunting season since the national forest is also a popular game land with hunters. Rattlesnakes have been known to slither around in the Uwharries so be wary! Finally, this area of North Carolina is near the Sandhills and can be hot and humid during the summer months. Water and rest your horse often.

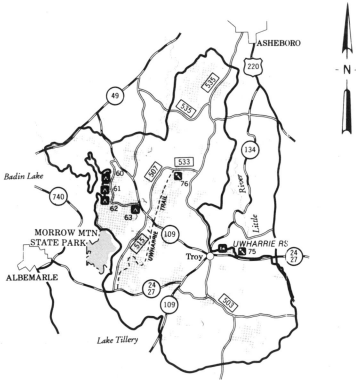

Uwharrie National Forest
Reprinted courtesy of The National Forest Service

RULES/REQUIREMENTS: Horses are not permitted on the hiking trails. Maximum stay is 14 days.

HIGHLIGHTS: scenic views from mountaintops, nice forests and flora (huge pine trees, ferns), wildlife, Badin Lake and Yadkin River

GENERAL/HISTORICAL NOTES: Uwharrie National Forest is named for the Uwharrie Mountains in this area. These are eroded, rounded mountain peaks that reach elevations of 900-1,000 feet. Pine and hardwood trees comprise the 46,000-acre national forest. The Yadkin, Pee Dee, and Uwharrie Rivers and Badin Lake are all near this area and offer excellent water recreational activities.

Indians were the earliest inhabitants of this region. During the 1700s, European immigrants explored and settled within the "haunted" Uwharrie Mountains. Numerous ghost stories about the Uwharries were passed down through the generations by those early settlers and are preserved in a book entitled *Ghost Tales of the Uwharries* by Fred T. Morgan. (John F. Blair, Publisher, 1406 Plaza Drive, Winston-Salem, NC 27103-1470, (336) 768-1374 or 1-800-222-9796; $7.95.)

The Uwharries were also popular for loggers and miners. Mining for gold, silver, lead and zinc in its ridges began after the discovery of gold near this region in 1799. The slate belts of Cabarrus City were among the first gold mines in America.

OTHER ACTIVITIES: hiking, fishing, hunting, camping, boating, canoeing, picnicking, mountain biking

NEAREST CITIES/FACILITIES: Troy, Asheboro, Albemarle

Drinking water is available at Badin Lake Campground and Uwharrie Hunt Camp within Uwharrie National Forest.

4B Farm is a privately-owned and operated equestrian campground adjacent to Uwharrie National Forest near Eldorado. It is located off Mullinix Rd (SR-1154) on the right before the forest service's horse camp within Uwharrie. Larry and Helen Blackburn are the owners of 4B Farm and can be contacted at 346 Mullinix Rd, Troy, NC 27371; telephone (910) 572-CAMP or (910) 572-BARN for fees and more information.

Facilities offered include camping, electric hookup, and a heated bathhouse with separate men's and women's restrooms that contain flush toilets, three shower stalls, and have electricity. Horses can be boarded overnight either in box stalls, a round pen, ring, or you may choose to tie your horse to the trailer. A current negative Coggins test is required and no alcoholic beverages are allowed. Please call ahead to reserve horse stalls.

Eldorado Outpost is located 0.7 mile south of Mullinix Rd (SR-1154) on NC-109. Groceries, gas, horse tack, hunting and fishing supplies, antiques/crafts, and a restaurant are available here. Hitching posts are located near the store for riders to tie their horses up. Future plans call for a trail to be cut from the store/restaurant to 4B Farm, allowing riders to travel cross-country and stay off the highway. Eldorado Outpost can be reached at (910) 572-FISH (3474).

Morrow Mountain State Park is located on the west side of the Pee Dee River and offers 15 miles of horseback riding (no horse camping).

CHAPTER 7

NATIONAL PARKS

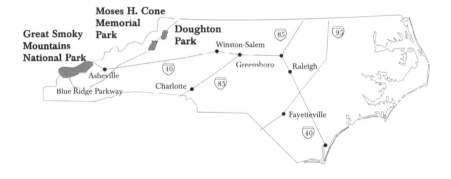

BLUE RIDGE PARKWAY

The Blue Ridge Parkway is a 469-mile scenic highway built along the crest of the Blue Ridge Mountains in western North Carolina and Virginia providing beautiful views of the mountains, highland meadows and valleys. It is managed by the National Park Service and joins the Great Smoky Mountains National Park in North Carolina to the Shenandoah National Park in Virginia. This area is rich in history and folklore of the early settlers that lived in the Blue Ridge Mountains.

There are several bridle trails located near the Blue Ridge Parkway, most of which are included in the national forests. Horseback riding is not permitted along the Parkway. The areas of the Parkway allowing horseback riding within park boundaries are Moses H. Cone Memorial Park and Doughton Park. Near Blowing Rock at Blue Ridge Parkway milepost 294, Moses Cone has beautiful, wide carriage roads through the gorgeous Blue Ridge Mountains. Blowing Rock Stables is located nearby and provides an excellent equine facility offering guided trail rides on rental horses within the park. Overnight camping and boarding of your own mount is also permitted at this stable.

Doughton Park is a scenic area of high mountain bluffs and forested foothill coves located between Sparta and North Wilkesboro. Horseback riding is allowed along a service road within the park that climbs to a mountaintop and ends upon reaching the Parkway. There are no other bridle trails although the park has several miles of hiking trails.

More general information concerning the Blue Ridge Parkway may be obtained at: Superintendent, Blue Ridge Parkway, 700 Northwestern Plaza, Asheville, NC 28801; (828) 259-0701. To report fires, accidents, and emergencies call 1-800-PARKWATCH (1-800-727-5928). Exploring these two very different areas of the Blue Ridge Mountains on horseback is exciting and fun. Both parks provide an excellent place to ride in addition to outstanding scenery and wildlife.

DOUGHTON PARK

County: Wilkes

Address: District Ranger, Rt. 1, Box 263
Laurel Springs, NC 28644
Telephone: (336) 372-8568

LOCATION: The main park entrance and information center is located on the Blue Ridge Parkway at milepost 241.1. However, the bridle trailhead is on the southeastern side of the park on gravel road SR-1730 (Longbottom Road). From the west entrance of Stone Mountain State Park it is 5.5 miles west and from Absher the trailhead is 2.5 miles west.

The gated Grassy Gap Fire Road (trailhead) is located on the northwest side of Longbottom Rd (SR-1730) near the Basin Creek bridge. Horse trailers may be parked along the side of Longbottom Rd. A parking area is also located directly across from the trailhead on the southeastern side of Longbottom Rd. However this area is designated as a hunters' primitive campground. It is regulated by the N.C. Wildlife Resources Commission and not by Doughton Park or the National Park Service. It is gated and subject to being closed without notice at any time.

SEASON: open daily year round

FACILITY REVIEW
TYPE: day use only
HORSE CAMPING FACILITIES: none
RESTROOMS: none
DAY RIDERS FEE: none
PARK ENTRANCE FEE: none

TRAIL REVIEW
TRAIL NAME: Grassy Gap Trail (also called Grassy Gap Fire Road; this area is commonly referred to as "Basin Creek")
TYPE: marked
TERRAIN: rolling hills-mountainous
DIFFICULTY: moderate
LENGTH: 6.5 miles (one-way)
WATER: yes
TRAIL MAP: Doughton Park Trails
TRAIL NOTES: Grassy Gap Trail is actually an old roadbed through dense forests and coves leading to the top of a mountain. It is used as a service road by

the park rangers. The wide trail begins on the northwest side of SR-1730 (Longbottom Rd) at a gated road.

It climbs from a valley and follows along Basin Creek for approximately 1.5 miles. The trail passes Basin Cove primitive campsite for backpackers on the left. Proceed up the trail and pass trailheads for two hikers' paths (Basin Creek and Bluff Ridge) on the right. The trail curves to the left and begins to follow alongside Cove Creek. Grassy Gap Trail continues for five more miles on a winding road up the mountain ridge. It crosses the Bluff Mountain Trail (hikers only) before reaching the mountaintop and its terminus at the Blue Ridge Parkway. Horseback riders must backtrack to the trailhead.

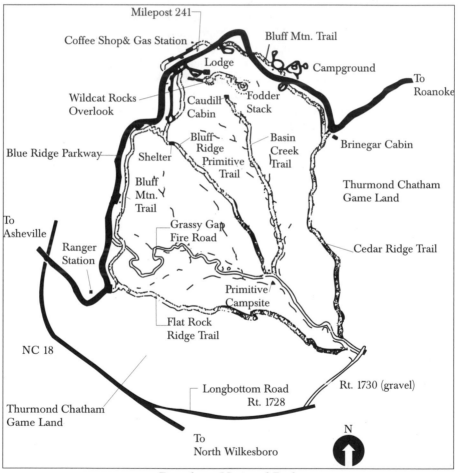

Doughton National Park
Reprinted courtesy of The National Park Service

View of Doughton Park from the Blue Ridge Parkway

RULES/REQUIREMENTS: No horses are permitted on the numerous hiking trails that connect to Grassy Gap Trail. No horse camping is allowed at Basin Cove backpacker's primitive campground located along the trail.

HIGHLIGHTS: dense forests and mountain flora, mountain streams and cascades, a good area to view deer and other wildlife

GENERAL/HISTORICAL NOTES: Doughton Park is named for Robert L. Doughton, a congressman in the mid 1900s. He introduced into Congress the bill for the development of the Blue Ridge Parkway. Doughton was a strong supporter of the scenic highway.

The 6,000-acre Doughton Park is an area noted for its highland meadows, mountain bluffs, and coves. Two pioneer cabins, the Brinegar Cabin and the Caudill Cabin, are located within the park along hiking trails and provide excellent examples of mountain culture. On the north side of the Grassy Gap Trail near the junction of the Bluff Ridge Trail and Basin Creek Trail (across from Basin Cove primitive campsite) stands a tombstone marker for Alice Caudill. She was a 15 year old child-bride who drowned in a major flood in this area in 1916.

OTHER ACTIVITIES: hiking, backpacking, backpack camping, trout fishing

NEAREST CITIES/FACILITIES: Elkin, State Road, Sparta, and North Wilkesboro

McGrady Grocery Store is located 4.9 miles east on Longbottom Road (SR-1737). The west entrance to Stone Mountain State Park is 5.5 miles east on Longbottom Road and offers additional bridle trails. Thurmond Chatham game lands are also located adjacent to the park. See the chapter "North Carolina Game Lands" for more information on horseback riding within the game lands.

MOSES H. CONE MEMORIAL PARK

County: Watauga

Stables: Blowing Rock Stables   Owner: Carl Underwood
Address: P.O. Box 26 Blowing Rock, NC 28605
Telephone: Stables: (828) 295-7847
Park information: (828) 295-3782; Ranger office: (828) 295-7591 In case of emergency call 1-800-PARKWAY

LOCATION: From Boone, take US-321 South to Blowing Rock. Turn right onto US-321 Business in Blowing Rock and go to US-221. Turn right onto US-221 and go for 2 miles. Look for the "Blowing Rock Stables" sign. Stables are on the left on Laurel Lane. Horsemen using the park for day use often park alongside US-221 near Laurel Lane and the Bass Lake entrance for quicker access to the trails. Day use parking is also allowed at Blowing Rock Stables. Main park entrance to the Cone Manor house is on the Blue Ridge Parkway at milepost 294.

SEASON: open daily year round   Horse rentals: April-December

FACILITY REVIEW
TYPE: day use and/or overnight horse camping (camping is permitted at Blowing Rock Stables but is prohibited within Moses Cone Park)
HORSE CAMPING FACILITIES: modern (electrical and water hookups)
CAMPING FEE: $4.00/night
HOT SHOWERS: yes (at barn)

Moses Cone Manor House

RESTROOMS: flush toilets (at barn)
STABLE FACILITIES: 365 box stalls
STABLING FEE: $6.00/night
DAY RIDERS FEE: $5.00/day (if parking truck and trailer at Blowing Rock Stables)
PARK ENTRANCE FEE: none

TRAIL REVIEW
TRAIL NAMES and DESCRIPTIONS: (one-way mileages)
1. Rich Mountain Carriage Road: 4.3 miles/moderate
2. Flat Top Mountain Carriage Road: 3.0 miles/moderate
3. Watkins Carriage Road: 3.3 miles/easy-moderate
4. Black Bottom Carriage Road: 0.5 mile/easy
5. Bass Lake Carriage Road: 1.7 miles/easy
6. Deer Park Carriage Road: 0.8 mile/moderate
7. Maze Carriage Road: 2.3 miles/moderate
8. Duncan Carriage Road: 2.5 miles/moderate
9. Rock Creek Bridge Carriage: 1.0 mile/easy
10. Trout Lake Trail: 1.0 mile loop/easy

TYPE: mapped; guided trail rides on rental horses ($15.00/hour)
TERRAIN: rolling hills-hilly
DIFFICULTY: easy-moderate
LENGTH: 27 miles
WATER: yes
TRAIL MAP: Cone Park Carriage Trails
TRAIL NOTES: Wide carriage roads provide great views of the Blue Ridge Mountains and valleys in this 3,500-acre park. These trails form a variety of loops, connecting paths and backtracking trips through woods, highland meadows and around a lake. Also included are moderate climbs to mountaintops that are occasionally rocky in the higher elevations. These are excellent trails for the novice horse and rider.

A favorite trail is the Flat Top Mountain Trail. It gradually ascends to a beautiful, view-filled meadow and the Cone family gravesite. The trail continues on to reenter the forest and climb its way through switchbacks to the forested summit of Flat Top Mountain. A fire tower is located here and provides good views of the surrounding countryside.

RULES/REQUIREMENTS: Blowing Rock Stables requires a negative Coggins test within the past twelve months. You must call ahead and make reservations for trail rides on rental horses. Minimum age for riders on rental horses is at least 9 years. No reservations are required for day use of the park's trails. However, if planning to camp overnight at the stables, it is wise to phone ahead and reserve stall space.

Park rules are as follows: Horses must be kept at a slow walk when passing hikers, joggers and skiers. Do not tie horses to the fence in front of Cone Manor house. No camping, littering, swimming, intoxication, disorderly conduct, or fires are allowed within the park boundaries. Stay on the designated trails and do not take shortcuts. Do not remove or destroy any natural or historical objects. Horses should always be kept under physical control and pets must be kept on a leash.

HIGHLIGHTS: excellent views of the Blue Ridge Mountains with a combination of meadows and mountains, wildlife, good family-type atmosphere

Above: Flat Top Mountain Trail
Below: Blowing Rock Stables

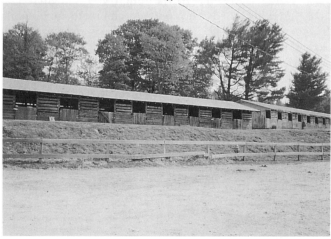

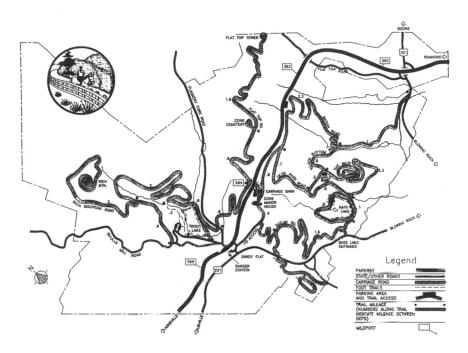

Moses H. Cone Memorial Park
Reprinted courtesy of The National Park Service

GENERAL/HISTORICAL NOTES: Moses Cone Memorial Park is supervised by the National Park Service. Blowing Rock Stables is a privately operated stable near the park that offers guided trail rides on rental horses into the park boundaries. The park was once the estate and summer home of Moses H. Cone, a textile pioneer from Greensboro, North Carolina. Cone's hobbies included tending acres of apple orchards and building miles of carriage roads throughout his property.

The Park Service received the land in 1950 as a donation from the Cone family for use as a public "pleasuring ground." The Manor House is located on a mountainside overlooking a beautiful valley and the 22-acre Bass Lake. It now serves as a craft center for the Southern Highlands Handicraft Guild. An old carriage barn with hitching rails is located northeast of the house.

OTHER ACTIVITIES: hiking, jogging, cross-country skiing, craft center at the Manor House

NEAREST CITIES/FACILITIES: Blowing Rock, Boone

GREAT SMOKY MOUNTAINS NATIONAL PARK

The Great Smoky Mountains National Park lies in western North Carolina and eastern Tennessee. The Cherokee Indians, the first inhabitants of this vast land, called the region "Shaconage" which means "Land of the Blue Smoke." The Smoky Mountains received its name from the smoky haze sometimes covering the mountain ridges. Although many mountains in other areas of the world also have haze around them, none has a thicker covering than the Great Smokies due to the large amount of rainfall and the millions of trees and shrubs within the park. The vast vegetation gives off water vapor and oil into the atmosphere that seems to cling to the mountain peaks.

The park is truly a natural wonder including great forests, heath balds with gorgeous views, beautiful waterfalls and mountain streams, awesome displays of wildflowers and shrubs, and an abundance of wildlife. As you travel from the lower to the higher elevations within the park, the plant life changes due to the temperature difference. In the high elevations, Canadian types of vegetation and birds can be seen. Because of this change in plant and animal life, traveling from the foothills to the crest of the Smokies is similar to traveling from Georgia to Canada.

Within the park are sixteen mountain peaks more than 6,000 feet high. Many streams and creeks flow down from these ridges into the foothills and valleys, called "coves." It is here that the history of the Appalachian pioneers comes alive. Remnants of their mountain culture can still be seen today through the few homesteads and old buildings that have been preserved by the Park Service. A favorite area of the Smokies is a 4,000-acre valley within Tennessee called Cades Cove. This valley and the Cataloochee Valley in the North Carolina side of the park are two of the prettiest sections in the Smoky Mountains. Horseback riding in these areas provides a memorable experience. In addition to the old pioneer homesteads found in the two valleys, wildlife is more often seen there than anywhere else in the Smokies.

The national park is a wildlife and nature preserve with more than fifty species of mammals living within its boundaries. Hunting and firearms are not allowed in the Great Smokies, but fishing is permitted in the several hundred miles of mountain streams. Bears are numerous and frequently encountered, more often than anywhere else in the state. Be wary and take the necessary precautions. Refer to the chapter entitled "Safety Guidelines." The park's trail map contains information regarding bears, and a diagram depicting the proper way to store your food when camping. The proper storage of food is essential to discourage bears. Violators are subject to a heavy fine.

The Smoky Mountains consist of over 520,000 acres, approximately 800 square miles of protected land. It is the most popular park in America with more than eight million visitors each year. Managed by the National Park Service, a division of the U.S. Department of the Interior, the park is open daily year-round.

During the wintertime, bad weather may cause the closing of some mountain roads.

Congress authorized the formation of this national park in 1926. Through the combination of state, federal and private funding, the park was officially dedicated in 1940 by President Franklin D. Roosevelt. Civilian Conservation Corps operated several camps in the Smoky Mountains during the 1930s. Their work included the building of visitor facilities and the upgrading or rerouting of many trails from old railroad grades and roads that were formerly used by logging companies.

Hikers and backpackers are allowed use of all trails but horseback riding is limited to designated trails. Currently, there are more than 850 miles of hiking trails in the entire park, and over 350 miles of trails in the North Carolina side permit horse travel. The bridle trails vary greatly in terrain, from old roadbeds in bottomlands and forested coves to steep climbs along mountain ridges. Due to the frequent rainfall and large amount of horse traffic, areas of some trails are boggy. Muddy going and hilly climbs are not uncommon.

Trails in the Great Smokies are marked with signs. However, park rangers report a high incidence of vandalism of these signs so do not rely on the trails to always be well-marked. Be sure to carry a trail map and compass whenever traveling in the Smoky Mountains.

The guidelines in the chapter "Rules and Regulations" should be followed while enjoying this scenic recreational area. Specific rules and regulations regarding horse use and camping in the park can be obtained from the Backcountry Reservations Office by calling (423) 436-1231. Office hours are from 8 a.m. to 6 p.m. seven days a week. A trail map and informational brochure can also be requested.

There are three types of horse camping within the park: auto access horse camps, backcountry campsites and shelters. Five auto access horse camps are available offering convenient, drive-in camping areas and easy access to the backcountry trails. They are usually open seasonally from April to November. Call the Backcountry Reservations Office to make reservations for the auto access horse camps since open spaces are filled on a "first-come, first-served" basis. If you do not have reservations, you must contact a ranger before setting up camp. Maximum stay is seven consecutive nights. Self-pay stations are located at each horse camp where a $2.00 per day stall fee is required.

The backcountry areas (campsites and shelters) are open all year. A backcountry use permit must be obtained if you are camping overnight. This is to help protect the park's natural resources, as well as contributing to your own personal safety. You can self-register for the free permit at any ranger station or visitor center. However, you must also make advance reservations with the Backcountry Reservations Office if you plan to use any of the rationed backcountry campsites and shelters.

The backcountry campsites are designated tent camping areas usually located within the woods along the backcountry trails. The shelters are lean-tos made of

Reprinted courtesy of The National Park Service

82

stone located along the Appalachian Trail. They usually have bunks for the overnight campers and are made bearproof with the use of wire. Pit toilets may be found at most shelters.

Camping is only allowed in designated areas. Anyone found camping in the backcountry at an undesignated site and without a registration permit is subject to a fine. Camping parties are limited to a maximum of eight people. Reservations for all three types of horse camping can be made one month in advance of your trip. If there are any changes in your plans, you must contact the Backcountry Reservations Office at least one week before arrival date. Refunds are not available. You may camp no longer than three consecutive nights at the same backcountry campsite and only one night at a shelter.

Hitching racks are available at most campsites that permit horses. If stalls are full or not available, cross tie your horse between trees but do not tie directly to trees. Keep horses out of the sleeping and cooking areas of the campsites and away from the trail shelters. Be sure to clean out the stalls and haul manure and excess hay to a designated area when breaking camp. In the backcountry, manure should be scattered away from the campsites. All livestock feed and hay must be packed in and out of the backcountry. Grazing is not allowed.

Other rules include the use of fires only in designated areas of the campsites. Do not damage trees or vegetation in any way. Open containers of alcohol are prohibited except in campsites. Keep your camp clean and do not leave trash, especially metal and glass, in the fireplace. Pack out all trash or place it in receptacles where provided. The horse camps allow pets but they must be kept on a leash no longer than six feet. Pets are prohibited in the backcountry.

Horses must stay on bridle trails only and are not permitted on hiking trails. However, hikers are permitted on all bridle trails. Horseback riders should be courteous and pass hikers at a slow walk. Keep horses under physical control at all times.

The Appalachian National Scenic Trail is a 2,100-mile hiking trail from Maine to Georgia, passing through the Great Smokies along the way. It is the second-longest footpath in the world. The trail is maintained by private clubs including the National Park Service, U.S. Forest Service and the Appalachian Trail Conference. Seventy-one miles of the Appalachian Trail is in the Great Smoky Mountains National Park and horse travel is permitted on 35 miles. The portions of the trail allowing horseback travel are listed in the appropriate Great Smoky Mountains National Park area of this book.

Several horseback riding stables are located near the park that offer guided trail rides into the Great Smokies on rental horses. See the "Riding Stables Within Great Smoky Mountains National Park" section for a listing of contacts. Call for hourly rates, seasonal dates and more details. There are three visitor centers within the park: Cades Cove in Tennessee, Sugarlands near Gatlinburg, Tennessee, and Oconaluftee near Cherokee, North Carolina. For any additional general park information the headquarters office can be contacted at: GSMNP, Gatlinburg, TN 37738; telephone: (423) 436-5615.

GREAT SMOKY MOUNTAINS NATIONAL PARK

HORSE CAMPS, BACKCOUNTRY CAMPSITES AND SHELTERS
(maximum rationed capacities are in parentheses)

NORTH CAROLINA

Cataloochee/Big Creek Area
2 Auto Access Horse Camps:
    Big Creek Area (20 horses)
    Cataloochee Area (28 horses)

BCC #36-Upper Walnut Bottoms (20 horses)
BCC #39-Pretty Hollow
BCC #41-Caldwell Fork
BCC #42-Spruce Mountain
Cosby Knob Shelter (12 horses)
Davenport Gap Shelter (12 horses)

Oconaluftee Area
2 Auto Access Horse Camps:
    Round Bottom (20 horses)
    Towstring (20 horses)

BCC #44-McGhee Spring
BCC #49-Cabin Flats
BCC #50-Lower Chasteen Creek (15 horses)
Pecks Corner Shelter (12 horses)
Laurel Gap Shelter (14 horses)
Tricorner Knob Shelter (12 horses)
Kephart Shelter (14 horses)

Deep Creek Area
BCC #52-Newton Bald
BCC #55-Pole Road (15 horses)
BCC #56-Burnt Spruce
BCC #57-Bryson Place (12 horses)

BCC #58-Nicks Nest Branch
BCC #60-Bumgardner Branch

Noland Creek Area
BCC #61-Bald Creek (6 horses)
BCC #62-Upper Ripskin
BCC #63-Jerry Flats
BCC #64-Mill Creek
BCC #65-Bear Pen Branch
BCC #67-Goldmine Branch

Forney Creek Area
BCC #70-Jonas Creek
BCC #71-CCC (12 horses)
BCC #73-Bear Creek
Silers Bald Shelter (12 horses)

Hazel Creek Area
BCC #81-North Shore
BCC #82-Calhoun
BCC #83-Bone Valley (10 horses)
BCC #85-Sawdust Pile
BCC #86-Proctor

Twentymile Area
BCC #88-Pinnacle Creek
BCC #90-Lost Cove
BCC #91-Upper Lost Cove
BCC #92-Upper Flats
BCC #95-Dalton Branch
Birch Spring Gap Shelter (12 horses)
Mollies Ridge Shelter (12 horses)
Russell Field Shelter (14 horses)
Spence Field Shelter (12 horses)

Chambers Creek Area
BCC #76-Kirkland Creek
BCC #77-Pilkey Creek
BCC #98-Chambers Creek

TENNESSEE

Cades Cove Area
Auto Access Horse Camp:
    Anthony Creek (12 horses)

BCC #1-Cooper Road
BCC #3-Hesse Creek
BCC #4-Kelly Gap
BCC #7-Ace Gap
BCC #9-Anthony Creek
BCC #10-Ledbetter Ridge (8 horses)
BCC #11-Beard Cane
BCC #13-Sheep Pen Gap (8 horses)
BCC #14-Flint Gap
BCC #15-Rabbit Creek

Elkmont/Tremont Area
BCC #18-West Prong
BCC #19-Upper Henderson
BCC #20-King Branch
BCC #27-Lower Jakes Gap
BCC #28-Marks Cove

Greenbrier/Cosby Area
BCC #35-Gilliland Creek

RIDING STABLES WITHIN
GREAT SMOKY MOUNTAINS NATIONAL PARK

1. Cades Cove Stables
    Cades Cove Area in Tennessee
    (423) 448-6286

2. Cosby Stables (near Cosby Campground)
    Rt. 2
    Newport, TN 37821
    (423) 623-6981

3. Deep Creek Riding Stables
    P.O. Box 1096
    Bryson City, NC 28713
    (828) 488-2681

4. McCarter's Riding Stables
    Newfound Gap Road
    Gatlinburg, TN 37738
    (423) 436-5354
    located 1.5 miles from Gatlinburg on US-441 South near Sugarlands
    Visitor Center; open early spring to late fall

5. Smokemont Riding Stables
    P.O. Box 72
    Cherokee, NC 28719
    (828) 497-2373
    located on US-441 (Newfound Gap Highway) near Smokemont
    Campground in the Oconaluftee Area, five miles north of Cherokee

6. Smoky Mountain Stables
    Box 26
    Gatlinburg, TN 37738
    (423) 436-5634
    located on TN-321 near Gatlinburg, four miles from traffic light #3; open
    daily dawn to dusk from mid-March through Nov.

OTHER RIDING STABLES NEAR
THE GREAT SMOKIES AREA

1. Cataloochee Ranch
   Rt. 1, Box 500F
   Maggie Valley, NC 28751
   (828) 926-1401 or 1-800-868-1401; Barn: (828) 926-8700

2. Fontana Riding Stables
   Fontana Dam, NC 28733
   (828) 479-8911 or 1-800-849-2258 ext. 272

3. Hemphill Mountain Campground
   Waynesville, NC 28786
   (828) 926-0331

4. Nantahala Village Riding Stables
   Rt. 1, Box 67
   Bryson City, NC 28713
   (828) 488-9649

CATALOOCHEE/BIG CREEK AREA

County: Haywood

Address: Cataloochee Ranger Station, GSMNP
Rt. 2, Box 555, Waynesville, NC 28786

Big Creek Ranger Station, GSMNP
Star Rt., Newport, TN 37821

Telephone: Cataloochee Ranger Station-no telephone
Big Creek Ranger Station (828) 486-5910

LOCATION: Cataloochee: A winding gravel road is the main access to this remote area of the GSMNP. From I-40 (Exit 20) in Cove Creek, take US-276. The first paved road on the right is Little Cove Rd (SR-1331). Turn here and go 1.3 miles, following the signs to Cove Creek Missionary Church. The road becomes gravel past the church and is Old NC-284, also named Cataloochee Rd (SR-1395). It is 4.5 miles to Cove Creek Gap at the park boundary. Go 1.8 miles to a paved road and turn left (the Big Creek area is 16 miles ahead and can be accessed by continuing on this winding road). Go 2.7 miles and veer left across the Cataloochee Creek bridge. It is 0.7 mile to the Cataloochee Ranger Station. The horse camp is approximately one mile beyond the ranger station on the right.

Big Creek: From Interstate-40 near the NC state line at Waterville, take exit #451. Cross the Pigeon River bridge and turn left onto Waterville Rd (SR-1332). This road passes through the Waterville community and eventually turns to gravel. Go 2 miles to a junction with Old NC-284 Rd, also called Mt. Sterling Rd (SR-1397; the Cataloochee area can be accessed by turning left here and following this gravel road south for 16 miles). The ranger station is straight across the road in 0.2 mile. The horse camp is on the right one mile past the ranger station.

SEASON: open daily year round
auto access horse camps open April-November

FACILITY REVIEW
TYPE: day use and/or overnight horse camping
HORSE CAMPING FACILITIES: auto access primitive horse camps and backcountry camping
    Cataloochee Horse Camp-limit of 28 horses
    Big Creek Horse Camp-limit of 20 horses

CAMPING FEE: none; reservations recommended for camps, free permit required for backcountry camping
HOT SHOWERS: none
RESTROOMS: Cataloochee-pit privy
    Big Creek-flush and pit toilets
OTHER FACILITIES: Big Creek-grills, picnic tables, pay telephone
STABLE FACILITIES: hitching racks
STABLING FEE: $2.00/day in auto access horse camps
DAY RIDERS FEE: none

TRAIL REVIEW
TRAIL NAMES and DESCRIPTIONS:
1. Big Creek: 5 miles/moderate; connects to #2,5/BCC #36

2. Low Gap: 2.5 miles in NC (2.5 miles in TN goes to Greenbrier/Cosby Area and ranger station)/moderate; connects to #1,4,AT/BCC #36

3. Appalachian Trail: 16.3 miles/moderate-difficult/continues into Oconaluftee Area; connects to #2,4 and trails in Oconaluftee Area/Davenport Gap Shelter, Cosby Knob Shelter

4. Camel Gap: 5 miles/moderate; connects to #1,2,AT/BCC #36 at junction of Trails #1,2,4

5. Swallow Fork: 4 miles/difficult; connects to #1,6,8

6. Mount Sterling Ridge: 5.4 miles/difficult; connects to #5,7,8,11 and Balsam Mountain Trail in Oconaluftee Area

7. Mount Sterling Trail: 1.8 miles/difficult; connects to #6,11

8. Pretty Hollow Gap: 5.3 miles/difficult; connects to #5,6,9,10 and the Cataloochee Rd/BCC #39

9. Palmer Creek: 3.3 miles/difficult; connects to #8,10 and to Balsam Mountain Rd on its western end

10. Little Cataloochee: 5.2 miles/moderate; connects to #9,11

11. Long Bunk: 3.7 miles/moderate; connects to #6,7,10

12. Rough Fork: 6.5 miles/difficult; connects to #13,15,17; its northern trailhead is located near #15

13. Polls Gap: 5.5 miles/difficult; connects to #12,17/BCC #42

14. Caldwell Fork: 6.5 miles/moderate; connects to #12,15,16,17 BCC #41

15. Big Fork Ridge: 3.1 miles/moderate; connects to #14,16; its northern trailhead is located near #12

16. McKee Branch: 2.3 miles/difficult; connects to #14,15,18

17. Hemphill Bald: 8.5 miles/moderate; connects to #12,13,14,18

18. Cataloochee Divide: 6.4 miles/moderate; connects to #16,17

TYPE: mapped
TERRAIN: mountainous
DIFFICULTY: moderate-difficult
LENGTH: 96+ miles combined
WATER: yes
TRAIL MAP: Great Smoky Mountains Trail Map
TRAIL NOTES: These trails follow old railroad grades, logging and jeep roads through forests, ridges and valleys on the park's eastern side. Balsam Mountain Range lies between the Cataloochee/Big Creek Areas and the Oconaluftee Area.

Big Creek Trail (#1) follows an old railbed as it goes to Walnut Bottoms, an old logging camp. Low Gap Trail (#2) junctions with Big Creek Trail near Walnut Bottoms. It leads northwest up the mountain ridge to where it crosses over the Appalachian Trail. This trail can be followed for another 2.5 miles into the Cosby Area of Tennessee.

The Appalachian Trail (#3) follows the crest of the Smokies and crisscrosses the NC-TN state line several times as it passes through the national park. The portion of the AT within the Big Creek and Oconaluftee Areas allows horse travel and consists of 21.6 miles of trail. Various combinations of loop trails can be made by including the AT since it junctions with a few trails in these two areas of the park.

Camel Gap Trail (#4) begins beyond the junction of Big Creek Trail (#1) and Low Gap Trail (#2). It proceeds in a broad U-shape to join with the AT near Camel Gap and offers scenic views of the valley. Swallow Fork Trail (#5) leads south from the Big Creek Trail. It ascends Mount Sterling Ridge on its way to a junction with Mount Sterling Ridge Trail (#6) and Pretty Hollow Gap Trail (#7) in Pretty Hollow Gap.

Pretty Hollow Gap Trail goes south from here as it descends Mount Sterling Ridge and follows along Pretty Hollow Creek. It is a major connector trail between the Big Creek and Cataloochee Areas. After 4 miles on Pretty Hollow Gap Trail, Palmer Creek Trail (#9) branches off to the right. Palmer Creek Trail goes west 3.3 miles to its end on Balsam Mountain Rd (also called Straight Fork

Rd). One-half mile further on Pretty Hollow Gap Trail is the trailhead for Little Cataloochee Trail (#10). Pretty Hollow Gap Trail continues on for 0.8 mile towards the Cataloochee Horse Camp and its southern trailhead on the Cataloochee Road.

Mount Sterling Ridge Trail (#6) goes west along Big Cataloochee Mountain (elev. 6,122 ft) from its junction at Pretty Hollow Gap with Swallow Fork Trail and Pretty Hollow Gap Trail. At 4.0 miles, it connects with the Balsam Mountain Trail in the Oconaluftee Area. To the northeast, the trail begins the ascent to the summit of Mount Sterling Ridge (elev. 5,835 ft). Near the end of the trail is an open grassy area where Mount Sterling Trail (#7) bears off to the right. Follow Mount Sterling Ridge Trail (#6) for another 0.3 mile to the Mount Sterling firetower on the summit of Mount Sterling. Beyond here is the beginning of the hiking trail, Baxter Creek, where horse travel is not permitted. Backtrack 0.3 miles to the junction with Mount Sterling Trail (#7).

Mount Sterling Trail is an old jeep road that descends the ridge on its way to end on gravel road Old NC 284 at Mount Sterling Gap. At 0.5 mile before the end of Mount Sterling Trail, Long Bunk Trail (#11) begins on the right. It leads south paralleling Old NC-284 along the way to junction with Little Cataloochee Trail (#10). Little Cataloochee Trail goes east from here for 1 mile to its end at graveled road Old NC-284. Going west on Little Cataloochee Trail at the junction leads to the Little Cataloochee Valley. Remnants of former settlements still exist today and can be seen along the trail. Little Cataloochee Trail proceeds past Noland Mountain and crosses over Davidson Gap on its way to Big Cataloochee and a junction with Pretty Hollow Gap Trail (#8).

Rough Fork Trail (#12) begins from a gated road at the end of the gravel Cataloochee Road west of the Cataloochee Ranger Station. It leads southwest into the Cataloochee Valley along Big Fork Ridge. After 3 miles, Caldwell Fork Trail (#14) branches off to the east. Rough Fork Trail continues on from here for 3.5 miles to junction with Polls Gap Trail (#13).

Polls Gap Trail goes north from here for 5.5 miles on its way to the top of Spruce Mountain (elev. 5,590 ft) and the old Spruce Mountain firetower. The trail dead-ends here and horseback riders must backtrack.

Caldwell Fork Trail (#14) goes east from the junction with Rough Fork Trail. At 1.7 miles, Hemphill Bald Trail (#17) begins on the right and goes for 3.0 miles to Double Gap and the park boundary. Hemphill Bald Trail continues south from Double Gap for 5.5 miles and Cataloochee Divide Trail (#18) goes north for 6.4 miles. Hemphill Bald Trail and Cataloochee Divide Trail follow the Cataloochee Divide and the park's southeastern boundary. Hemphill Bald (elev. 5,540 ft) offers great views of this area.

At the junction of Caldwell Fork Trail and Hemphill Bald Trail, Caldwell Fork Trail continues northeast. At 1.5 miles is a junction with McKee Branch Trail (#16) on the right. McKee Branch Trail leads southeast for 2.3 miles to Purchase Gap and a junction with Cataloochee Divide Trail (#18).

Continue on Caldwell Fork Trail for 150 yards to a junction with Big Fork Ridge Trail (#15) to the west. Caldwell Fork Trail goes north from here for 3.3 miles to its end on the Cataloochee Road near the Cataloochee campground. Big Fork Ridge Trail crosses over Big Fork Ridge as it proceeds for 3.1 miles to its end on the gravel Cataloochee Road. The northern trailhead for Rough Fork Trail (#12) is also just ahead to the left.

HIGHLIGHTS: several options for various combinations of loop trails, beautiful mountain ridges and valleys, pioneer history and old settlements, wildlife, nice forests

GENERAL/HISTORICAL NOTES: Cataloochee is a Cherokee word meaning "waves of mountains or ridges" and represents the terrain of this area. This is a remote, peaceful area of the GSMNP, consisting of 29 square miles of valley and forest. It is an excellent area to view wildlife, especially deer.

The Cherokee once roamed this land while hunting and fishing. White settlers began to move into the area in the early 1800s. Their population reached 1,200 people in the early 1900s, the largest community within the park. More than 200 buildings were once located in this valley. A few of the early settlers' homesites, cabins, barns and churches still exist along the trails near the Cataloochee area.

Noland Mountain, located near Little Cataloochee Trail, separates Big Cataloochee from Little Cataloochee. The Little Cataloochee Valley was also once inhabited by settlers. Hemphill Bald Trail and Cataloochee Divide Trail were once the pathway over the mountains for the settlers to reach Maggie Valley.

OTHER ACTIVITIES: hiking, backpacking, camping, fishing

NEAREST CITIES/FACILITIES: Waterville, Maggie Valley, Newport, Tennessee

Smoky Mtn. Outfitters is located at Waterville, NC, adjacent to the park boundary near the Big Creek Area. They offer a completely-furnished cabin (sleeps 6 people) and a 5-stall barn for rental by the day, weekend, or week. You can bring your own horses or they will provide them for guided or unguided trail riding into the Smokies. Trout fishing and bear hunting are also available through them. Call (828) 648-2313 or (828) 646-8934 or 1-800-532-4631 for more information or to make reservations.

Cataloochee Ranch is a guest ranch/resort near Maggie Valley that offers guided trail rides on rental horses and pack trips into the GSMNP. No personal horses or private camping is allowed. Call 1-800-868-1401 or (828) 926-1401 for more information.

CHAMBERS CREEK AREA

County: Swain

Address: Deep Creek Ranger Station, GSMNP
970 Park Rd. Bryson City, NC 28713
Telephone: (828) 488-3184

LOCATION: The Lakeshore Trail is accessed only from trails in other areas. Eastern access is from the trails in the Noland Creek and Forney Creek Areas. Western access is from trails in the Twentymile and Hazel Creek Areas. See these areas for more information. The nearest vehicle access is by taking Lakeview Drive (SR-1364; also called Fontana Rd) from Bryson City (see Noland Creek Area).

SEASON: open daily year round

FACILITY REVIEW
TYPE: day use and/or overnight horse camping
HORSE CAMPING FACILITIES: backcountry camping
CAMPING FEE: none; free permit required
HOT SHOWERS: none
RESTROOMS: none
STABLE FACILITIES: hitching racks
STABLING FEE: none
DAY RIDERS FEE: none

TRAIL REVIEW
TRAIL NAME: Lakeshore Trail
TYPE: mapped
TERRAIN: hilly-mountainous
DIFFICULTY: moderate
LENGTH: 12.9 miles (in this area; continues for 28.6 miles into other areas)
WATER: yes
TRAIL MAP: Great Smoky Mountains Trail Map
TRAIL NOTES: The Lakeshore Trail's eastern trailhead is in the Noland Creek Area near the gate at the end of Lakeview Drive. Go 5.2 miles west (3.8 miles if traveling the Tunnel Trail), passing through Forney Creek Area along the way. Near BCC #74 (for hikers only), the Lakeshore Trail leads west along old roads that weave through the forest and along coves and low ridges. It generally follows the northern Fontana Lake shoreline.

BCC #76, 77 and 98 allow backcountry camping with horses and are located along the trail within the Chambers Creek Area. Views of Fontana Lake are the best along this stretch of trail where the backcountry campsites are located. After BCC #77, the Lakeshore Trail continues west into Hazel Creek Area. There are no major trail connections for 24.8 miles of the Lakeshore Trail from Forney Creek Area until it reaches Hazel Creek Trail in Hazel Creek Area. From Hazel Creek Area, the trail continues west into Twentymile Area and its eventual end at the Appalachian Trail north of Fontana Dam.

HIGHLIGHTS: old pioneer settlements, wildlife, Fontana Lake

GENERAL/HISTORICAL NOTES: The coves of this area were once inhabited mainly by miners, loggers and their families. Several old settlements and cemeteries can be seen today along the trail.

OTHER ACTIVITIES: hiking, backpacking, backcountry camping, fishing

NEAREST CITY/FACILITIES: Bryson City

A cantilever barn, part of a pioneer homestead in the Great Smokies.

DEEP CREEK AREA

County: Swain

Address: Deep Creek Ranger Station, GSMNP
970 Park Rd Bryson City, NC 28713
Telephone: (828) 488-3184

LOCATION: Take US-19 to Bryson City downtown. Turn north on Everette St. at the Swain County Courthouse and cross the bridge over the Tuckasegee River. From here follow the signs to the Deep Creek access. Go 0.2 mile and turn right on Depot St. At Ramseur St. turn left then make another turn to the right. Follow this road to the Deep Creek Ranger Station and campground, four miles north of Bryson City. A gravel road on the left 150 yards beyond the park boundary leads to the horse trailer parking area and Deep Creek Trail (#1) access.

SEASON: open daily year round

FACILITY REVIEW
TYPE: day use and/or overnight horse camping
HORSE CAMPING FACILITIES: backcountry camping
CAMPING FEE: none; free permit required
HOT SHOWERS: none
RESTROOMS: none
STABLE FACILITIES: hitching racks
STABLING FEE: none
DAY RIDERS FEE: none

TRAIL REVIEW
TRAIL NAMES and DESCRIPTIONS:
1. Deep Creek: 6.6 miles/difficult; connects to #2,3,4,6,8; BCC #55,56,57,58,60

2. Pole Road Creek: 3.3 miles/difficult; connects to #1,3 and Noland Creek Trail in Noland Creek Area

3. Noland Divide: 11.8 miles/difficult; connects to #1,2 and Noland Creek Trail in Noland Creek Area

4. Indian Creek: 4.7 miles/difficult; connects to #1,5,6,7,8,11

97

5. Stone Pile Gap: 1.0 mile/moderate; connects to #4,8

6. Loop: 1.0 mile/moderate; connects to #1,4,7

7. Sunkota Ridge: 8.7 miles/difficult; connects to #4,6,8,9,12

8. Martins Gap: 1.5 miles/moderate; connects to #1,4,7

9. Thomas Divide: 8.6 miles/difficult; connects to #4,5,10,11,12

10. Indian Creek Motor: 2.0 miles/moderate-difficult; connects to #9,11

11. Deeplow Gap: 8.7 miles/moderate; connects to #9,10,12

12. Newton Bald: 6.0 miles/difficult; connects to #7,9,11 and leads to US-441 near Smokemont Campground and the Hughes Ridge Trail in the Oconaluftee Area/BCC #52

TYPE: mapped
TERRAIN: mountainous-rugged
DIFFICULTY: moderate-difficult
LENGTH: 64+ miles combined
WATER: yes
TRAIL MAP: Great Smoky Mountains Trail Map
TRAIL NOTES: These trails consist of old roadbeds and jeep roads through hardwood and evergreen forests in the Deep Creek basin. They basically run from north to south and can be combined to form various combinations of loops. The high elevations provide awesome views of the surrounding mountain ridges.

Deep Creek Trail (#1) runs along Deep Creek and provides an access for several trails in this area. From its trailhead west of the Deep Creek campground on Deep Creek Road, the trail goes north for 13.9 miles almost to the crest of the Smokies to end at Newfound Gap Road. However, horse travel is only permitted on the initial 6.6 miles of the trail and not beyond BCC #55.

Several trails branch off Deep Creek Trail as it ascends from the Deep Creek valley. After 0.7 mile from the southern trailhead, Indian Creek Trail (#4) leads to the right. After 1.2 miles, the Loop Trail (#6) also branches off to the right. At 6.5 miles along Deep Creek Trail is Bryson Place, BCC #57, and the junction of Martins Gap Trail (#8) to the east. Pole Road Creek Trail (#2) provides a connector between Deep Creek Trail and Noland Divide Trail (#3). The eastern trailhead is near BCC #55. Pole Road Creek Trail goes west for 3.3 miles to join with the Noland Divide Trail.

Noland Divide Trail's (#3) southern trailhead junctions with the Deep Creek Trail west of the campground and ranger station on Deep Creek Road. Noland Divide Trail follows the Noland Divide Ridge and goes to Clingman's Dome Rd near Clingman's Dome, changing the most in elevation of any trail in the eastern Smoky Mountains (4,155 ft). Horseback riders must backtrack the last 3.8 miles of this trail, where there is a junction with Pole Road Creek Trail (#20) to the east and Noland Creek Trail of the Noland Creek Area to the west. Noland Creek Trail proceeds southwest 9.5 miles along Noland Creek and down the ridge to join with Lakeview Drive.

Indian Creek Trail (#4) is accessed from the south by following Deep Creek Trail for 0.7 mile from its trailhead on Deep Creek Road. Indian Creek Trail goes northeast on an old roadbed that follows along Indian Creek. At 0.5 mile from the beginning of Indian Creek Trail is the Stone Pile Gap Trail (#5). This trail goes east for 1 mile to junction with the Thomas Divide Trail (#9).

Continuing northeast on Indian Creek Trail, at 0.8 mile the Loop Trail (#6) joins on the left and goes 0.5 mile west to the Sunkota Ridge Trail (#7). It is another 0.5 mile west on the Loop Trail to its junction with Deep Creek Trail. Indian Creek Trail goes beyond its junction with the Loop Trail for another 2.2 miles where Deeplow Gap Trail (#11) branches off to the east. Go an additional 2.0 miles north as the Indian Creek Trail ascends Sunkota Ridge on its way to Martins Gap. At this gap is an intersection with Sunkota Ridge Trail (#7) and Martins Gap Trail (#8). Sunkota Ridge Trail descends south from here for 3.8 miles to join with the Loop Trail (#6) and goes northeast for 4.9 miles to connect to the Thomas Divide Trail (#9). Martins Gap Trail (#8) leads west from the gap and descends Sunkota Ridge for 1.5 miles to its junction with Deep Creek Trail at Bryson Place.

Thomas Divide Trail (#9) can be accessed on its southern end via the Indian Creek (#4) and Stone Pile Gap Trails (#5). From the Stone Pile Gap Trail/Thomas Divide Trail junction, Thomas Divide Trail goes south for 1.1 miles to end on the Deep Creek Road east of the Deep Creek campground and ranger station. To the northeast, Thomas Divide Trail follows along the Thomas Ridge line for 7.5 miles to its junction with Sunkota Ridge Trail (#7). Horses are not permitted beyond this point as it becomes a hiking trail.

Sunkota Ridge Trail goes southwest from here for 4.9 miles to Martins Gap and a junction with the Martins Gap and Indian Creek Trails. From the junction of Thomas Divide and Sunkota Ridge Trails is the western trailhead for Newton Bald Trail (#12). Newton Bald Trail goes east, ascending the ridge of Newton Bald. After 0.5 mile, Deeplow Gap Trail (#11) branches off to the right and descends south for 6.6 miles to join the Thomas Divide Trail.

From Newton Bald, the Newton Bald Trail leads east for 5.5 miles to its end on Newfound Gap Road (US-441) near the Smokemont campground. The southern trailhead for Hughes Ridge Trail in the Oconaluftee Area can be accessed near here and used to connect the trails in the Deep Creek Area with the trails in the Oconaluftee Area.

The western end of Deeplow Gap Trail (#11) is accessed from the Indian Creek Trail (#4) 3.0 miles from the southern trailhead of Indian Creek Trail. It leads to the east along an old roadbed. At 3.0 miles to the right is the Indian

Creek Motor Trail (#10). This trail goes south for 2 miles to provide a connector to Thomas Divide Trail (#9). Deeplow Gap Trail continues on for 8.7 miles to its end at Newton Bald. Along the way it crosses Thomas Divide Trail.

HIGHLIGHTS: excellent combinations of loop trails, beautiful scenic ridges and valleys, waterfalls and cascades, wildlife, flora

GENERAL/HISTORICAL NOTES: The Deep Creek area was once the site of an ancient Cherokee Indian village named Kituhwa. Bryson Place is the backcountry area along Deep Creek Trail that was once a camp for Horace Kephart, a famous conservationist. It is named for the Bryson family, the early leaders of Bryson City, and owners of a cabin in this area. Today several backcountry campsites are located here.

Newton Bald, along Newton Bald Trail (#9), is now overgrown with trees and no longer considered a bald mountain. Since at one time, many years ago, the mountain was a grassy bald, this is a good example of how the forest can reclaim an area.

The Thomas Divide Ridge, along which Thomas Divide Trail follows, is named for William Thomas. He was a white man raised by the Cherokees who later became a strong leader and champion of their rights. Thomas is the one who found the famous Cherokee chief, Tsali, in these hills and persuaded him to surrender to the U.S. government. In 1838, Tsali had hidden his family from the "Trail of Tears" on a ridge now called the Thomas Divide Ridge. The Cherokee Indian Reservation was established near here with the help of William Thomas.

OTHER ACTIVITIES: hiking, backpacking, fishing, tubing

NEAREST CITY/FACILITIES: Bryson City

Deep Creek Campground is a modern campground located near the ranger station (family camping only; no horses). Services include flush toilets and drinking water.

Deep Creek Riding Stables offers guided trail rides on rental horses. Call (828) 488-2681 or write P.O. Box 1096, Bryson City, NC 28713 for details.

Double Eagle Farm in Bryson City offers overnight boarding and several other services (see section on "North Carolina Private Stables and Outfitters"). Contact Greg or Karen Crisp at (828) 488-9787 for information and reservations.

FORNEY CREEK AREA

County: Swain

Address: Deep Creek Ranger Station, GSMNP
970 Park Rd. Bryson City, NC 28713
Telephone: (828) 488-3184

LOCATION: Access the trails in this area only by traveling trails from other areas: Noland Creek Area in the east, Hazel Creek Area and Chambers Creek Area in the west. To reach the nearest vehicle access, take US-19 to Bryson City. From downtown at the County Courthouse, go north on Everette St. This road becomes Lakeview Drive (SR-1364; also called Fontana Rd). Go 3 miles to the park boundary; continue for 5.7 miles on Lakeview Drive to a parking area and access to the Tunnel and Lakeshore Trails in the Noland Creek Area (see Noland Creek Area).

SEASON: open daily year round

FACILITY REVIEW
TYPE: day use and/or overnight horse camping
HORSE CAMPING FACILITIES: backcountry camping
CAMPING FEE: none; free permit required
HOT SHOWERS: none
RESTROOMS: none
STABLE FACILITIES: hitching racks
STABLING FEE: none
DAY RIDERS FEE: none

TRAIL REVIEW
TRAIL NAMES and DESCRIPTIONS:
1. Lakeshore Trail: 1.6 miles/moderate; connects to #4,5; This trail continues into Noland Creek, Chambers Creek, Hazel Creek and Twentymile Areas for 40 additional miles.

2. Forney Creek: 3 miles/difficult; connects to #3,4,5,6/BCC #70,71

3. Jonas Creek: 4.5 miles/difficult; connects to #2 and Welch Ridge trail in the Hazel Creek Area/BCC #70

4. White Oak Branch: 2 miles/moderate-difficult; connects to #1,2

5. Bear Creek: 6.3 miles/difficult; connects to #1,2 and the junction of Cold Spring Gap Trail and Welch Ridge Trail in the Hazel Creek Area/BCC #73

6. Springhouse Branch: 7.0 miles/difficult; connects to #2 and Noland Creek Trail in Noland Creek Area

TYPE: mapped
TERRAIN: mountainous-rugged
DIFFICULTY: moderate-difficult
LENGTH: 24.4 miles combined
WATER: yes
TRAIL MAP: Great Smoky Mountains Trail Map

Trails in the Great Smokies provide beautiful views
of the most popular national park in America.

TRAIL NOTES: These trails consist of some old railroad grades and roadbeds that follow and cross several creeks through the forest along ridgelines. They lie between Forney Ridge in the east and Welch Ridge in the west.

The Lakeshore Trail's (#1) eastern trailhead is in the Noland Creek Area near the gate at the end of Lakeview Drive. Go 5.2 miles west (3.8 miles if traveling the Tunnel Trail). The Tunnel Trail provides the quickest access from Lakeview Drive to the Forney Creek Area (see Noland Creek Area). The Tunnel Trail begins at the gated road on Lakeview Drive and proceeds 0.7 mile west to junction with Lakeshore Trail (#1). The Lakeshore Trail leads west along Fontana Lake through several areas of the park to its end north of Fontana Dam in Twentymile Area.

At 6.7 miles on the Lakeshore Trail (5.3 miles if the Tunnel Trail was traveled), White Oak Branch Trail (#4) leads north on an old road to join Forney Creek Trail (#2). Lakeshore Trail continues 1.1 miles west to junction with Bear Creek Trail (#5). Bear Creek Trail joins with Forney Creek Trail near BCC #73 after traveling 0.5 mile from its southern trailhead at the Lakeshore Trail. This trail goes northwest over Jumpup Ridge to its end at a junction with Welch Ridge and Cold Spring Gap Trails in Hazel Creek Area at the open area called Bearwallow Bald.

Forney Creek Trail (#2) goes north along Forney Creek. At 1 mile along Forney Creek Trail, White Oak Branch Trail (#4) joins to the east and leads south for 2 miles to create a loop back to Lakeshore Trail. Continuing north on Forney Creek Trail at 2.0 miles is the junction with Springhouse Branch Trail (#6). Springhouse Branch Trail goes east over Forney Ridge to join with Noland Creek Trail of the Noland Creek Area in Solola Valley.

Forney Creek Trail continues from its junction with Springhouse Branch Trail for another mile to connect to Jonas Creek Trail (#3). At this point, Forney Creek Trail heads northeast towards Clingman's Dome and horses are prohibited on this section of the trail. Jonas Creek Trail leads northwest to a junction with Welch Ridge Trail in Hazel Creek Area. Jonas Creek Trail (#3) and Bear Creek Trail (#5) are both over 3,000 ft and have the highest elevation change of the trails in this area.

HIGHLIGHTS: scenic views, excellent loop trail possibilities

OTHER ACTIVITIES: hiking, backpacking, backcountry camping, fishing

NEAREST CITY/FACILITIES: Bryson City

HAZEL CREEK AREA

County: Swain

Address: Twentymile Ranger Station, GSMNP
Fontana, NC 28733
Telephone: (828) 498-2327

LOCATION: Access the trails in this area by beginning on trails from other areas: Forney Creek and Chambers Creek Areas in the east, and Twentymile Area in the west. See these areas for more information regarding vehicular access.

SEASON: open daily year round

FACILITY REVIEW
TYPE: day use and/or overnight horse camping
HORSE CAMPING FACILITIES: backcountry camping
CAMPING FEE: none; free permit required
HOT SHOWERS: none
RESTROOMS: none
STABLE FACILITIES: hitching racks
STABLING FEE: none
DAY RIDERS FEE: none

TRAIL REVIEW
TRAIL NAMES and DESCRIPTIONS:
1. Hazel Creek: 3.6 miles/moderate-difficult; connects to #2,3,6 BCC #82,83

2. Lakeshore Trail: 11.9 miles in this area/moderate; connects to #1. This trail continues on into other GSMNP areas for 29.6+ additional miles. BCC #81,85,86

3. Cold Spring Gap: 4 miles/difficult; connects to #1,4 and to the Bear Creek Trail in the Forney Creek Area

4. Welch Ridge: 6.5 miles/moderate-difficult; connects to #3, AT and to Jonas Creek Trail and Bear Creek Trail in Forney Creek Area

5. Appalachian Trail: 3.5 miles/moderate-difficult; connects to #4/Silers Bald Shelter

6. Bone Valley: 1.5 miles/easy; connects to #1

TYPE: mapped
TERRAIN: mountainous-rugged
DIFFICULTY: easy-difficult
LENGTH: 31+ miles combined
WATER: yes
TRAIL MAP: Great Smoky Mountains Trail Map

TRAIL NOTES: These trails consist of old roadbeds and railroad grades that follow along several creeks. From its junction in the east with Bear Creek Trail of the Forney Creek Area, the Lakeshore Trail (#2) goes west 20.3 miles without any major trail connections. It follows along the northern shoreline of Fontana Lake within the Chambers Creek and Hazel Creek Areas. After reaching BCC #77 near Pilkey Creek, the Lakeshore Trail continues west into Hazel Creek Area. It parallels Fontana Lake for an additional 7.4 miles to BCC #86 at Proctor, a former lumber settlement. Here the trail turns away from Fontana Lake and heads northeast.

At 4.5 miles from BCC #86, the Lakeshore Trail junctions with Hazel Creek Trail (#1), the first major trail connection for 24.8 miles since the Lakeshore Trail and Bear Creek Trail junction in Forney Creek Area. At this point near BCC #84, Lakeshore Trail continues west into Twentymile Area and its eventual end at the Appalachian Trail north of Fontana Dam.

Wildlife is frequently seen in the Great Smokies.

Hazel Creek Trail (#1) leads northeast from BCC #84. At 0.7 mile near BCC #83, Bone Valley Trail (#6) branches to the north. This short trail follows along Bone Valley Creek near Forrester Ridge and leads to the historic Crate Hall Cabin where it dead ends. Hazel Creek Trail continues beyond the Bone Valley Trail junction for another mile to connect with Cold Spring Gap Trail (#3). At this point, Hazel Creek Trail leads northeast for an additional 1.9 miles to BCC #82. The trail continues beyond here to eventually junction with Welch Ridge Trail (#4) 1.5 miles south of the AT. However, horses are not permitted beyond BCC #82.

Cold Spring Gap Trail (#3) goes east from its junction with Hazel Creek Trail. It passes through the beautiful scenic area called High Rocks (elev. 5,190 ft). Views from here include the North Shore Area, Steoah Mountain Range south of Fontana Lake, and the Little Tennessee River Valley. At 4.0 miles, Cold Spring Gap Trail connects with Welch Ridge Trail (#4) and Bear Creek Trail in the Forney Creek Area. Bear Creek Trail leads southeast for 5.8 miles to junction with Lakeshore Trail.

Welch Ridge Trail continues north from Cold Spring Gap Trail along Welch Ridge. At 4.5 miles along Welch Ridge Trail, Jonas Creek Trail of the Forney Creek Area branches off to the right and leads southeast to join with Forney Creek Trail. Welch Ridge Trail goes north an additional 2.0 miles to end at the Appalachian Trail.

The Appalachian Trail (#5) runs east to west from its junction with Welch Ridge Trail. Clingman's Dome, the highest point in the Smokies (elev. 6,643 ft) and the third tallest mountain peak in eastern America, is located 4.2 miles east along the AT from here. However, horse traffic is not allowed on this section of the AT. From the junction of the AT and Welch Ridge Trail, horse travel is permitted on the AT 3.5 miles to the west and offers nice views of the Smokies. At 0.7 mile, Silers Bald Shelter is located just beyond Silers Bald. Continuing along the AT leads to Buckeye Gap (elev. 4,820 ft) and Cold Spring Knob. Horses are not allowed beyond Cold Spring Knob, so riders must backtrack.

HIGHLIGHTS: scenic vistas from mountain ridges, High Rocks, old historic settlements, wildlife

OTHER ACTIVITIES: hiking, backpacking, fishing, backcountry camping

NEAREST CITIES/FACILITIES: Fontana Village, Bryson City

NOLAND CREEK AREA

County: Swain

Address: Deep Creek Ranger Station, GSMNP
970 Park Rd. Bryson City, NC 28713
Telephone: (828) 488-3184

LOCATION: Take US-19 to Bryson City. From downtown at the County Courthouse, go north onto Everette Street. This becomes Lakeview Drive (SR-1364; also called Fontana Rd). It is 3 miles on this road to the park boundary. Go another 5 miles to the Noland Creek trailhead (#1). Access to a parking area and the other trails in this area is 0.7 mile farther west on Lakeview Drive.

SEASON: open daily year round

FACILITY REVIEW
TYPE: day use and/or overnight horse camping
HORSE CAMPING FACILITIES: backcountry camping
CAMPING FEE: none; free permit required
HOT SHOWERS: none
RESTROOMS: none
STABLE FACILITIES: hitching racks
STABLING FEE: none
DAY RIDERS FEE: none

TRAIL REVIEW
TRAIL NAMES and DESCRIPTIONS:
1. Noland Creek: 10.5 miles/difficult; connects to Springhouse Branch Trail in Forney Creek Area and Noland Divide Trail in the Deep Creek Area. BCC #61,62,63,64,65

2. Lakeshore: 3.6 miles (in this area)/moderate; connects to #3,4 and continues into other areas of the park for an additional 37.9 miles

3. Tunnel Trail: 0.7 mile/moderate; connects to #2

4. Gold Mine Loop: 6.1 miles/moderate; connects to #2/BCC #67

TYPE: mapped
TERRAIN: mountainous-rugged

DIFFICULTY: moderate-difficult

LENGTH: 21+ miles combined

WATER: yes

TRAIL MAP: Great Smoky Mountains Trail Map

TRAIL NOTES: Noland Creek Trail (#1) is an old roadbed that lies between the ridgelines of Noland Divide in the east and Forney Ridge in the west. From the parking area on Lakeview Drive, the trail heads south for 1 mile towards Fontana Lake to a dead end at BCC #66 (for hikers only). Noland Creek Trail leads northeast for 9.5 miles along Noland Creek to its eventual end and junction with the Noland Divide Trail in the Deep Creek Area at Sassafras Gap. Five backcountry campsites are located along this trail as it ascends Noland Divide. At 4.7 miles north in Solola Valley and at BCC #64, Noland Creek Trail junctions with Springhouse Branch Trail of the Forney Creek Area. Springhouse Branch Trail leads west over Forney Ridge.

After passing the Noland Creek trailhead on Lakeview Drive, it is 0.7 mile west to the end of the road. Lakeshore Trail (#2) begins here on the left before the gate. It forms a U-shape as it loops south and then heads north along Tunnel Ridge before joining with the western end of the Tunnel Trail (#3). The Lakeshore Trail continues on to the west through the Forney Creek, Chambers Creek, Hazel Creek and Twentymile areas for an additional 37.9 miles.

The Tunnel Trail begins straight beyond the gated road on the paved Lakeview Drive and follows the road for 0.7 mile. It passes through a 200-yard tunnel along the way and then the pavement ends. The Tunnel Trail provides a shorter access to the trails in the Forney Creek Area and junctions with the Lakeshore Trail at its western terminus.

At 0.5 mile from the Lakeshore Trail's eastern trailhead, the Gold Mine Loop Trail (#4) branches off and leads south towards Fontana Lake. It forms a U-shape as it loops back north beyond BCC #67 to rejoin the Lakeshore Trail after 6.1 miles.

HIGHLIGHTS: scenic areas, connects with trails in several other areas of the park, Solola Valley (a former settlement)

GENERAL/HISTORICAL NOTES: Lakeview Drive is also called "the Road to Nowhere." In 1943, an agreement was made by the National Park Service to build a road within the park that spanned from Bryson City to Fontana Dam along the northern shore of Fontana Lake. Only 6 miles of the proposed 50 mile route have been completed of the Northshore Road. By 1968, the park service abandoned the project due to the lack of necessity for the road and public pressure to retain the wilderness environment of the park.

Today, Lakeview Drive comprises the portion of the Northshore Road that was completed by 1968. It leads to the trailheads of Noland Creek, Lakeshore and Tunnel Trails. The Tunnel Trail was also once a part of the proposed

Northshore Road. The pavement ends soon after passing through the 200-yard tunnel.

OTHER ACTIVITIES: hiking, backpacking, backcountry camping

NEAREST CITY/FACILITIES: Bryson City

OCONALUFTEE AREA

County: Swain

Address: Smokemont Ranger Station, GSMNP
Box 4, Park Circle Cherokee, NC 28719
Telephone: (828) 497-9147

LOCATION: Go north on US-411 (called Newfound Gap Rd inside the GSMNP) from Cherokee for 5.7 miles to the ranger station. Towstring Horse Camp is on a road to the right off US-441, 1.2 miles before the ranger station.

Round Bottom Horse Camp can be accessed by going north on US-441 from Cherokee for approximately 2.5 miles. Turn right onto Big Cove Rd and go for 8.9 miles to Straight Fork Rd (this road is also the east end of Heintooga/Round Bottom Rd, and becomes gravel). Turn right and go approximately 5 miles. The horse camp is on the left.

SEASON: open daily year round, auto access horse camps open April-November

FACILITY REVIEW
TYPE: day use and/or overnight horse camping
HORSE CAMPING FACILITIES: auto access primitive horse camps and backcountry camping
>   Round Bottom Horse Camp-limit of 20 horses
>   Towstring Horse Camp-limit of 20 horses

CAMPING FEE: none; reservations recommended for camps, free permit required for backcountry camping
HOT SHOWERS: none
RESTROOMS: pit toilets
STABLE FACILITIES: hitching racks
STABLING FEE: $2.00/day in auto access horse camps
DAY RIDERS FEE: none

TRAIL REVIEW
TRAIL NAMES and DESCRIPTIONS:
1. Hughes Ridge: 12 miles/difficult; connects to #2,3,4,AT and leads to US-441 and the Newton Bald Trail in the Deep Creek Area/Pecks Corner Shelter

2. Bradley Fork: 6.9 miles/easy-moderate; connects to #1,3

3. Chasteen Creek: 4.1 miles/difficult; connects to #1,2/BCC #50

4. Enloe Creek: 3.6 miles/moderate; connects to #1,3,5

5. Hyatt Ridge: 4.2 miles/difficult; connects to #4,6 and Straight Fork Rd/BCC #44

6. Beech Gap: 5.3 miles/difficult; connects to #5,7 and to Straight Fork Rd (this road leads to Pin Oak Gap and Palmer Creek Trail in Cataloochee Area).

7. Balsam Mountain: 10.8 miles/moderate-difficult; connects to AT, Mount Sterling Ridge Trail (in Cataloochee/Big Creek areas) and Straight Fork Rd (this road leads to Trails #5 & 6 and Palmer Creek Trail in Cataloochee Area)/Laurel Gap Shelter

8. Cabin Flats: 0.7 mile/easy-moderate; connects to #9/BCC #49

9. Dry Sluice Gap: 3.8 miles/difficult; connects to #2,8,AT

10. Grassy Creek: 2.5 miles/difficult: connects to #9,11/Kephart Shelter

11. Kephart Prong: 2.0 miles/easy; connects to #10/Kephart Shelter

12. Appalachian Trail: 5.3 miles/moderate-difficult; connects to #1,7,9 and continues into the Big Creek Area for 16.3 more miles/Tricorner Knob Shelter, Pecks Corner Shelter

TYPE: mapped
TERRAIN: mountainous-rugged
DIFFICULTY: easy-difficult
LENGTH: 61+ miles combined
WATER: yes
TRAIL MAP: Great Smoky Mountains Trail Map
TRAIL NOTES: These trails follow mainly old roads along several creeks around Hughes Ridge. The Oconaluftee River is to the southwest. Hughes Ridge Trail (#1) proceeds north from near the Smokemont campground to the Appalachian Trail. Along the way Bradley Fork Trail (#2), Chasteen Creek Trail (#3) and Enloe Creek Trail (#4) branch off it. From its southern trailhead, Hughes Ridge Trail leads to US-441 (Newfound Gap Rd) to join with Newton Bald Trail in the Deep Creek Area. These two trails can be used to connect trails in the Deep Creek and Oconaluftee Areas.
     Bradley Fork Trail (#2) begins north of the Oconaluftee campground and leads north along Richland Mountain. Dry Sluice Gap Trail (#9) connects to Bradley Fork Trail (#2) and ascends Richland Mountain as it leads north to the Appalachian Trail. This portion of the AT does not allow horse traffic so riders must backtrack. Cabin Flats Trail (#8) is a short path that branches off Dry Sluice

Gap Trail just above its junction with Bradley Fork Trail. Chasteen Creek Trail (#3) provides a north to south connector route between Hughes Ridge Trail and Bradley Fork Trail as it follows along Chasteen Creek.

Hyatt Ridge Trail (#5) begins 0.9 mile west of the Round Bottom Horse Camp off Straight Fork Rd. It leads north along Hyatt Ridge. Enloe Creek Trail (#4) branches off from it after 1.8 miles and goes west along Enloe Creek and over Hughes Ridge towards its junction with Hughes Ridge Trail (#1).

The trailhead for Beech Gap Trail (#6) is near the Round Bottom Horse Camp. It leads west to join with the Hyatt Ridge Trail and goes east to a junction with Balsam Mountain Trail (#7). Balsam Mountain Trail follows Balsam Mountain Ridge through fir and spruce forests on its way to the Appalachian Trail and the crest of the Smokies. Laurel Gap Shelter is located near Balsam High Top Mountain (elev. 5,640 ft) along this trail.

To the east from Balsam Mountain Trail is a junction with Mount Sterling Ridge Trail that continues eastward into the Cataloochee/Big Creek areas. A nice loop can be made by combining this trail with Pretty Hollow Gap Trail and Palmer Creek Trail in the Cataloochee/Big Creek areas. Palmer Creek Trail can be ridden west for 3.3 miles to its end on Straight Fork Rd. Straight Fork Rd can then be followed west to the Round Bottom Horse Camp.

Grassy Creek Trail (#10) and Kephart Prong Trail (#11) lie on the west side of Richland Mountain. Grassy Creek Trail begins on the left from the Dry Sluice Gap Trail, 1.3 miles before the junction of the Appalachian Trail and Dry Sluice Gap Trail. Grassy Creek Trail leads southwest to a junction with the Kephart Prong Trail and the Kephart Shelter. Kephart Prong Trail follows along the creek named Kephart Prong and then dead ends at US-441 (Newfound Gap Rd).

The Appalachian Trail (#12) follows along the crest of the Smoky Mountains as it passes through the park. From the Hughes Ridge Trail (#1) in the Oconaluftee area to the point where the AT crosses the park boundary in the Big Creek area, horse travel is permitted. This is a 21.6-mile stretch of the AT that can be utilized to create various combinations of loops since it junctions with trails in these areas.

HIGHLIGHTS: excellent system of trails with several possibilities for loops; a few trails connect to the Appalachian Trail along the crest of the Smokies; nice forests, mountain streams and cascades

GENERAL/HISTORICAL NOTES: This area is near the Oconaluftee River, and was named by the Cherokee Indians. Oconaluftee means "by the riverside." The Smokemont Campground area was once a sawmill community managed by the logging company, Champion Fibre. This area was formerly named Bradley-town after the pioneers that lived in this area. Also located here is the Balsam Mountain Ridge, the only mountain connecting the Blue Ridge Mountains to the Great Smokies. Kephart Shelter, located near the junction of Grassy Creek Trail and Kephart Prong Trail, is named for the famous author and conservationist, Horace Kephart.

OTHER ACTIVITIES: hiking, backpacking, fishing, camping

NEAREST CITY/FACILITIES: Cherokee
Smokemont Campground (family camping only; no horses) is located near the ranger station. It is open all year and offers flush toilets and drinking water. Oconaluftee Visitor Center is on US-441 North near Cherokee. Drinking water for people is also available here. Smokemont Riding Stables offers guided trail rides on rental horses. Call (828) 497-2373 for more information.

TWENTYMILE AREA

County: Swain

Address: Twentymile Ranger Station, GSMNP
Fontana, NC 28733
Telephone: (828) 498-2327

LOCATION: Take NC-28 to Fontana Village and go west for 6 miles. The Twentymile Access and the Twentymile Ranger Station are on the right. The trailhead for Twentymile Trail (#1) is just beyond the ranger station at a gated road. Parking for trucks and trailers is available on the left side of NC-28, across the road from the Twentymile Access. An additional parking area is located beyond the Twentymile Access, around the curve on NC-28.

The trailhead for the western terminus of Lakeshore Trail (#4) is located north of Fontana Dam. From NC-28 east of Fontana Village, go north on the road that leads to the dam and visitor center. After 1.2 miles, cross over Fontana Dam, then turn right. Follow this road for another 1.1 miles to the end of the road and the trailhead. The Appalachian Trail is also accessed here but this section is for hikers only.

SEASON: open daily year round

FACILITY REVIEW
TYPE: day use and/or overnight horse camping
HORSE CAMPING FACILITIES: backcountry camping
CAMPING FEE: none; free permit required
HOT SHOWERS: none
RESTROOMS: none (toilets at Fontana Dam visitor center)
STABLE FACILITIES: hitching racks
STABLING FEE: none
DAY RIDERS FEE: none

TRAIL REVIEW
TRAIL NAMES and DESCRIPTIONS:
1. Twentymile: 5 miles/difficult; connects to #2,3,6,AT

2. Long Hungry Ridge: 4.5 miles/difficult; connects to #1/BCC #92

3. Lost Cove: 3.5 miles/difficult; connects to #1,4,AT/BCC #91

4. Lakeshore: 11.5 miles in this area/moderate; connects to #3,5, AT. This trail continues into Hazel Creek, Chambers Creek, Forney Creek and Noland Creek Areas for 30 additional miles/BCC #88,90

5. Jenkins Ridge: 6 miles/difficult; connects to #4, AT

6. Wolf Ridge: 6.5 miles/difficult; connects to #1,7/BCC #95

7. Gregory Bald: 3.1 miles in NC (4 miles in TN)/difficult; connects to #6, AT and the Hannah Mountain Trail in the Cades Cove Area of TN; BCC #13 is just inside the TN state line

8. Appalachian Trail: 10.5 miles (in this area)/moderate-difficult; connects to #1,3,5,7/Birch Spring Gap, Mollies Ridge, Russell Field, Spence Field Shelters

TYPE: mapped
TERRAIN: mountainous-rugged
DIFFICULTY: moderate-difficult
LENGTH: 51+ miles combined
WATER: yes
TRAIL MAP: Great Smoky Mountains Trail Map
TRAIL NOTES: From the gated gravel road beyond the ranger station, go 0.5 mile on the Twentymile Trail (#1). At this point, Wolf Ridge Trail (#6) branches off to the left and goes north on an old road for 6.5 miles. It ascends Wolf Ridge to reach Parson Bald at 5.8 miles. At Sheep Pen Gap and BCC #13, the trail ends and junctions with Gregory Bald Trail (#7). To the northwest, Gregory Bald Trail goes 4.0 miles to Parson Branch Road, which leads to the Cades Cove Area in TN. To the east, the trail climbs the summit of the grassy Gregory Bald, offering great views of the surrounding mountains (elev. 4,948 ft).

Gregory Bald Trail continues east and junctions with Long Hungry Ridge Trail (#2) near Rich Gap after 1.1 miles. Gregory Bald Trail goes east for an additional 2.0 miles to its end and junction with the Appalachian Trail (#8). Long Hungry Ridge Trail (#2) leads south from its junction with Gregory Bald Trail, descending an old roadbed on Long Hungry Ridge for 4.5 miles to join with the Twentymile Trail (#1).

From its western trailhead and junction with Wolf Ridge Trail (#6), the Twentymile Trail (#1) continues northeast and follows along Twentymile Creek for 2.5 miles to a junction with Twentymile Loop Trail (for hikers only) and Long Hungry Ridge Trail (#2). Long Hungry Ridge Trail climbs north 4.5 miles to the Smokies' crest and a junction with Gregory Bald Trail (#7). Twentymile Trail continues east beyond the junction with Long Hungry Ridge Trail for 2 miles to connect to the Appalachian Trail (#8) and Lost Cove Trail (#3) at Sassafras Gap.

The AT leads north and south from this point. The southern section of the AT is for hikers only and leads down to Fontana Dam. Going north on the AT follows the crest of the Smokies and horses are allowed on this portion of the trail. At Doe Knob, 3.0 miles north, is a junction with Gregory Bald Trail (#7) that leads west. Continuing on the AT in a northeast direction leads to several trail shelters. After 10.5 miles just beyond Spence Field Shelter, horse travel is not permitted any farther on the AT. Horseback riders must take Jenkins Ridge Trail (#5) that leads south for 6.0 miles along Jenkins Ridge to junction with Lakeshore Trail (#4).

Lakeshore Trail runs east and west from here. Going east, it is 2.5 miles to a junction with Hazel Creek Trail of the Hazel Creek Area. The Lakeshore Trail continues from this junction for an additional 30 miles into the areas north of the Fontana Lake shoreline. Going west leads to a junction with Lost Cove Trail (#3). Lost Cove Trail goes 3.5 miles west following along Lost Cove Creek to join with the AT at Sassafras Gap. Lakeshore Trail continues southwest from its junction with Lost Cove Trail for 5.5 miles to end at the parking area north of Fontana Dam.

HIGHLIGHTS: excellent possibilities for loop trails, scenic views from mountain balds, Gregory Bald, Fontana Lake, azaleas and other flora, Appalachian Trail

GENERAL/HISTORICAL NOTES: This area is 20 miles from the Tennessee junction of the Little Tennessee River and Tuckasegee River, hence its name "Twentymile." Fontana Village was once a community for the construction workers that built Fontana Dam. The 480-feet high dam on the Little Tennessee River is the highest dam in the Tennessee Valley Authority system and east of the Rocky Mountains. It was constructed in the early 1940s to supply electricity for the production of aluminum by ALCOA. America was fighting World War II at the time, and aluminum was in great demand for the manufacturing of airplanes.

Today, the dam is still in use and Fontana Village is a resort area popular with fishermen. The Appalachian Trail, the second longest hiking trail in the world, enters the national park when it crosses over Fontana Dam. The famous footpath continues northeast as it traverses the crest of the Smokies for 71 miles.

The high mountain balds of the Twentymile Area were once grazing fields for cattle and sheep. Such is the case for Gregory Bald. It is named for Russell Gregory, a legendary settler from Cades Cove that hunted and maintained herds on the bald during the mid 1800s. He built a stone cabin on top of Gregory Bald because he enjoyed the area and wilderness so much. He was tragically killed in 1864 during the Civil War by Confederate troops. Gregory remained loyal to the Union and led a group of settlers in Cades Cove who defended their homes against a band of Confederates. The defeated soldiers later returned for revenge and murdered Gregory.

Today, Gregory Bald is best known for the beautiful azaleas that cover the area and bloom each year during the middle of June. It is one of only two balds within the Smokies that the Park Service is maintaining through the use of special practices. All other balds in the park will some day no longer exist as the forest grows and reclaims them.

Parson Bald is located nearby along Wolf Ridge Trail. It is an open area where grass and shrubs grow. This bald was a popular place during the 1800s where people congregated for revivals, hence the name "Parson."

OTHER ACTIVITIES: hiking, backpacking, fishing, camping

NEAREST CITIES/FACILITIES: Fontana Village, Bryson City, Robbinsville

Call (828) 498-2211 or 1-800-849-2258 for more information on services and facilities available in Fontana Village Resort.

Fontana Stables at Fontana Dam can be contacted at (828) 479-8911 or 1-800-849-2258 ext. 272 regarding horseback riding and guided trail rides.

Fontana Campground is the nearest developed campground (family camping only; no horses) and offers hot showers. It is located 5 miles east of the ranger station at the base of Fontana Dam.

Anthony Creek Ranger Station and Horse Camp (auto access) is located in the Cades Cove Area of Tennessee, 4.8 miles from the Russell Field Shelter along the Appalachian Trail.

Double Eagle Farm in Bryson City offers overnight boarding and several other services (see section on "North Carolina Private Stables and Outfitters"). Contact Greg or Karen Crisp at (828) 488-9787 for information and reservations.

View of Fontana Lake

CHAPTER 8

NATIONAL SEASHORES

There are two national seashores in North Carolina: Cape Hatteras and Cape Lookout. They are located along the Atlantic Ocean and are managed by the National Park Service. Cape Hatteras allows horseback riding on the beach, a 75-mile stretch of coastline along the Outer Banks from Bodie Island to Ocracoke Island. It is an historical area of North Carolina, including some of the early colonial settlements, wild ponies of Ocracoke, famous lighthouses, and numerous stories and legends of pirates and shipwrecks.

Cape Lookout National Seashore is in Carteret County near Beaufort, North Carolina. It consists of isolated barrier islands accessed only by ferry or private boat. Cape Lookout National Seashore is not included in this trail guide since horseback riding is currently not permitted within its boundaries.

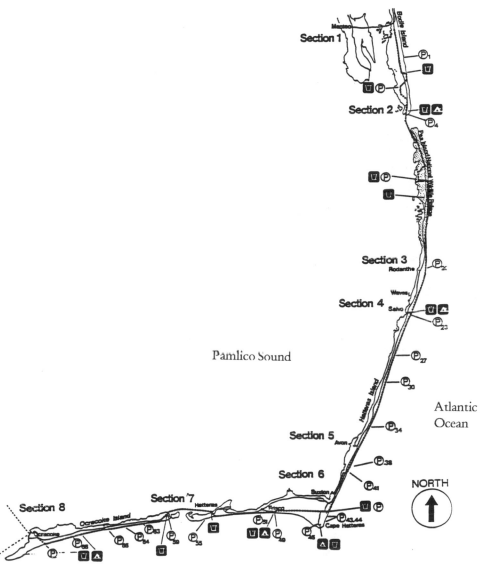

Riding trail that runs over Bodie, Hatteras, and Ocracoke Islands
Reprinted courtesy of Cape Hatteras National Seashore

CAPE HATTERAS NATIONAL SEASHORE

Counties: Dare and Hyde

Address: Superintendent
Rt. 1, Box 675 Manteo, NC 27954
Telephone: (252) 473-2111

LOCATION: Take US-158 South from Elizabeth City to the northern trailhead at Whalebone Junction Information Station near Nags Head and Bodie Island. Parking is available near here at Coquina Beach. Contact the park office for information on the location of additional designated vehicular beach accesses.

Ocracoke Island can only be reached by ferry from either Swan Quarter, Cedar Island, Hatteras or Portsmouth, NC. Information on ferry schedules is included in the "North Carolina Roadmap" that can be found in most service stations.

SEASON: open daily year round

FACILITY REVIEW
TYPE: day use
HORSE CAMPING FACILITIES: none (you may camp at the National Park Service's family campgrounds, however horses must be stabled overnight at a local private barn)
HOT SHOWERS: none (cold showers only at NPS campgrounds)
RESTROOMS: flush toilets (at NPS campgrounds)
DAY RIDERS FEE: none

TRAIL REVIEW
TRAIL NAME: Cape Hatteras Beach Trail
TYPE: unmarked
TERRAIN: flat and sandy
DIFFICULTY: easy
LENGTH: 75.8 miles
WATER: yes
TRAIL MAP: Cape Hatteras
TRAIL NOTES: Horseback riding is permitted on the beach section of the seashore trail. Numerous parking areas and beach accesses are found along the way in the park. The trail is divided into eight sections as it crosses over three islands: Bodie, Hatteras and Ocracoke. These islands are commonly called the Outer Banks. They are joined together by NC-12 and the Hatteras Inlet Ferry.

Be aware that some sections of the national seashore allow off-road vehicle use. Some beach sections may be closed during the year. Contact the park office for additional information.

Be sure to wear insect repellent during the warm months to ward off mosquitoes and biting insects that are present along the coast.

Section 1: Nags Head to Oregon Inlet-8 miles
Section 2: Oregon Inlet to Rodanthe-17.9 miles
Section 3: Rodanthe to Salvo-3 miles
Section 4: Salvo to Avon-13 miles
Section 5: Avon to Cape Hatteras Lighthouse-9.4 miles
Section 6: Cape Hatteras Lighthouse to Cape Hatteras Village-10 miles
Section 7: Cape Hatteras Village to Ocracoke Campground-8 miles
Section 8: Ocracoke Campground to Ocracoke Town-6.5 miles

RULES/REQUIREMENTS: Horses can be ridden on the beach only on the oceanside of the sand dunes and on vehicular beach access routes. Riding along the road shoulders and crossing paved roads at designated vehicular beach access areas is only allowed for access to the beach. Horses are permitted on the beach sections of the trail except in Pea Island National Wildlife Refuge, where horseback riding is prohibited. Do not enter posted bird nesting areas during the nesting season months of May and June. The National Park Service campgrounds prohibit horses.

HIGHLIGHTS: beach, coastal history, birds and wildlife, wild ponies of Ocracoke

GENERAL/HISTORICAL NOTES: These barrier islands comprise America's first national seashore, set aside by Congress in 1937. The Outer Banks has been called the "Graveyard of the Atlantic" due to the many shipwrecks in its shallow shoals and turbulent, stormy sea. At Coquina Beach is the ruins of the Laura A. Barnes, shipwrecked in 1921. The three unique, historic lighthouses located along the trail are Bodie, Cape Hatteras and Ocracoke. They were all built in the 1800s.

Ocracoke Island is an isolated island and harbor village now popular as a fisherman's haven. It is home to a famous band of wild ponies. Their exact origin is unknown but numerous theories exist. Possibly the most popular belief is the ponies were accidentally shipwrecked off the North Carolina coast during Spanish explorations. They swam ashore and roamed free on the island for several hundred years. Ocracoke once served as a hideout for Blackbeard and other pirates.

OTHER ACTIVITIES: fishing, hiking, family camping, surfing, swimming, sunbathing, sailing, beachcombing

NEAREST CITIES/FACILITIES: Nags Head, Hatteras, numerous small villages are located along the route.

The five National Park Service campgrounds (family camping only; no horse camping) are Oregon Inlet, Salvo, Cape Point, Frisco and Ocracoke. They each provide drinking water, cold showers, flush toilets, picnic tables and fire grills, but no utility hookups. No reservations are required; first-come, first-served basis. Their operating seasons are usually from April or May to September or October.

Contact the Dare County Tourist Bureau, P.O. Box 399, Manteo, NC 27954, telephone (252) 473-2138; or the Outer Banks Chamber of Commerce, P.O. Box 1757, Kill Devil Hills, NC 27948, telephone (252) 441-8144 (North Beaches), or (252) 995-4213 (Hatteras Island) for a vacation guide on commercial campgrounds, motels, tourist activities and boarding stables along the Outer Banks.

Buxton Stables, Inc. is located on Hatteras Island off NC-12. Services include overnight boarding, trail rides through the Buxton Woods maritime forest, and beach rides. It is best to call ahead and make reservations. For additional information contact at P.O. Box 545, Buxton, NC 27920; (252) 995-4659.

Seaside Stables in Ocracoke Village on Ocracoke Island offers overnight boarding and guided rides on rental horses. Contact at P.O. Box 669, Ocracoke, NC 27960; (252) 928-3778 for more information.

CHAPTER 9

NORTH CAROLINA STATE PARKS, FORESTS AND NATURAL AREAS

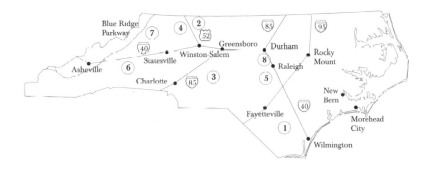

1. Bladen Lakes State Forest
2. Hanging Rock State Park
3. Morrow Mountain State Park
4. Pilot Mountain State Park
5. Raven Rock State Park

6. South Mountains State Park
7. Stone Mountain State Park
8. W. B. Umstead State Park

North Carolina offers a variety of terrain in the state properties, from the sandy ridges in the Sandhills region to the rugged South Mountains near Morganton. The Division of Parks and Recreation manages the thirty-four state parks and natural areas in North Carolina. Five forests are maintained by the Division of Forest Resources. Both divisions are part of the North Carolina Department of Environment, Health and Natural Resources.

Ten state parks allow horseback riding along trails and/or roads. South Mountains State Park is currently the only one that allows overnight camping with your horse. However, camping is limited to pack-in sites a few miles away from your truck and trailer. The other state parks permit only day use of the facilities. North Carolina's parks have a limited amount of bridle trails, slightly less than 100 miles with all parks combined. Weymouth Woods-Sandhills Nature Reserve has only a few miles of of service roads open to horses. Two parks, Medoc Mountain State Park near Roanoke Rapids and Crowder's Mountain State Park in King's Mountain, currently have only three miles or less of bridle trails. This short distance is probably not worth the time it takes to transport your horse. Therefore, Weymouth Woods-Sandhills, Medoc Mountain, and Crowder's Mountain are not included in this book.

The state parks open at 8:00 a.m. daily year round except for Christmas Day. Closing hours vary according to the season of the year. Currently the parks close at 6:00 p.m. from November-February, 7:00 p.m. in March and October, 8:00 p.m. in April, May and September, and 9:00 p.m. June-August.

Each state park has a map and brochure available that includes general park regulations. Follow these rules in addition to the "Rules and Regulations" in Chapter 1. Call the park for more information regarding facilities and trails. For general information on all of the state parks and recreational areas, contact: North Carolina Department of Environment, Health and Natural Resources, Division of Parks and Recreation, P.O. Box 27687, Raleigh, NC 27611-7687, or call (919) 733-PARK.

The state forests are part of a commercial operation where the forest resources are managed and harvested for profit. Bladen Lakes State Forest covers over 32,000 acres and is the largest of the five state forests in North Carolina. Riding is currently allowed along the roads within Bladen Lakes. The other four forests consist of 300 acres or less, have no designated bridle trails, and do not allow horses to enter.

Horsemen need to unite and request the development of horse camping facilities and more equestrian trails within the state parks from the Division of Parks and Recreation. Several parks have included the improvement of equestrian facilities within their master plans. These upgrades are tentatively scheduled within the next several years, but the serious lack of funding is definitely a limiting factor. The State Parks Bond Referendum that was passed by North Carolina voters in November 1993 should help alleviate some of the financial burden. Hopefully, some of these allocated funds will be used to create or improve horse trailer parking areas, upgrade and renovate existing trails, and help purchase additional land for new bridle trails. However, it may be quite some time before any changes are actually enacted.

Many park rangers welcome assistance with trail maintenance from horsemen and volunteer groups. Simple tasks include marking and blazing trails, ensuring that existing trails are passable and in good condition, and picking up trash along the trails left by careless trail users. These acts are greatly appreciated by park rangers and all trail users benefit from them.

Equestrian groups and organizations are encouraged to contact a local state park and find out what kind of volunteer work can be done in their area. Rangers have many good ideas for trails and park facilities but often lack the amount of time and funding needed to support their suggestions. Volunteers can really make a worthwhile difference by donating a few hours' worth of work and showing an interest in helping to protect our trails.

Horsemen can also join the North Carolina Horse Council to help work toward the goal of establishing more bridle trails in the state. The Horse Council is dedicated to this project and can be contacted for more information about membership at P.O. Box 12999, Raleigh, NC 27605; phone (919) 821-1030; fax (919) 828-9322.

BLADEN LAKES STATE FOREST

County: Bladen

Address: Forest Supervisor, Rt. 2, Box 942
Elizabethtown, NC 28337
Telephone: (910) 588-4964

LOCATION: From Elizabethtown, take US-701 and go north 1.1 miles to NC-242. Go north for 3 miles on NC-242. The forest office is on the right. Horse trailer parking is allowed along the edge of the roads within the state forest.

SEASON: open daily year round; office hours are Monday-Friday from 8:00 a.m.-5:00 p.m.

FACILITY REVIEW
TYPE: day use and/or overnight horse camping
HORSE CAMPING FACILITIES: primitive
CAMPING FEE: none
HOT SHOWERS: none
RESTROOMS: pit toilets
STABLE FACILITIES: none (trailer tie)
DAY RIDERS FEE: none; obtain free permit to ride
PARK ENTRANCE FEE: none

TRAIL REVIEW
TYPE: unmarked
TERRAIN: flat
DIFFICULTY: easy
LENGTH: 100 miles
WATER: yes
TRAIL MAP: Bladen Lakes State Forest
TRAIL NOTES: Horseback riding is allowed on numerous secondary and primitive roads and jeep trails throughout the forest. The terrain mostly consists of sandy areas, swamps and bays. A major portion of this state forest is also managed as a game land and hunting is permitted within the boundaries during season. Be wary and wear blaze orange when horseback riding during hunting season.

RULES/REQUIREMENTS: You must obtain a free permit at the forest office during office hours before riding. Do not tie horses to trees in the seed orchards. No littering.

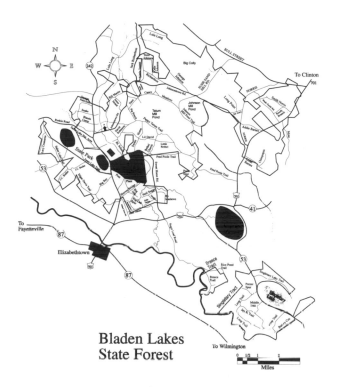

Bladen Lakes
State Forest

Reprinted courtesy of the North Carolina Forest Service

HIGHLIGHTS: nice coastal forest areas, forestry management, numerous primitive roads for trail riding

GENERAL/HISTORICAL NOTES: Consisting of 32,237 acres, this is the largest state forest in NC. It is located north of the Cape Fear River and contains Salters Lake, Jones Lake and Singletary Lake within its boundaries. Forest resources are managed and maintained for commercial profit. During the 1930s, the Civilian Conservation Corps (CCC) built numerous roads and buildings within the forest.

OTHER ACTIVITIES: hiking, picnicking, educational exhibits, hunting

NEAREST CITY/FACILITIES: Elizabethtown
Jones Lake State Park and Singletary Lake State Park are located nearby. They offer family camping and recreational areas (no horse camping).

HANGING ROCK STATE PARK

County: Stokes

Address: P.O. Box 186 Danbury, NC 27016
Telephone: (336) 593-8480

LOCATION: Take NC-66 to Moores Spring Rd (SR-1001) and turn right. Follow Moores Spring Rd for 6 miles to its end. The main park entrance is on the right on Hanging Rock Rd (SR-1001).

The horse trailer parking area is located in a different area of the park. Go 0.5 mile on Moores Spring Rd and turn right onto Mickey Rd (SR-2011). Go 0.9 mile to Charlie Young Rd (SR-2028) and turn right. Tory's Den parking lot for horse trailers is at the end of Charlie Young Rd. The bridle trail crosses this road, 0.2 mile west of the parking area.

SEASON: open 8 a.m.-dark daily year round; closed Christmas Day

FACILITY REVIEW
TYPE: day use (overnight horse camping available nearby)
HORSE CAMPING FACILITIES: none (see Nearest Cities/Facilities)
RESTROOMS: none accessible in areas where horses are permitted
STABLE FACILITIES: none (see Nearest Cities/Facilities)
DAY RIDERS FEE: none
PARK ENTRANCE FEE: none

TRAIL REVIEW
TRAIL NAME: Loop Trail
TYPE: marked
TERRAIN: rolling hills-hilly
DIFFICULTY: moderate
LENGTH: 6 miles (connects to 25+ miles of trails in this area)
WATER: yes
TRAIL MAP: Hanging Rock State Park
TRAIL NOTES: The Loop Trail passes through the forest and an abundance of mountain flora including rhododendron and laurel as it makes a loop through the state park. An occasionally narrow pathway, the Loop Trail is best ridden clockwise (more scenic). Along the way is an overlook that provides an excellent view of Sauratown Mountain and the distant Blue Ridge Mountains.

HIGHLIGHTS: good views of the distant Blue Ridge Mountains and Sauratown Mountain, mountain flora, bridle trail connects to the Sauratown Trail

GENERAL/HISTORICAL NOTES: Hanging Rock State Park currently consists of 6,192 acres. It is a part of the ancient Sauratown Mountain Range that includes nearby Pilot Mountain and Sauratown Mountain, which reach elevations of 1700-2500 feet. The cliffs and bare rock formations of Moores Knob, Hanging Rock, etc. are made of erosion-resistant quartzite, a similar geological composition of Sauratown Mountain and Pilot Mountain. Hanging Rock is a rock formation whose summit juts, or "hangs," 200 feet out of the Sauratown Mountains. Several beautiful waterfalls and cascades can be seen along some of the park's hiking trails. A man-made 12-acre lake is located within the park and was built by the CCC during the mid 1930s.

OTHER ACTIVITIES: fishing, swimming, picnicking, hiking, family and group camping, rental cabins, rock climbing

NEAREST CITIES/FACILITIES: Danbury, King, Pilot Mountain, Winston-Salem

The western trailhead for Sauratown Trail (see "Regional Trails" chapter) is just off NC-66 North on Rock House Road. Trailer parking and a picnic area are available here. Sauratown Mountain Stables is located within riding distance of the trail and offers a family campground and overnight stabling in a 20-stall barn. Contact Tim McKinney at (336) 994-2182 for more information and to make reservations.

Pilot Mountain State Park is also located nearby and offers additional bridle trails.

MORROW MOUNTAIN STATE PARK

County: Stanly

Address: Rt. 5, Box 430 Albemarle, NC 28001
Telephone: (704) 982-4402

LOCATION: Take NC-740 from Albemarle to Morrow Mountain Rd (SR-1798). Go 2.5 miles to the park entrance. Go 0.2 mile beyond the information center and park entrance and turn right onto a gravel road. The horse trailer parking area is at the end of this road.

SEASON: open 8 a.m.-dark daily year round; closed Christmas Day

FACILITY REVIEW
TYPE: day use only
HORSE CAMPING FACILITIES: none
RESTROOMS: flush toilets within the park (none at the horse trailer parking area)
DAY RIDERS FEE: none
PARK ENTRANCE FEE: none

TRAIL REVIEW
TYPE: marked (blazed red)
TERRAIN: rolling hills-hilly
DIFFICULTY: easy-moderate
LENGTH: 15 miles
WATER: yes
TRAIL MAP: Morrow Mountain State Park
TRAIL NOTES: The wooded bridle trails wind through the small valleys and follow the mountain ridges in this 4,693-acre state park. They consist of wide roadbeds and narrow pathways that can be combined to form a large loop around the entire park. One trail loops around the base of Morrow Mountain. Other trails pass near Mountain Creek, Lake Tillery and the Pee Dee River. Mountain Creek is one of the best areas to view beautiful wildflowers within the park. These bridle trails offer a variety of terrain and scenery.

HIGHLIGHTS: views of Morrow Mountain, Lake Tillery, Pee Dee River, nice woodlands, wildlife

GENERAL/HISTORICAL NOTES: Morrow Mountain State Park is part of the ancient Uwharrie Mountains, one of the oldest mountain ranges in the eastern United States. The park consists of rounded ridges less than 1,000 feet in elevation due to the effects of erosion. Morrow Mountain has the highest elevation in the park at 936 feet. Other prominent peaks include Sugarloaf, Hattaway and Fall.

Indians and European settlers once inhabited the Pee Dee River area. Many artifacts have been recovered from these early settlements. The Kron House is a restored home from the 1800s located within the park. It is the estate of the first practicing medical doctor in the area, Dr. Francis Kron, a man who traveled by horseback to treat his patients. Also restored at this site is the doctor's office, infirmary and greenhouse.

OTHER ACTIVITIES: fishing, swimming, boating, hiking, family and group camping, rental cabins, picnicking, nature museum

NEAREST CITIES/FACILITIES: Albemarle, Badin

Uwharrie National Forest is located on the eastern side of the Yadkin River and offers additional bridle trails and overnight horse camping.

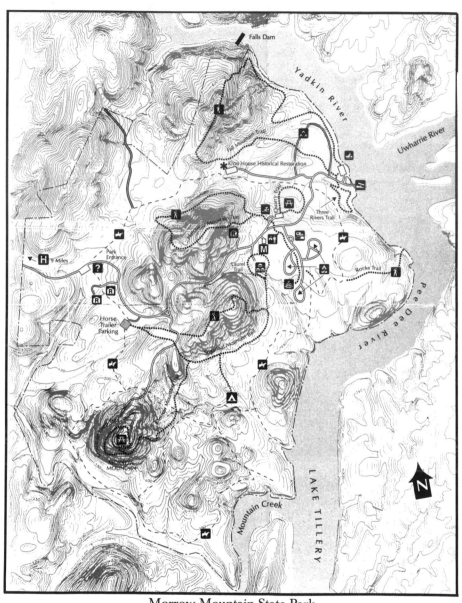

Morrow Mountain State Park
Reprinted courtesy of NC Division of Parks and Recreation

PILOT MOUNTAIN STATE PARK

Counties: Surry and Yadkin

Address: Rt. 1, Box 21 Pinnacle, NC 27043
Telephone: (336) 325-2355

LOCATION: The main park entrance is located between Winston-Salem and Mount Airy off US-52. Various parking areas and bridle trail accesses are described in more detail below.

SEASON: open 8 a.m.-dark daily year round; closed Christmas Day

FACILITY REVIEW
TYPE: day use only
HORSE CAMPING FACILITIES: none (See Nearest Cities/Facilities)
RESTROOMS: pit toilets (at Horne Creek picnic area)
DAY RIDERS FEE: none
PARK ENTRANCE FEE: none

TRAIL REVIEW
TRAIL NAMES and DESCRIPTIONS:
1. Yadkin River Trail: 0.6 mile/easy-moderate; blazed red
2. Corridor Trail: 5.5 miles/moderate, blazed white
3. Grassy Ridge Trail: 1.5 miles/moderate; blazed white
4. Mountain Trail: 2.5 miles/difficult; blazed red

TYPE: marked
TERRAIN: hilly-mountainous
DIFFICULTY: easy-difficult
LENGTH: 10 miles (combined; one-way)
WATER: yes
TRAIL MAP: Pilot Mountain State Park
TRAIL NOTES: The Yadkin River Trail (#1) begins at the River Section South in Yadkin Islands Park near East Bend, NC. It passes through the forest for a short distance before crossing the Yadkin River at a shallow area. Horseback riders travel across the two small river islands along the way. This trail ends on the north side of the Yadkin River where it connects to the Corridor Trail (#2). Be aware the park rangers do not have any equipment or capability to maintain the trail on the islands. During times of heavy rains and high water, use care if attempting to cross the river.

133

State Parks, Forests, & Natural Areas

Crossing the Yadkin River
Courtesy of Tyler Cox

The Corridor Trail is a wide woodland pathway connecting the river section of Pilot Mountain State Park to the mountain section. The trail often follows old farm roads as it passes through evergreen and hardwood forests. It crosses three paved roads along the way. The Corridor Trail can be accessed from either the River Section North of the park or at Pinnacle Hotel Rd (SR-2061).

Grassy Ridge Trail (#3) begins at Pinnacle Hotel Rd. It is a wooded trail that leads to the park office. Horseback riders must backtrack.

The Mountain Trail (#4) also begins at Pinnacle Hotel Rd. This trail is discouraged for horse use because it is a rough, narrow pathway. It gradually climbs up the mountain through the dense forest and some rocky sections. The trail ends at Ledge Spring Trail, a hiking trail. Horseback riders must backtrack from here.

TRAIL ACCESSES:

All three parking areas within this state park have been significantly improved and enlarged.

1. Yadkin River Trail: Follow NC-67 to East Bend, NC. Take Main Street into town. Turn right on Fairground Rd (SR-1541) and go 0.5 mile. Turn right on Shady Grove Church Rd (SR-1538) and go 0.4 mile. Turn right on Shoals Rd (SR-1546) and go 2.5 miles to Yadkin Islands Park and parking area.

2. Corridor Trail (southern access): From US-52 take the Pinnacle exit (SR-1147) and go 1.2 miles to Stony Ridge Rd (SR-2048). Turn right and go 2.8 miles. Turn left on Shoals Rd (SR-2069) and go 1.4 miles. Turn left onto Caudel Rd (SR-2070) and go 1.9 miles. Turn right onto Hauser Rd (SR-2072, gravel road) and go 1 mile to the Corridor Trail access and parking area on the left. This is 0.2 mile beyond the log shed and park entrance gate to the Horne Creek picnic area.

3. Grassy Ridge Trail and Mountain Trail (also the northern access of the Corridor Trail): From Pinnacle, take Surry Line Rd (becomes Pinnacle Hotel Road in Surry County, SR-2061). Turn left onto Culler Rd (SR-2063). Parking area is immediately after the junction on the right. The Grassy Ridge Trail begins on the north side of Pinnacle Hotel Road at the junction with Culler Road. The Mountain Trail starts on the north side of Pinnacle Hotel Road directly across from the "Pilot Mountain Corridor" sign and parking area.

Pilot Mountain

RULES/REQUIREMENTS: Horses are only allowed on designated bridle trails. No alcoholic beverages permitted.

HIGHLIGHTS: views of Pilot Mountain, nice woodlands, mixture of Piedmont and mountainous flora, Yadkin River, wildlife

GENERAL/HISTORICAL NOTES: This 3,703-acre state park encompasses Pilot Mountain, a part of the ancient Sauratown Mountain Range that includes Sauratown Mountain and Hanging Rock. It has an elevation of 2,420 feet that is a distinct contrast to the Piedmont countryside of 900 feet. The isolated mountain peak, called a monadnock in geological terms, was formed by the effects of erosion. Made of quartzite, the rounded knob is named the Big Pinnacle and reaches 200 feet high from its base. The Little Pinnacle connects to it by a saddle in the mountain.

Pilot Mountain is highly visible for many miles from several surrounding counties. The mountain served as a guide and natural landmark to the Indians, hunters and early settlers. The Saura Indians called it "Jomeokee," which means Great Guide or Pilot.

OTHER ACTIVITIES: hiking, family and youth group camping, canoeing and canoe camping, fishing, rock climbing, picnicking

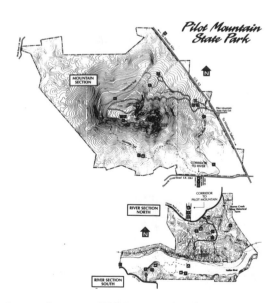

Reprinted courtesy of NC Division of Parks and Recreation

NEAREST CITIES/FACILITIES: Pinnacle, Pilot Mountain, East Bend

Pit toilets and drinking water are available at the Horne Creek picnic area near the north shore of the Yadkin River. No horses are allowed in this area.

Pioneer Village Family Campground is nearby off Shoals Rd (SR-2069) and offers overnight horse camping, showers and water. Contact: Rt. 2, Box 155A, Pinnacle, NC 27043, or call (336) 325-2582 for more information.

Serenity Stables is located within riding distance of the trails in Pilot Mountain State Park. It offers weekend and pasture boarding, camping, RV hookups, and trail rides by appointment. No alcohol or drugs allowed at this family-oriented stable. Contact Bill or Pam Stowers at 1144 Shoals Rd, Pinnacle, NC 27043; telephone (336) 325-2229.

RAVEN ROCK STATE PARK

County: Harnett

Address: Rt. 3, Box 1005 Lillington, NC 27546
Telephone: (910) 893-4888

LOCATION: The park's main entrance is located on SR-1314, 3 miles north of US-421 and 9 miles west of Lillington. The bridle trails and horse trailer parking area are on the north side of the Cape Fear River and not accessible from the park's main entrance. From US-421 in Lillington, take US-401 North and go 3.3 miles. Turn left onto SR-1412. Go 3 miles and turn left on SR-1418 (turns to gravel). Go approximately 1.5 miles to the horse trailer parking area and picnic area on the left.

SEASON: open 8 a.m.-dark daily year round; closed Christmas Day

<u>FACILITY REVIEW</u>
TYPE: day use only
HORSE CAMPING FACILITIES: none
RESTROOMS: pit toilets
OTHER FACILITIES: picnic area
DAY RIDERS FEE: none
PARK ENTRANCE FEE: none

<u>TRAIL REVIEW</u>
TYPE: marked
TERRAIN: rolling hills-hilly
DIFFICULTY: easy-moderate
LENGTH: 7 miles
WATER: yes
TRAIL MAP: Raven Rock State Park
TRAIL NOTES: The bridle trails are located on the north side of the 2,847-acre state park and Cape Fear River. The trails wind through woodlands and form two major loops. From the parking area, the large East Loop extends all the way to the eastern boundary of the park. The West Loop makes a large circle to return to the picnic and parking area. Along the way it crosses Avents Creek. A short spur trail leads from the West Loop to the northern bank of the Cape Fear River near the Northington Lock and Dam remains.

RULES/REQUIREMENTS: No horses are allowed on hiking trails. Do not trespass on posted private property adjoining the park. No alcoholic beverages permitted within the park.

HIGHLIGHTS: Cape Fear River, Raven Rock, nice flora and woodlands

GENERAL/HISTORICAL NOTES: The park is located on the fall line between the Piedmont and Coastal Plains. The harder rocks and soil of the foothills are divided from the softer coastal soil. Rock outcroppings are a prime example of this separation. Raven Rock, one such formation, is a 150-foot high rock that hangs out along the Cape Fear River for over a mile. It is named for the ravens that used to roost on top. In the 1700s and early 1800s, it was formerly named Patterson's Rock. A canoer named Patterson discovered the unusual formation after seeking shelter when his canoe capsized on the Cape Fear River.

A family named Northington owned several thousand acres of land in this area during the late 1700s and early 1800s, a time when the Cape Fear River was used extensively as a major trade route. Several locks and dams were built along the river to make navigation easier. The remains of the Northington lock and dam can still be seen today.

OTHER ACTIVITIES: fishing, hiking, picnicking, canoeing; family, group, backpack and canoe camping

NEAREST CITIES/FACILITIES: Lillington, Sanford

SOUTH MOUNTAINS STATE PARK

County: Burke

Address: Rt. 1, Box 206 Connelly Springs, NC 28612
Telephone: (828) 433-4772

LOCATION: Take exit 105 off I-40 near Morganton. Go south on NC-18 for 10.5 miles to Sugar Loaf Rd (SR-1913). Turn right and go 3.8 miles. Turn left onto Old NC-18 (SR-1924) and go 2.4 miles. Turn right on Ward's Gap Rd (SR-1902) and go 1.3 miles. Turn right on South Mountains State Park Rd (SR-1904) and go 1.6 miles to the park entrance. Horse trailer parking area is located on the left along the park road, 1.1 miles from the entrance gate. The park office is 0.4 mile farther on the right.

SEASON: open 8 a.m.-dark daily year round; closed Christmas Day

FACILITY REVIEW
TYPE: day use and/or overnight horse camping
HORSE CAMPING FACILITIES: backcountry horse camping
    A pack-in area is located in an open field about 5 miles from the parking area off Headquarters Trail. You must leave vehicles and trailers in the designated parking area. Additional pack in sites #9-11 on Fox Trail and #12-14 on Sawtooth Trail may be utilized by request. One group allowed per site (maximum of six campers.)
CAMPING FEE: $5.00/night; permit required
HOT SHOWERS: none
RESTROOMS: pit toilet at pack-in area
OTHER FACILITIES AT PACK-IN AREA: rock fire ring, trash can, nearby stream for watering livestock
STABLE FACILITIES: hitching racks
STABLING FEE: none
DAY RIDERS FEE: none; must register before riding
PARK ENTRANCE FEE: none

TRAIL REVIEW
TYPE: marked
TERRAIN: hilly-mountainous
DIFFICULTY: moderate-difficult
LENGTH: 29 miles

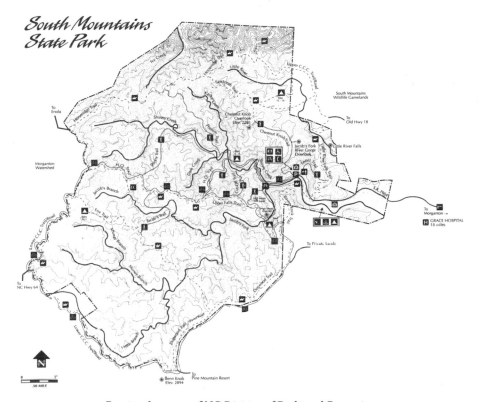

Reprinted courtesy of NC Division of Parks and Recreation

WATER: yes

TRAIL MAP: South Mountains State Park

TRAIL NOTES: The trails consist of old road beds and CCC (Civilian Conservation Corps) roads now used for horseback riding, hiking and mountain biking in this 7,225-acre state park. Trails can be combined to form various combinations of loops. Some are fairly steep and rugged.

Be aware that mountain bikers share 18 miles of trails on the park's south side. No mountain bikes are allowed on the north side. Several miles of trails are accessible to off road vehicle use. Stay alert for the possibility of encounters with ATVs and motorbikes. Two trails, Raven Rock Trail and Upper CCC Trail, cross private property. Be courteous and stay on the trails. Upper CCC Trail crosses the Somo Wildlife Game Lands. Proceed with caution in this area during hunting season.

This is a popular area for horseback riding on the weekends. The horse trailer parking area has an approximate capacity of 25 trucks and trailers. You should arrive early to ensure a parking space.

Two bridle trailheads:
1. Little River Falls Trail: begins on the north side of the entrance road, 0.1 mile west of the horse trailer parking area

2. Raven Rock Trail: begins at the west end of the horse trailer parking area, near the trail signboard display

RULES/REQUIREMENTS: No firearms, alcoholic beverages or unleashed dogs allowed. No horses are permitted past the main parking area, park office or picnic area. No horses are to be ridden along the main entrance road except to access the trailhead for the Little River Falls Trail.

One person from each party must fill out a registration form before riding. These forms can be found at the trail signboard display in the horse trailer parking area. This is for your own safety and in case of an emergency. Camping is by permit only. You must self-register if backpack horse camping. No horse trailer camping is available at this time.

HIGHLIGHTS: undeveloped and remote, wilderness-type environment, nice forests, several creeks and cascades, excellent system of interconnecting trails and old roads

GENERAL/HISTORICAL NOTES: The South Mountains are steep, rugged ridges that reach elevations of 1,200-2,894 feet. Benn Knob, located near the southern boundary, is the highest point in the park. The mountains created a natural barrier between the Cherokee and Catawba Indians that once inhabited the area. Gold was discovered at Brindle Creek in 1828, and miners came seeking their fortunes.

In the 1930s the Civilian Conservation Corps (CCC) built numerous roads and trails through the forest and mountain ridges. The park rangers are currently in the process of establishing several miles of new trails within the park. Horsemen are welcome to submit suggestions and comments for the park and equestrian facilities.

OTHER ACTIVITIES: mountain biking, hiking, backpacking, primitive camping, picnicking, fishing

NEAREST CITY/FACILITIES: Morganton
Several convenience stores and gas stations are located along NC-18.

STONE MOUNTAIN STATE PARK

Counties: Alleghany and Wilkes

Address: Star Rt. 1, Box 17 Roaring Gap, NC 28668
Telephone: (336) 957-8185

LOCATION: The main entrance is located halfway between Sparta and Elkin. Follow US-21 North to Traphill Rd (SR-1002). Take Traphill Rd West and go 4.3 miles to John P. Frank Parkway (SR-1784). Follow the parkway north to the main park entrance. Designated parking area for horse trailers is on the left 2.5 miles beyond the hiker's parking lot (becomes a gravel road.)

An alternate route provides an easier access to the horse trailer parking lot via the park's west entrance. From US-21 take Traphill Rd (SR-1002) for 5.1 miles. Turn right onto Longbottom Rd (SR-1737). Go 3 miles and turn right at the park's sign onto the gravel road. Horse trailer parking area is 0.4 mile on the right.

SEASON: open 8 a.m.-dark daily year round; closed Christmas Day

FACILITY REVIEW
TYPE: day use only
HORSE CAMPING FACILITIES: none
RESTROOMS: flush and pit toilets (none at the horse trailer parking area)
DAY RIDERS FEE: none
PARK ENTRANCE FEE: none

TRAIL REVIEW
TYPE: marked occasionally
TERRAIN: rolling hills-hilly
DIFFICULTY: easy-moderate
LENGTH: 6+ miles (one-way)
WATER: yes
TRAIL MAPS: Stone Mountain State Park
TRAIL NOTES: Access the bridle trail by riding northeast on the park's gravel road for approximately 0.3 mile from the horse trailer parking area. Turn right, crossing a small wooden bridge over the East Prong Roaring River. The horse trail begins on the right.

This is a fairly wide wooded trail through hardwood and evergreen forests. The trail also passes through a large open grassy field and crosses a few small streams and Big Sandy Creek. Backtrack to the trailhead or turn left at its terminus

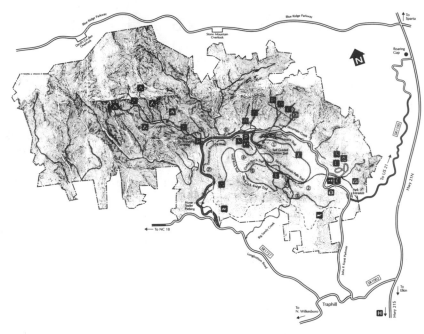

Stone Mountain State Park
Reprinted courtesy of NC Division of Parks and Recreation

and ride the park road (John P. Frank Parkway) back to the main park entrance
to create a loop.

During the wintertime the bridle trail provides good views of Stone Mountain, especially as it follows along Blackjack Ridge. Views are limited other times
of the year due to the dense foliage.

HIGHLIGHTS: Stone Mountain, nice forests and mountain streams, Piedmont
and mountain flora, wildlife habitat including deer, bear, bobcat and wild goats

GENERAL/HISTORICAL NOTES: Stone Mountain is a 600-foot tall granite
dome nestled at the southern edge of the Blue Ridge Mountains. In 1975, it was
designated as a National Natural Landmark. Two smaller granite exposures
within the park are Wolf Rock and Cedar Rock, located southwest of Stone
Mountain. A combination of Piedmont and mountain plant life contributes to
the uniqueness and beauty of this area.

Three dazzling waterfalls are located along hiking trails in the 13,000-acre
park. The largest and best known is Stone Mountain Falls (also called Beauty
Falls) that cascades 200 feet down a granite stone. The earliest inhabitants in this

area included the Catawba Indians. Loggers and farmers later moved and settled here long before it was designated as a state park. Land donations from the North Carolina Granite Corporation and R. Philip Hanes, Jr. in the 1960s and early 1970s led to the creation of the state park in 1969.

OTHER ACTIVITIES: hiking, backpacking, rock climbing, picnicking, trout fishing; family, group and backpack camping

NEAREST CITIES/FACILITIES: Elkin, Traphill, Sparta

Stone Mountain Grocery/Cafe is near the main park entrance on Traphill Road. McGrady Grocery Store is west on Longbottom Rd (SR-1737), 0.6 mile from the Stone Mountain State Park west entrance.

Doughton Park, a part of the Blue Ridge Parkway and managed by the National Park Service, is located nearby. It offers an additional trail of 6.5 miles (one-way) beginning from Longbottom Road (SR-1737, becomes gravel road SR-1730 en route) 5.5 miles from the west entrance of Stone Mountain State Park. See "Doughton Park" within the National Park chapter for more detailed information.

Stone Mountain

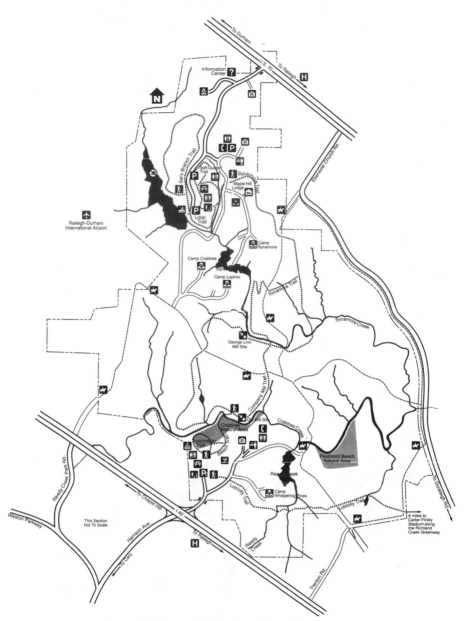

William B. Umstead State Park
Reprinted courtesy of NC Division of Parks and Recreation

146

WILLIAM B. UMSTEAD STATE PARK

County: Wake

Address: Rt. 8, Box 130 Raleigh, NC 27612
Telephone: (919) 787-3033

LOCATION: The park has two main entrances. The Reedy Creek section is off I-40, 3 miles west of Raleigh. The Crabtree Creek section is located on US-70, 2 miles northwest of Raleigh.

The park does not have a designated parking area for horse trailers within its boundaries. Trailer parking is allowed along the gravel roads of Ebenezer Church Rd and Reedy Creek Park Rd.

Bridle trails have 3 accesses:
1. Reedy Creek Park Road off I-40
2. On Trenton Rd from Duraleigh Rd
3. Ebenezer Church Rd off US-70

SEASON: open 8 a.m.-dark daily year round; closed Christmas Day

FACILITY REVIEW
TYPE: day use only
HORSE CAMPING FACILITIES: none
RESTROOMS: flush toilets are located within the park but are not accessible from the bridle trails
DAY RIDERS FEE: none
PARK ENTRANCE FEE: none

TRAIL REVIEW
TYPE: marked
TERRAIN: rolling hills
DIFFICULTY: easy
LENGTH: 16 miles
WATER: yes
TRAIL MAP: William B. Umstead State Park
TRAIL NOTES: The wide bridle trails consist of gravel roads that pass through some of the more remote areas in this 5,337-acre state park. They cross numerous creeks and bridges throughout the woodlands. The gravel roads form various combinations of loops as they connect both sections of the park, Reedy Creek and Crabtree Creek. Trails are shared with bicyclists and hikers.

RULES/REQUIREMENTS: Horses must stay on bridle trails and are not permitted in any other areas of the park. No alcoholic beverages allowed.

HIGHLIGHTS: excellent trails for the novice horse and/or rider, nice woodlands and creeks, lakes, natural areas, wildlife

GENERAL/HISTORICAL NOTES: This area was once a great wilderness where Indians lived. Wildlife such as bison and elk inhabited the vast forests. Settlers later used the land for farming and logging until their poor techniques

Trails of Umstead State Park

led to erosion. The Civilian Conservation Corps (CCC) began work in 1938 to restore the area, and built several visitor's facilities including the lakes and trails.

The park was originally divided into two separate state parks and called Reedy Creek State Park and Crabtree Creek State Park. The Reedy Creek section was once set aside for blacks only. The parks were eventually joined in 1966 and renamed after the former North Carolina governor, William B. Umstead. Today, this park lies within the heart of the Raleigh-Durham area. Raleigh, North Carolina's capital city, is one of the fastest growing cities in America. The Raleigh-Durham International Airport is located just northwest of the park's boundary.

OTHER ACTIVITIES: hiking, bicycling, fishing, family and group camping, picnicking, rental boats and canoes

NEAREST CITIES/FACILITIES: Raleigh, Durham

J & H Stables is located off Ebenezer Church Road and offers guided trail rides on rental horses within the state park. Call (919) 782-9830 to make reservations.

CHAPTER 10

NORTH CAROLINA GAME LANDS

The North Carolina Wildlife Resources Commission manages two million acres of game land in North Carolina, consisting of publicly and privately owned tracts. All national forests are also designated as state game lands.

The game lands are specifically for the activities of public hunting, trapping and fishing. Any other use of the land, including horseback riding, is secondary. Landowners of the private tracts have the authority to control and prohibit use of the land except for game purposes. Camping is only allowed on the game lands in specifically designated areas. The landowner also has complete control of the camping areas.

A few game lands completely prohibit horses, while others allow horseback riding only during specific times of the year. It is highly recommended not to ride horses in any of the game lands during hunting season. Blaze orange should be worn at all times to minimize the chance of an accident.

CURRENT REGULATIONS:

1. Horseback riding is prohibited at any time of year within the Butner-Falls of Neuse, Jordan, and Guilford County Farm Game Lands.
2. Thurmond Chatham and Caswell Game Lands only allow horseback riding during June, July and August, and on Sundays except during turkey and deer hunting seasons. Horses may be ridden only on the roads and trails open to vehicles. Horsemen must possess a game lands license in order to ride in these areas. Be aware of the fact that most of the roads in the Thurmond Chatham game lands are only open during hunting season.

Game land maps and a regulations digest can be obtained by contacting the North Carolina Wildlife Commission at 512 N. Salisbury St., Raleigh, NC 27604-1188; telephone (919) 733-7191. These booklets contain annually updated information including hunting seasons, current regulations and restrictions, and general locations and boundaries of each game land.

There has been much debate over the past few years on the admittance of horses within the game lands. In 1992, the game lands of Jordan and Butner-Falls of Neuse near Raleigh were closed to horseback riding by the N.C. Wildlife Commission. The North Carolina Horse Council has worked, so far unsuccessfully, to reopen these lands. Horsemen should support the council to help maintain access of our current trails before they too disappear.

LISTING OF GAME LANDS

Alcoa: 6,909 acres in Davie, Davidson, Montgomery, Rowan and Stanly Counties; 1,617 acres in Rowan and Davidson Counties

Angola Bay: 21,134 acres in Duplin and Pender Counties

Anson: 2,886 acres in Anson County

Bachelor Bay: 9,446 acres in Washington and Bertie Counties

Bladen Lakes State Forest: 31,640 acres in Bladen County

Brushy Mountains: 2,493 acres in Alexander and Caldwell Counties

Butner-Falls of Neuse: closed to horseback riding; 43,554 acres in Durham, Granville and Wake Counties

Camden: 1,445 acres in Camden County

Carson Woods: 960 acres in Ashe County

Caswell: 16,010 acres in Caswell County; horseback riding permitted but with certain restrictions

Catawba: 2,353 acres in Catawba and Iredell Counties

Chatham: 571 acres in Chatham County

Cherry Farm: 1,400 acres in Wayne County

Chowan Swamp: 8,884 acres in Gates County

Croatan National Forest: 157,000 acres in Craven, Jones and Carteret Counties

Dare: 45,149 acres in Dare County

Dysartsville: 7,536 acres in McDowell and Rutherford Counties

Elk Knob: 1,638 acres in Watauga and Ashe Counties

Elk Ridge: 1,140 acres in Ashe County

Gardner-Webb: 2,654 acres in Cleveland County

Goose Creek: 7,599 acres in Beaufort and Pamlico Counties

Green River: 20,843 acres in Henderson, Rutherford and Polk Counties; 7,536 acres in McDowell and Rutherford Counties

Green Swamp: 14,296 acres in Brunswick County

Guilford County Farm: closed to horseback riding; 756 acres in Guilford County

Gull Rock: 19,436 acres in Hyde County

H.M. Bizzell, Sr.: 415 acres in Lenoir County

Hofmann Forest: 20,121 acres in Jones and Onslow Counties

Holly Shelter: 48,795 acres in Pender County

Huntsville Community Farms: 844 acres in Yadkin County

Jordan: closed to horseback riding; 40,324 acres in Chatham, Durham, Orange and Wake Counties

Lantern Acres: 1,825 acres in Washington and Tyrrell Counties

Lee: 2,421 acres in Lee County

Moore: 1,169 acres in Moore County

Nantahala National Forest: 516,000 acres in Cherokee, Clay, Graham, Jackson, Macon and Swain Counties

New Lake: 394 acres in Hyde County

North River: 8,730 acres in Currituck County

Northwest River Marsh: 1,251 acres in Currituck County

Pee Dee River: 12,577 acres in Anson and Richmond Counties, 645 acres in Montgomery and Stanly Counties

Person: 7,938 acres in Person County

Pisgah National Forest: 495,000 acres in Avery, Buncombe, Burke, Haywood, Henderson, Madison, McDowell, Mitchell, Transylvania and Yancey Counties

Pungo River: 614 acres in Hyde County

Roanoke River Wetlands and Roanoke River National Wildlife Refuge: 19,485 acres in Bertie, Halifax and Martin Counties

Sandhills: 60,203 acres in Richmond, Scotland and Moore Counties

Sauratown Plantation: 3,258 acres in Stokes County

Shearon Harris: 4,361 acres in Wake County; 3,429 acres in Chatham County

South Mountains: 7,307 acres in Burke and Cleveland Counties

Sutton Lake: 3,322 acres in New Hanover County

Thurmond Chatham: 6,231 acres in Wilkes County; horseback riding permitted but with certain restrictions

Toxaway: 14,720 acres in Transylvania County

Uwharrie National Forest: 46,390 acres in Montgomery, Randolph and Davidson Counties

Vance: 841 acres in Vance County

Yadkin: 998 acres in Caldwell County

1. Biltmore Saddle & Bridle Club
2. Cane Creek Park
3. Cedarock County Park
4. Las Praderas
5. Latta Plantation Park
6. Leatherwood Mountains

7. Love Valley
8. Old College Farm Trail
9. Sauratown Trail
10. Springmaid Mountain
11. Tanglewood Park

CHAPTER 11

REGIONAL TRAILS

North Carolina has numerous privately maintained horse trails in addition to federal and state lands. Several facilities offer overnight camping and/or guided trail rides on rental horses. Included in these listings of regional trails are county parks, private clubs, camps and resorts.

Many facilities have their own set of rules and requirements, so be sure to read this section in addition to "Basic Trail Guidelines." Obey their rules to ensure the continued access of private facilities to horsemen. In these days of decreasing national and state lands that permit horseback riding, we have to rely on privately managed trails to meet our recreational activity needs.

The Sertoma Trails Network closed and has been deleted from this book, while the Sauratown Trail has been added. A new section, "North Carolina Private Stables and Outfitters," is located at the end of the chapter.

BILTMORE SADDLE & BRIDLE CLUB

County: Buncombe

Address: P.O. Box 15072 Asheville, NC 28813
Telephone: (828) 274-6943 or (828) 274-3757

Manager: Jane Howell

LOCATION: Must contact Jane Howell for directions. Reservations are required.

SEASON: open daily year round

FACILITY REVIEW
TYPE: day use and/or overnight horse camping
HORSE CAMPING FACILITIES: primitive
CAMPING FEE: $5.00/night
HOT SHOWERS: none
RESTROOMS: flush toilets (at barn)
STABLE FACILITIES: box stall (limited), trailer tie
STABLING FEE: $15.00/day box stall
DAY RIDERS FEE: $15.00/day
CLUB ENTRANCE FEE: none

TRAIL REVIEW
TYPE: marked
TERRAIN: rolling hills; flat and sandy along river bottoms
DIFFICULTY: easy-moderate
LENGTH: 100+ miles
WATER: yes
TRAIL MAP: yes
TRAIL NOTES: Well-maintained, very wide and smooth carriage roads. These trails form a vast network of loops and connecting paths throughout the dense forest. One beautiful trail follows the French Broad River bottoms. Excellent trails for the novice horse and rider.

RULES/REQUIREMENTS: You must contact Jane Howell (barn manager) to make reservations for trail riding and stabling. Proof of a current negative Coggins test within the past twelve months is required. No campfires or firearms. No carousing or cowboying is allowed on the trails.

Biltmore Bridle & Saddle Club

HIGHLIGHTS: wide trails, nice forests, French Broad River, secluded. The Biltmore House is visible from the top of the hill at the indoor riding ring.

GENERAL/HISTORICAL NOTES: In 1887, George Vanderbilt visited the Asheville area and purchased 125,000 acres for his estate. The Biltmore House was built in the late 1800s and modeled after the French chateaux. The largest private home in the U.S., it is named after the old English word "more," which means rolling hills. The House is surrounded by beautiful gardens, stables and the historic Biltmore Forest. A portion of the original estate is now part of the Pisgah National Forest. It is here that Vanderbilt began the first practices of forestry management in America.

OTHER ACTIVITIES: dressage and hunter/jumper shows, indoor arena is available for schooling, annual NATRC competitive trail ride in August

NEAREST CITY/FACILITIES: Asheville
    A modern campground is approximately 15 miles away from the Biltmore Saddle & Bridle Club. Call the Club for details. Lake Powhatan Campground (family camping only: no horses) is located near Bent Creek in the Pisgah National Forest and offers hot showers and public telephones. Call (828) 667-8429 for more information.

CANE CREEK PARK

County: Union

Address: Union County Parks and Recreation
5213 Harkey Rd Waxhaw, NC 28173
Telephone: (704) 843-3919

LOCATION: From the junction of NC-16 and NC-75 in Waxhaw, go 0.3 mile on NC-75 West. Go south on Providence Rd (SR-1117; becomes Old Waxhaw-Monroe Rd) for 1.6 miles. Turn right and go 4.5 miles on Providence Rd. Follow the signs to the "Day Use Area" on the north side of Cane Creek Lake. Turn left on Harkey Rd (SR-1121) and go 0.8 mile to the park entrance (Day Use Area) on the right. Horse trailer parking area is in a gravel lot at the ballfield on the left, 0.2 mile past the operations center.

Camping is permitted on the south side of the lake. On Providence Rd, go one mile beyond the junction with Harkey Rd. Turn left on Cane Creek Rd and go 1.5 miles. Go straight after the campground entrance towards the Group Camping Area. Horse overnight camping is allowed in a grassy field on the left, 0.3 mile after the entrance.

SEASON: open year round
DAILY HOURS: dawn to sunset

FACILITY REVIEW
TYPE: day use and/or overnight horse camping
HORSE CAMPING FACILITIES: primitive
CAMPING FEE: $10.00/site minimum; over 5 persons=$2.00/person
Must be paid in advance. Check out time: 3:00 pm
HOT SHOWERS: yes (bathhouse)
RESTROOMS: flush toilets in family and group campgrounds
STABLE FACILITIES: none (trailer tie)
DAY RIDERS FEE: $1.00
PARK ENTRANCE FEE: $1.00

TRAIL REVIEW
TYPE: marked (various colors of paint blazes)
TERRAIN: rolling hills
DIFFICULTY: easy
LENGTH: 14 miles
WATER: yes
TRAIL MAP: yes

TRAIL NOTES: The wooded bridle trails wind along wide pathways in this 1,050-acre county park. Various trails can be combined to form loops. The park's forests and meadows surround the 350-acre Cane Creek Lake. Trails are located on the north (day use area) and south (camping) sides of the lake. One trail crosses over the lake's dam to provide a link to the park's north and south sides. Bridle trails are shared with hikers and bicyclers.

RULES/REQUIREMENTS: Horseback riding is not allowed in the family camping area, picnic areas or along roadways. All campers must register and pay fees at campstore.

HIGHLIGHTS: nice views of Cane Creek Lake, natural woodland areas, good trails for the novice horse or rider

OTHER ACTIVITIES: hiking, bicycling, backpacking, fishing, boating, canoeing, family and group camping, lake swimming, recreational areas, picnicking

NEAREST CITIES/FACILITIES: Waxhaw, Monroe, Charlotte
   The park has a camp store that provides concessions, firewood, ice, picnic and fishing supplies.

CEDAROCK COUNTY PARK

County: Alamance

Address: Rec & Parks Dept. 217 College St. Graham, NC 27253
Telephone: (336) 570-6760

LOCATION: At the junction of I-85/NC-49 in Burlington, go 6.5 miles south on NC-49. Turn left onto Friendship-Patterson Mill Rd (SR-1130). Go 0.3 mile to Cedarock Park Rd (SR-2409) and the park entrance on the left. Horse trailer parking area and bridle trailhead is on the right, past the Garrett House Office.

SEASON: open year round
DAILY HOURS: 8:00 a.m.-8:00 p.m.; closed Mondays

FACILITY REVIEW
TYPE: day use and/or overnight horse camping
HORSE CAMPING FACILITIES: primitive
CAMPING FEE: none
HOT SHOWERS: none
RESTROOMS: flush and pit toilets
STABLE FACILITIES: none (trailer tie)
DAY RIDERS FEE: none
PARK ENTRANCE FEE: none

TRAIL REVIEW
TYPE: marked (blazed orange)
TERRAIN: rolling hills
DIFFICULTY: easy
LENGTH: 4 miles
WATER: yes
TRAIL MAP: yes
TRAIL NOTES: Trails pass through woods and open fields with several creek crossings in this 414-acre county park.

RULES/REQUIREMENTS: Must make arrangements and register with a ranger for overnight camping. Horseback riders must stay on designated trails and are not allowed in other areas of the park.

HIGHLIGHTS: nature preserve, historical areas

GENERAL/HISTORICAL NOTES: This park is located in the foothills of the Cane Mountain range. It is named for the numerous cedar trees and rock formations found in the park. German immigrants were among the first settlers to live in the area. Remnants and artifacts of their settlements, including an old mill site and a rock dam, are visible today.

OTHER ACTIVITIES: fishing, hiking, recreation areas, primitive family camping

NEAREST CITIES/FACILITIES: Alamance, Burlington, Liberty

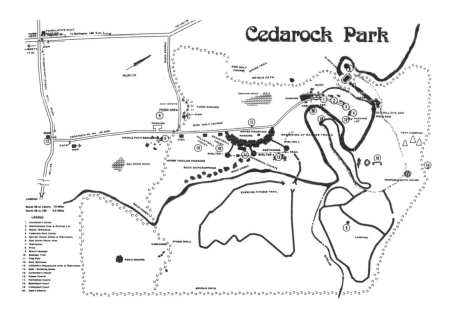

Reprinted courtesy of Alamance Co. Parks & Recreation

LAS PRADERAS

County: Buncombe

Address: See Off Road
Rt. 1, Box 12A
Brevard, NC 28712

Telephone: For cottage rates and reservations: (828) 883-3375, Nancy Searles, owner. For stabling and trail riding information: (828) 884-6375, Orr's Equine Enterprises/Roy and Wayne Orr.

LOCATION: From I-26 in Asheville, take exit #9 (airport exit.) Follow NC-280 west to the intersection of Broad and Main streets in Brevard, approximately 18 miles from the airport. Go 7.1 miles south on US-276. Turn left onto See Off Mountain Road and go 1.7 miles to Las Praderas sign. Turn right and follow the signs.

SEASON: open daily year round
DAILY HOURS: 8 a.m.-5 p.m.

FACILITY REVIEW
TYPE: day use and/or overnight accommodations
HORSE CAMPING FACILITIES: no horse camping available; overnight accommodations include four furnished cottages with full kitchen, heating and air conditioning
COTTAGE FEE: call for rates and reservations
HOT SHOWERS: yes
RESTROOMS: yes
OTHER FACILITIES: laundry, cable TV and VCR, outdoor gas grill, boarding kennel for pets
STABLE FACILITIES: 27 box stalls, indoor wash stall, 60 ft. covered round pen, outdoor riding ring
STABLING FEE: $15.00/night (includes hay, feed, bedding, stall cleaning, use of arenas and trails)
DAY RIDERS FEE: $20.00/day-by appointment only; must be guided
RESORT ENTRANCE FEE: none

TRAIL REVIEW
TYPE: unmarked; no rental horses
TERRAIN: hilly-mountainous
DIFFICULTY: moderate

LENGTH: 30-50 miles
WATER: yes
TRAIL MAP: none
TRAIL NOTES: Scenic trails wind through woods and pass by waterfalls on 15,000 acres of privately owned land. Well-maintained and picturesque, Las Praderas' trails offer a variety of terrain for the vacationer from fairly level to mountainous.

RULES/REQUIREMENTS: Reservations are required. There is a minimum stay of two days in cottages. A current negative Coggins test is required on all horses before unloading.

HIGHLIGHTS: beautiful mountain setting; excellent vacation spot near the Pisgah Ranger District of Pisgah National Forest and a variety of activities in western North Carolina

GENERAL/HISTORICAL NOTES: Las Praderas is a 32-acre farm and resort located 9 miles south of Brevard. Spanish for "the meadows," Las Praderas also raises, trains and sells Paso Fino and Appalachian Singlefoot horses in the highland meadows and mountains of North Carolina.

OTHER ACTIVITIES: motor home camping, long term boarding and overnight stabling

NEAREST CITIES/FACILITIES: Brevard, Asheville
    A tack shop and gift shop are located at the resort.

LATTA PLANTATION PARK

County: Mecklenburg

Address: Rt. 3, Box 882 Huntersville, NC 28078
Telephone: Park: (704) 875-1391
    Rick Hunning (Equestrian Center): (704) 875-0808

LOCATION: From the south, take I-77 North towards Statesville. Take Sunset Rd exit (16B West) and go 0.5 mile to Beatties Ford Rd (SR-2074). Turn right and go 5 miles. Turn left on Sample Rd (SR-2125) and go 0.7 mile to the park entrance. Parking area for horse trailers is on the right, 0.4 mile past the entrance gate and beyond the Equestrian Center.

From the north, take I-77 South towards Charlotte. Take NC-73 West (exit 28). Turn right and go 4.8 miles. Turn left on Beatties Ford Rd and go 4.6 miles. Turn right on Sample Rd and go 0.7 mile into the park entrance.

SEASON: open year round (Closed on Mondays during winter)
DAILY HOURS: 9 a.m.-dark weekdays; 7 a.m.-dark weekends

FACILITY REVIEW
TYPE: day use
HORSE CAMPING FACILITIES: none
RESTROOMS: flush toilets
STABLE FACILITIES: box stalls (can board overnight or longer)
DAY RIDERS FEE: none
PARK ENTRANCE FEE: none

TRAIL REVIEW
TYPE: marked; guided trail rides on rental horses
TERRAIN: rolling hills
DIFFICULTY: easy
LENGTH: 6 miles
WATER: yes
TRAIL MAP: yes
TRAIL NOTES: The bridle trails are wide pathways through the woods that weave across the park on the north and south sides of the main park road. Various combinations of loops and backtracking trips are possible. Trails are shared with hikers and bicyclers. There are no campgrounds nearby. If boarding your horse overnight, you must stay at a local motel.

Gar Creek Trail follows along Gar Creek on the southeastern side of the park. The Raptor Trail loops around the Carolina Raptor Center and connects to the

Powerline Trail on its west end. The Powerline Trail follows an old road along the powerline. Latta Place, an old plantation house, can be seen by riding Latta Trail. Buzzard Rock Trail is a short backtracking trip to a rock outcrop and scenic view of Mountain Island Lake.

Riding is also permitted along the paved park road but horses must be kept at a walk.

RULES/REQUIREMENTS: You must make an appointment for guided trail rides on rental horses. No camping or lake swimming is allowed. No horses are allowed in the picnic area beyond the rail fence or in Latta House area. Do not leave horses unattended. When watering your horse near the lake, dismount first. Walk while riding on the park road. No alcoholic beverages allowed within the park. Pets must be on a leash. Horses must be loaded on the trailer and ready to leave before the park's closing time.

HIGHLIGHTS: Latta Place, nice view of Mountain Island Lake, good beginner trails, excellent equestrian facility

GENERAL/HISTORICAL NOTES: This county park is a 760-acre nature habitat and has an equestrian center with 80 stalls and 2 arenas. Numerous equestrian events are held here throughout the year. The park is named for merchant, farmer and former owner James Latta. Latta Place is his restored plantation home near Mountain Island Lake and the Catawba River that was built in the 1800s.

OTHER ACTIVITIES: guided trail rides, riding lessons, horse shows, hiking, bicycling, canoeing, boating, picnic areas, Latta Place tours, Carolina Raptor Center (bird sanctuary)

NEAREST CITIES/FACILITIES: Charlotte, Cornelius, Huntersville

LEATHERWOOD MOUNTAINS

County: Wilkes

Address: 512 Meadow Rd Ferguson, NC 28624
Telephone: (336) 973-4142
Elk Creek Stables (336) 973-8635 or 1-800-462-6867

LOCATION: Leatherwood Mountains is located on Elk Creek Road (SR-1162) near the Blue Ridge Parkway. It is 20 miles from Wilkesboro off NC-268 West, 18 miles from Lenoir off NC-268 East and 15 miles from Boone off US-421, SR-1508 and SR-1166. Numerous signs are erected along the way.

SEASON: open daily year round

FACILITY REVIEW
TYPE: day use and/or overnight accommodations
HORSE CAMPING FACILITIES: no campground is available; cabins and private residences may be rented for overnight stays
FEE: Cabin rental fees vary; call for more information on current rates and minimum stay requirements
HOT SHOWERS: yes
RESTROOMS: flush toilets
STABLE FACILITIES: 60 box stalls (10 outside stalls)
STABLING FEE: $15.00/day
DAY RIDERS FEE: $5.00/day
RESORT ENTRANCE FEE: none

TRAIL REVIEW
TYPE: marked; horse rentals available
TERRAIN: hilly-mountainous
DIFFICULTY: easy-difficult
LENGTH: 100+ miles
WATER: yes (water is infrequent at higher elevations)
TRAIL MAP: yes
TRAIL NOTES: Horseback riding is permitted on gravel roads, wooded trails and old logging roads along mountain streams on over 30,000 acres of the scenic southern slopes of the Blue Ridge Mountains.

Most trails are wide pathways through the forest. One nice trail climbs a ridge to a rocky outcropping called Raven Rock and provides a gorgeous view of the foothills below. Along the way is a spur trail leading to a beautiful waterfall. Meadow Run is a pretty meadow area between the ridges of West Ridge,

Hawkrest and Elk Ridge. Numerous bridle trailheads span out from an area beyond Meadow Run where the Keys Cabin is located. An all day loop trail ride leads to a scenic view from near Dugger Mountain.

RULES/REQUIREMENTS: You must show proof of a negative Coggins test within the past twelve months. Horses must be stalled in the barn if staying overnight. Bring your own feed and hay if stabling overnight. Shirts are required at all times. No haltertops. No alcoholic beverages are allowed in public. You must call and make reservations for horse rentals. It is best to also call ahead for day use of the facility. Register at the stable before riding. A special parking area for day riders is provided. Boarding is available for $150.00/month. Horse rental rates: $15.00/one hour, $10.00 an hour/2 hours or more, $50.00/day.

HIGHLIGHTS: good views of the Blue Ridge Mountains from historic Elk Ridge and Dugger Mountain, wildlife, beautiful mountain streams, secluded environment, excellent trails for the novice horse and/or rider

GENERAL/HISTORICAL NOTES: This beautiful mountain area of the Blue Ridge has been owned by the R.B. Johnston family for several years. Small tracts of land are currently offered for sale in this unique private community. It is reported Daniel Boone passed through this area along Elk Ridge during his many wilderness travels.

OTHER ACTIVITIES: fishing, hiking, rental cabins, boarding

NEAREST CITIES/FACILITIES: Wilkesboro, Lenoir, Boone
Several recreational areas are located nearby. Call or write for more information.

LOVE VALLEY

County: Iredell

Address: P.O. Box 265 Love Valley, NC 28677
Telephone: (704) 592-7451; Andy Barker, mayor

LOCATION: Love Valley is located halfway between Statesville and North Wilkesboro. From I-40, go north on NC-115. Go 10 miles and turn left on Mountain View Rd (SR-1614). Follow the Love Valley signs from there. Go 2.5 miles and turn right onto SR-1611. Go 0.7 mile to the end of the paved road. The town of Love Valley is straight ahead along the gravel road.

Public trailer parking and camping area is located in the lower end of town near the rodeo arena. From the main road in town, turn left onto Tori Pass and go 0.1 mile. Turn right and the town's free campground is on the right.

SEASON: open daily year round

FACILITY REVIEW
TYPE: day use and/or overnight horse camping
HORSE CAMPING FACILITIES: primitive
CAMPING FEE: none at the town's campground; local private campgrounds charge various fees (see Nearest Cities/Facilities)
HOT SHOWERS: none at the town's free campground (see Nearest Cities/Facilities)
RESTROOMS: pit toilets
STABLE FACILITIES: trailer tie in the town's free campground (see Nearest Cities/Facilities)
DAY RIDERS FEE: none
TOWN ENTRANCE FEE: none

TRAIL REVIEW
TYPE: mostly unmarked; horse rentals available
TERRAIN: rolling hills-mountainous
DIFFICULTY: easy-moderate
LENGTH: 100+ miles
WATER: yes
TRAIL MAP: none
TRAIL NOTES: Trails wind through the Brushy Mountains and consist of wooded pathways and old logging roads. Many of these trails are on privately owned land. Numerous gravel roads in the area can be utilized as a connector

to the trails. Main street in town is named the Henry Martin Trail. At the end of the main street in town near the rodeo arena is a major trailhead.

RULES/REQUIREMENTS: On weekends when the rodeos are scheduled, the town's free campground is for parking only; no campers. Do not tie horses to the chain link fence in the town's campground.

HIGHLIGHTS: scenic foothills of the Brushy Mountains, "Old West" atmosphere

GENERAL/HISTORICAL NOTES: Love Valley, the self-proclaimed "Cowboy Capital," is located in a valley at the foothills of the Brushy Mountains. The town is modeled according to a western theme with weathered wooden buildings, board sidewalks, hitching rails and an arena where several rodeos are held throughout the year. The Ponder Leather Company is also located within the town. Love Valley was begun in 1954 by Andy Barker after he returned home from World War II. He developed plans for an "Old West" town while he was fighting in the European foxholes. Barker is the current mayor of Love Valley.

OTHER ACTIVITIES: rodeos, wagon trains, poker runs

NEAREST CITIES/FACILITIES: Statesville, Wilkesboro, Harmony, Union Grove

Stabling is available at Love Valley Stables which is located on the main road to Love Valley. This stable is open year round; by appointment in the wintertime. Overnight stabling, rental horses and riding lessons are offered. Contact (704) 592-2024 for more information.

Martha's Cowboy Campground is located one mile from the Love Valley town and offers primitive camping and hot showers. Contact Martha and John Webster at (704) 592-2013.

Ottare Farm is located on Brookhaven Rd (SR-1590), a short distance from Love Valley, and offers trailer parking and camping. Contact Joan Rash at (704) 592-2791 for information.

Horses may also be boarded at BMW Stables. Contact Benny and Gay Burr at (704) 592-5012 for information.

Additional areas that offer camping are: Betty and Ron Trivette at (704) 592-9431; and Dale Jolly at (704) 592-2053.

A new area in Love Valley is currently being developed with lots available for lease by the year. Weekend rentals are also available, including horses, stalls, hot showers, bed and breakfast, and overnight parking. Contact Mike and Cheryl Caruso at (704) 592-5517 for more information.

There are several restaurants located within or near Love Valley.

OLD COLLEGE FARM TRAIL

County: Cleveland

Address: Boiling Springs, NC

Information: Fred Blackley
504 South Dekalb St. Shelby, NC 28150
(704) 484-1731

LOCATION: Take NC-150 and go 3 miles south of Boiling Springs. The parking area is on the north side of the Broad River bridge. The trail can also be accessed from the northwest off Old College Farm Rd (SR-1195). Parking is allowed along the side of the gravel road.

SEASON: open daily year round

FACILITY REVIEW
TYPE: day use and/or overnight horse camping
HORSE CAMPING FACILITIES: primitive
CAMPING FEE: none
HOT SHOWERS: none
RESTROOMS: none
STABLE FACILITIES: none (trailer tie)
DAY RIDERS FEE: none

TRAIL REVIEW
TYPE: marked
TERRAIN: rolling hills-hilly
DIFFICULTY: moderate
LENGTH: 9+ miles
WATER: yes
TRAIL MAP: yes
TRAIL NOTES: The loop trail winds through the forest on old roadbeds, forest roads and narrow pathways. It provides scenic views of the Broad River and Jolly Mountain. Old College Farm Rd (SR-1195) is utilized as a connector for the trail. A primitive campsite is located on Jolly Mountain.

RULES/REQUIREMENTS: No motorized vehicles allowed on trails.

HIGHLIGHTS: nice forests and flora, Broad River, Jolly Mountain

GENERAL/HISTORICAL NOTES: This trail was developed by the Cleveland County Trails Association, the Broad River Group of the Sierra Club and the Boy Scout Troop 100 on private property owned by the Duke Power Company and Federal Paperboard Company.

OTHER ACTIVITIES: hiking, primitive camping

NEAREST CITY/FACILITIES: Boiling Springs

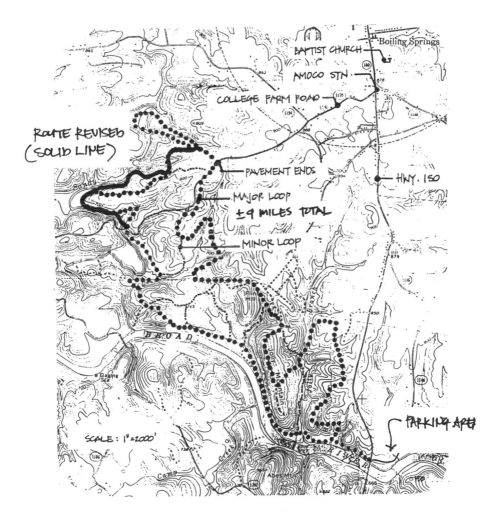

Old College Farm Trail
Reprinted courtesy of Old College Farm Trail

SAURATOWN TRAIL

County: Stokes

Stables: Sauratown Mountain Stables   Owner: Tim McKinney
Address: Rt. 1, Box 213 Westfield, NC 27053
Telephone: Sauratown Mountain Stables: (336) 994-2182
(336) 924-6072 Joy McNabb, President, Sauratown Trails Association;
(336) 983-4757 Beverly Duval

LOCATION: Two areas are available to access the trail:
1. Sauratown Mountain Stables: Take US-52 to Moore-RJR exit. Turn left and go 4.5 miles to NC-66. Turn left (follow the Hanging Rock State Park signs). Go 7 miles and turn right onto Moore Springs Rd (SR-1001). Go one mile and turn right at Sauratown Mountain Stables sign.
2. Sauratown Trails picnic area: Take US-52 to Moore-RJR exit. Turn left and go 4.5 miles to NC-66. Turn left and go 7.5 miles to the second entrance to Taylor Rd. Turn left and go 0.2 mile. Turn right on Rock House Rd and go 0.3 mile to the parking area and picnic shelter on the left (at the red gate).

SEASON: open daily year round

FACILITY REVIEW
TYPE: day use and/or overnight horse camping
HORSE CAMPING FACILITIES: primitive
CAMPING FEE: $6.00/person at Sauratown Mountain Stables; electric use $10.00/night; parking for truck and trailer $10.00/night; RV hookup available
HOT SHOWERS: none
RESTROOMS: pit toilet
STABLE FACILITIES: 20-stall barn at Sauratown Mountain Stables
STABLING FEE: $6.00/night at stables
DAY RIDERS FEE: none

TRAIL REVIEW
TYPE: marked (blazed with white circle dots); guided trail rides by reservation on the weekends $15.00/group; rental horses also available by appointment
TERRAIN: rolling hills-hilly
DIFFICULTY: moderate
LENGTH: total of 25+ miles including 3 loop trails available in this area; connects to 6-mile Loop Trail in Hanging Rock State Park
WATER: yes
TRAIL MAP: yes (available at the stables)

TRAIL NOTES: This single-track trail travels across privately-owned property. Property owners have signed a lease agreement with the Sauratown Trails Association, Inc. allowing horsemen to ride here. Sauratown Trail crosses four paved roads on its way to connect to the trailhead of the Loop Trail just off Charlie Young Rd (SR-2028) within Hanging Rock State Park.

Numerous creeks and streams are along the way. Three other loop trails are also available for horseback riding. Along Section 1 (the first part of the trail near the picnic area) is a short spur trail that leads to a pretty waterfall and a nice area to take a break from riding.

Sauratown Mountain Stables is a privately-owned family campground located in the middle of the Sauratown Trail. From the stables you can choose to ride toward Hanging Rock State Park or go in the opposite direction toward Pilot Mountain and stop at the Sauratown Trails picnic area on Rock House Rd. Currently this trail ends at the picnic area and does not extend to Pilot Mountain State Park.

RULES/REQUIREMENTS: Please stay on the trail and do not trespass onto private property. A negative Coggins test within the past twelve months is required at Sauratown Mountain Stables and also at the picnic area during organized trail rides. Reservations are suggested for the stables. A deposit of $20.00 is required for the stables and family campground, but it is refundable if a cancellation notice is given seven days in advance of arrival.

HIGHLIGHTS: connects to trail in Hanging Rock State Park, beautiful mountain flora, creeks, views of Moore's Knob

GENERAL/HISTORICAL NOTES: The Sauratown Trail is privately-maintained by the Sauratown Trails Association, Inc. It was newly-reopened to the public in June 1995. The master plan is for the trail to eventually connect to Pilot Mountain State Park on its western end. Upon completion, the entire trail will connect Pilot Mountain State Park to Hanging Rock State Park. Sauratown Trails Association, Inc. is a volunteer group that believes in preserving our heritage. Contact the above address and/or phone numbers for more information or membership details with the association.

OTHER ACTIVITIES: hiking, camping, annual trail ride (Morris Animal Foundation's Ride for Research) in November

NEAREST CITIES/FACILITIES: Danbury, King, Pilot Mountain

Serenity Stables, near Pilot Mountain State Park, has weekend and pasture boarding available along with camping, RV hookups, and trail rides by appointment. Contact Bill and Pam Stowers at 1144 Shoals Rd, Pinnacle, NC 27043; telephone (336) 325-2229.

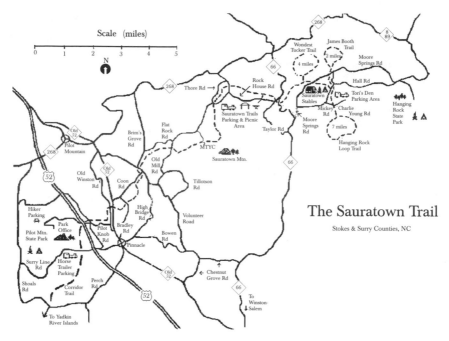

Scale (miles)

0   1   2   N   3   4   5

268

Wondest Tucker Trail   James Booth Trail   8 89

2 miles   Moore Springs Rd

4 miles

66

Rock House Rd   Hall Rd

Thore Rd →   268   Tori's Den Parking Area

Sauratown Stables

Hanging Rock State Park

Mickey Rd   Charlie Young Rd

Sauratown Trails Parking & Picnic Area   Moore Springs Rd

Flat Rock Rd   Taylor Rd   7 miles

Brim's Grove Rd

Pilot Mountain   268

Old 32

MTYC   Hanging Rock Loop Trail

Old Mill Rd   Sauratown Mtn.   66

Old Winston Rd   Old 32   Coon Rd

Old 52   Tillotson Rd

High Bridge Rd   Volunteer Road

Hiker Parking   **The Sauratown Trail**

Stokes & Surry Counties, NC

Park Office   Bradley Rd

Pilot Mtn. State Park   Pilot Knob Rd   Bowen Rd

Pinnacle

Surry Line Rd   Horse Trailer Parking

Shoals Rd   Perch Rd   Old 32   ← Chestnut Grove Rd

Corridor Trail   66

52   To Winston- ↓ Salem

To Yadkin River Islands

Reprinted courtesy of the Sauratown Trails Association, Inc.

*** *********

SPRINGMAID MOUNTAIN

County: Mitchell

Address: Rt. 3, Box 376 Spruce Pine, NC 28777
Telephone: (828) 765-2353 Manager: Alfred Breedin
Owner: Leroy Springs and Co.

LOCATION: Springmaid Mountain is located off the Blue Ridge Parkway, milepost 327.5 at McKinney Gap. An alternate access route is by taking the Marion exit from I-40. From Marion take NC-226 towards Spruce Pine. Turn right on Halltown Rd before reaching Spruce Pine. At the end of Halltown Rd, turn right on Altapass Rd. Turn left at the fire station and follow this road to Springmaid Mountain.

SEASON: open daily year round

FACILITY REVIEW
TYPE: day use and/or overnight horse camping
HORSE CAMPING FACILITIES: 26 modern campsites with electrical and water hookups; cabins are also available
CAMPING FEE: $8.00/each weekday; $10.00/each weekend night
HOT SHOWERS: yes; closed during winter months
RESTROOMS: flush toilets
STABLE FACILITIES: pasture board, trailer tie
STABLING FEE: $1.00/day
DAY RIDERS FEE: none
RESORT ENTRANCE FEE: none

TRAIL REVIEW
TYPE: well-marked; guided trail rides available
TERRAIN: mountainous-rugged
DIFFICULTY: moderate-difficult
LENGTH: 20+ miles
WATER: yes
TRAIL MAP: trail signboard display at camp
TRAIL NOTES: This 400-acre resort is near the North Toe River in the Blue Ridge Mountains. The mountainous trails are rocky and rugged in some sections.

RULES/REQUIREMENTS: Call to schedule guided trail rides.

HIGHLIGHTS: Blue Ridge Mountains, secluded

OTHER ACTIVITIES: fishing, swimming, hiking, volleyball, canoeing, rental cabins

NEAREST CITY/FACILITIES: Spruce Pine
   The Pisgah National Forest boundary is near this area.

TANGLEWOOD PARK

County: Forsyth

Address: P.O. Box 1040 Clemmons, NC 27012
Telephone: Equestrian Center: (336) 766-9540
Park Information: (336) 766-0591

LOCATION: Go 10 miles southwest of Winston-Salem on I-40 and take Exit 182. Go south 0.3 mile to US-158 (Clemmons Rd) and turn right. Go 0.4 mile to the park entrance on the left. Parking area for horse trailers is located on the right near the stables, 0.7 mile after the park entrance.

SEASON: open year round
DAILY HOURS: 8:00 a.m.-sunset

FACILITY REVIEW
TYPE: day use and/or overnight camping
HORSE CAMPING FACILITIES: modern and primitive family camping sites available (no horses allowed in campgrounds)
CAMPING FEE: $8.00-$16.00/night (over 4 persons=$1.50 each)
HOT SHOWERS: yes
RESTROOMS: flush toilets
STABLE FACILITIES: box stalls (limited)
STABLING FEE: $15.00/night
DAY RIDERS FEE: none
PARK ENTRANCE FEE: $2.00 per vehicle

TRAIL REVIEW
TYPE: marked; guided trail rides with rental horses available
TERRAIN: flat-rolling hills
DIFFICULTY: easy
LENGTH: 4 miles
WATER: yes
TRAIL MAP: none
TRAIL NOTES: Tanglewood's wide trails are along the woodlands and meadows of the Yadkin River bottoms. They provide an excellent route for the novice horse and rider. From the parking area at the stables, follow the gravel road behind the barns towards the steeplechase course and racetrack. The trails begin near here on the left. A gravel road can be used to form a loop back to the stables.

RULES/REQUIREMENTS: Proof of a negative Coggins test within the past twelve months is required. No horses are allowed in the campground areas. If camping overnight, horses must be stabled at the barn. It is best to call ahead and make stable reservations.

HIGHLIGHTS: beautiful landscape, Yadkin River, wildlife

GENERAL/HISTORICAL NOTES: Tanglewood was named by former owners Thomas and Margaret Griffith after Nathaniel Hawthorne's *Tanglewood Tales* due to the thick underbrush that grew along the Yadkin River. The land was later sold to Kate B. and William Neal Reynolds. In 1951 they donated their picturesque 1,200-acre piedmont estate to Forsyth County for the development of a park.

OTHER ACTIVITIES: annual steeplechase in May, riding lessons, boarding and training facilities, hay rides, carriage rides, bicycling, family camping, golf, swimming, boating, canoeing and paddleboats on a lake, fishing, tennis, picnicking, deer park, manor house bed and breakfast

NEAREST CITIES/FACILITIES: Winston-Salem, Clemmons

NORTH CAROLINA PRIVATE STABLES AND OUTFITTERS

1. Blowing Rock Stables
    Carl Underwood
    P.O. Box 26
    Blowing Rock, NC 28605
    (828) 295-7847

Offers guided trail rides on rental horses within Moses Cone Memorial Park along the Blue Ridge Parkway. Other facilities include overnight camping with electric and water hookups, hot showers, toilets, and overnight boarding.

2. Burnside Plantation "Bed and Barn"
    Agnes and George Harvin
    Rt. 10, Burnside
    Henderson, NC 27536
    (252) 438-7688; office: (252) 430-6161

Offers four 12'x14' stalls in restored 18th-century barn with board-fenced pastures, and miles of trails for use as a vacation or overnight layover spot. Nineteenth-century guest house has two bedrooms with private bath, living, dining, and kitchen facilities. Located near Kerr Lake for fishing, boating, swimming, etc. Reservations and a current negative Coggins test are required.

3. Buxton Stables, Inc.
    P.O. Box 545
    Buxton, NC 27920
    (252) 995-4659

Offers overnight boarding, trail rides through the Buxton Woods maritime forest, and beach rides on Hatteras Island.

4. Cataloochee Ranch
    Rt. 1, Box 500F
    Maggie Valley, NC 28751
    (828) 926-1401 or 1-800-868-1401; barn: (828) 926-8700

A guest ranch/resort near Maggie Valley that offers guided trail rides on rental horses and pack trips into the Great Smoky Mountains National Park. No personal horses or private camping is allowed. Offers meals, lodging, pool.

5. Clear Creek Guest Ranch
    100 Clear Creek Dr, Hwy 80 South
    Burnsville, NC 28714
    1-800-651-4510

Complete guest ranch offering horseback riding, meals, lodging, pool, spa, fishing, ranch activities and family entertainment. No personal horses, rental horses only.

6. Double Eagle Farm
    Greg and Karen Crisp
    50 Sawmill Creek Rd
    Bryson City, NC 28713
    (828) 488-9787

Offers overnight or long-term boarding; fourteen 12'x12' stalls, each with a window, skylight, and fan. Security system, indoor round pen, ample trailer parking space, and grain and hay available. Also offers training services, veterinarian and farrier on call. Located near hundreds of miles of trails within Nantahala National Forest and Great Smoky Mountains National Park. Provides trail maps and trail advice, and can arrange for trail guides. Also provides a list of lodging and campgrounds nearby. Call ahead to make reservations. Requirements include a flu shot at least 2-4 weeks before arrival and a negative Coggins test.

7. FENCE, Bed and Barn
    500 Hunting Country Rd
    Tryon, NC 28782
    (828) 859-9021

Offers a two-bedroom apartment in Foothills Equestrian Nature Center (FENCE) for use as a vacation or overnight layover spot; has eight 12'x14' stalls, paddock,

(FENCE continued)
riding ring, and several miles of riding and hiking trails in the scenic foothills of western North Carolina (between Asheville and Spartanburg, SC). Popular area for foxhunts and horse shows. Call for reservations and rates. Negative Coggins test and health papers are required.

8. 4B Farm, Inc.
    Larry and Helen Blackburn
    346 Mullinix Rd
    Troy, NC 27371
    (910) 572-CAMP or (910) 572-BARN

Offers camping and overnight stabling adjacent to Uwharrie National Forest. Has electric hookups and heated bathhouse. Annual memberships are available. Options for horses include box stalls, round pen, ring, or trailer tie. Call for rates and to reserve horse stalls. Negative Coggins test is required and no alcoholic beverages are allowed.

9. Horseplay Ranch
    Woodrow Place, Rt. 2, Box 727
    Lenoir, NC 28645
    (828) 757-9114

Offers indoor/outdoor stalls, new covered stalls, holding pens, primitive camping (with picnic tables, BBQ grill, campfire area), primitive log cabin, camper parking with water, and fishing. Located near several miles of trails. Reservations and negative Coggins test are required.

10. J & H Stables
     Raleigh, NC
     (919) 782-9830

Offers guided trail rides on rental horses within William B. Umstead State Park.

11. Ardie Keene
     514 Everett Farm Rd
     Pisgah Forest, NC 28768
     (828) 883-3241

(Ardie Keene continued)
Offers 8 acres of pasture and small indoor arena for use as a vacation or layover spot near Pisgah Ranger District of Pisgah National Forest. Near several miles of trails. A bed and breakfast is located within five minutes from farm. Reservations and negative Coggins test are required.

12. Misty Mountain Riding Center, Inc.
    1265 Dillingham Rd
    Barnardsville, NC 28709
    (828) 626-3644

Offers guided trail rides and horseback holidays within the Toecane Ranger District and Coleman Boundary Area of Pisgah National Forest.

13. Rose Creek Stables
    Patrice and Tim Strange
    70 Rose Creek Cove Rd
    Franklin, NC 28734
    (828) 524-6549 or 1-800-484-6188

Offers 12 indoor stalls, two paddock areas with small barns, pasture, outdoor arena, two-hour trail through mountains, and guest bedroom for use as a vacation or layover spot. Reservations and negative Coggins test are required.

14. Sauratown Mountain Stables
    Tim and Thelma McKinney
    Rt. 1, Box 213
    Westfield, NC 27053
    (336) 994-2182

Offers a family campground with electric and RV hookup possible, truck and trailer parking, and overnight stabling in a 20-stall barn near the Sauratown Trail and Hanging Rock State Park. Horse rentals and guided trail rides are available by appointment. Call for rates and reservations. A negative Coggins test within the past twelve months is required.

15. Seaside Stables
    P.O. Box 669
    Ocracoke, NC 27960
    (252) 928-3778

(Seaside Stables continued)
Offers overnight boarding and guided rides on rental horses on Ocracoke Island.

16. Serenity Stables
     Bill and Pam Stowers
     1144 Shoals Rd
     Pinnacle, NC 27043
     (336) 325-2229

A family-oriented stable located within riding distance of the trails in Pilot Mountain State Park. Offers weekend and pasture boarding, camping, RV hookups, and trail rides by appointment. No alcohol or drugs allowed.

17. Smokey Mtn. Outfitters
     Denny Russell
     Waterville, NC
     (828) 648-2313 or (828) 646-8934 or 1-800-532-4631

Offers completely-furnished cabin (sleeps six) and 5-stall barn adjoining GSMNP at Big Creek Area; bring your own horses or rental horses are available, guided or unguided trips, discounts for clubs. Also offers trout fishing and bear hunting, registered guides available. Located 10 minutes off I-40 at the Waterville exit, near the NC-TN border. Call for reservations. Currently in the process of expanding with two additional cabins and more stalls.

18. Tukanoshun Farms
     P.O. Box 54
     Scaly Mountain, NC 28775
     (828) 526-4196

Offers guided trail rides, cookouts, and picnic rides on beautiful mountain trails near North Carolina's Highlands/Cashiers area.

CHAPTER 12

LOCAL TRAILS OUTSIDE NORTH CAROLINA

The following list contains national forests, parks and public trails in states surrounding North Carolina where horseback riding is permitted. General information contacts are also included. Call or write for more detailed information on the facility and trails, much of which can be obtained for free.

Before traveling, be sure to check with each particular state's current requirements regarding Coggins testing and health certificates. Your local veterinarian should be knowledgeable in the current laws. Some facilities have requirements that differ from the state's policy on current Coggins tests. Check with the facility to find out its specific rules.

Camping at Mount Rogers National Recreation Area in Virginia.

GEORGIA

Georgia currently requires a negative Coggins test within the past twelve months for each horse before entering public parks and facilities.

NATIONAL PARKS AND FORESTS

1. National Forests Supervisor (Chattahoochee and Oconee)
   508 Oak St. N.W.
   Gainesville, GA 30501
   (770) 536-0541

2. Chattahoochee National Forest
   Chattooga Ranger District
   P.O. Box 196, Burton Road
   Clarkesville, GA 30523
   (706) 754-6221

Ladyslipper Trail: 6.2 miles; primitive camping

3. Chattahoochee National Forest
   Tallulah Ranger District
   P.O. Box 438
   Clayton, GA 30525
   (706) 782-3320

   Willis Knob Trail and Camp: 15 mile loop of trails; offers eight primitive campsites, toilet facilities (handicapped accessible), group campfire areas, grills, picnic tables, lantern posts, twenty horse stalls, and watering trough. Camping reservations are required and must be made at least 14 days in advance.
   This trail system can be combined with the Rocky Gap Trail and Camp in the Andrew Pickens Ranger District of Sumter National Forest in South Carolina to form 27.5 miles of bridle trails in the hills and valleys of the southern Blue Ridge Mountains and along the Chattooga River. Call the Rabun County Chamber of Commerce at (706) 782-4812 for more information on nearby motels and campgrounds.

4. Chickamauga and Chattanooga National Military Park
   Superintendent
   P.O. Box 2128
   Fort Oglethorpe, GA 30742
   (706) 866-9241

11 miles of trails for day use only, no camping
   Trails End Ranch is a riding stable located south of the park that allows overnight boarding of horses if space is available. Contact at P.O. Box 503, Chickamauga, GA 30707 or call (706) 375-4346.

5. Oconee National Forest
   Oconee Ranger District
   349 Forsyth Street
   Monticello, GA 31064
   (706) 468-2244

Burgess Mountain Trail: 1 mile; Kinnard Creek Trail: 4.1 miles; Ocmulgee River Trail: 2.8 miles; Wise Creek Trail; 2.5 miles; primitive camping

STATE PARKS

1. Georgia State Parks
   205 Butler St., Suite 1258 East
   Atlanta, GA 30334
   (404) 656-3530

2. F.D. Roosevelt State Park
   2970 Ga. Hwy. 190
   Pine Mountain, GA 31822
   (706) 663-4858

Offers guided trail rides on rental horses only; see City Slickers Trail Rides under "Regional Trails."

3. Hard Labor Creek State Park
   P.O. Box 247
   Rutledge, GA 30663
   (706) 557-3001

(Hard Labor Creek State Park continued)
Offers 15 miles of trails; Furlong Farms (see below) offers guided trail rides within
the park; facilities include stables, camping, water and electrical hookups, showers

REGIONAL TRAILS, PRIVATE STABLES AND OUTFITTERS

1. Burnt Pine Plantation
   2941 Little River Rd
   Madison, GA 30650
   (706) 342-7202 or (706) 342-2170

Offers novice and experienced horseback and/or wagon trails for individuals or
groups on 7,500 acres in Georgia; weekends can be reserved for saddle clubs and
guests; provides gourmet meals, overnight camping, lodging, use of rustic lodge,
Saturday night entertainment; open daily; call ahead to register the number of
riders in your party

2. City Slickers Trail Rides
   Wayne Wilkins
   (706) 628-4533

Offers guided trail rides on 12,000 acres around F.D. Roosevelt State Park, Pine
Mountain, GA; rental horses

3. Furlong Farms
   1868 Riden Road
   Madison, GA 30650
   office: (706) 342-4054; manager's residence: (706) 342-7044

Offers guided trail rides within Hard Labor Creek State Park; boarding, rental
horses, moonlight trail rides, cowboy cookout and campouts, barrel racing,
church group and organization rates

4. Gold City Corral
   owner: David Kraft
   Rt. 3, Box 510
   Dahlonega, GA 30533
   (706) 864-6456

(Gold City Corral continued)
Offers guided trail rides and camping; located near Forrest Hills Mountain Hideaway, 1-800-654-6313 or (706) 864-6456

5. Horseshoe Bend Stables
   At the Cornett Ranch
   (706) 276-3900

Offers guided trail rides along the Ellijay River in the North Georgia mountains; boarding, training and riding lessons also available

6. Oak Valley Stables and Exotic Game Reserve
   owners: Freddie and Rhonda Huckeba
   (706) 864-8576

Offers guided trail rides on rental horses or on your own personal horse; limited camping space available; located near the gold mining city of Dahlonega, Georgia on 2,000+ acres of scenic hills and valleys

7. Sunburst Stables
   owners: Kevin Craig and Richard Hayes
   Rt. 1, Box 1075
   Sautee, GA 30571
   (706) 878-2095

Offers guided trail rides, camping, boarding, training

8. Toccoa River Valley Cabins and Stables
   Dial, GA
   contact: Mike and Denise Cox
   185 Newport Rd
   Blue Ridge, GA 30513
   (706) 838-4706

Offers guided trail rides on your own horse in the north Georgia mountains; fully furnished air-conditioned cabins, jacuzzi, TV, VCR; training and limited boarding is also available; located 90 miles north of Atlanta

ADDITIONAL CONTACTS

1. Georgia Department of Industry, Trade and Tourism
   P.O. Box 1776
   Atlanta, GA 30301
   (404) 656-3590 or 1-800-VISIT GA

2. Georgia Horse Council
   P.O. Box 736
   Dahlonega, GA 30533-0736
   (706) 864-4654

SOUTH CAROLINA

All horses must have had a negative Coggins test within the past twelve months to enter public parks and facilities.

NATIONAL PARKS AND FORESTS

1. Kings Mountain National Military Park
   Blacksburg, SC 29702
   (864) 936-7921

In conjunction with Kings Mountain State Park, offers 20 miles of bridle trails (see "State Parks"). Group camping and stables are available within the state park.

2. National Forests Supervisor (Francis Marion and Sumter)
   1835 Assembly St., Room 333
   Columbia, SC 29201
   (803) 765-5222

3. Francis Marion National Forest
   Witherbee Ranger District
   HC 69, Box 1532
   Moncks Corner, SC 29461
   (803) 336-3248

The Jericho Trail consists of a 19-mile loop through the coastal plain forests of South Carolina. It is open year round free of charge. Trailhead parking and a primitive camping area (no facilities or water) are located at the north end of the loop off SC-48.

4. Sumter National Forest
   Andrew Pickens Ranger District
   112 Andrew Pickens Circle
   Mountain Rest, SC 29664
   (864) 638-9568

(Sumter National Forest, Andrew Pickens Ranger District continued)
Rocky Gap Trail and Whetstone Base Camp: 12 miles of trails; offers twenty primitive campsites (fourteen are available for group reservation and five are available on a first-come, first-served basis); toilet facilities (handicapped accessible), drinking water, grills, tables, lantern posts and hitching rails. Across the road from the camp is a day use parking area. This trail system can be combined with the Willis Knob Trail in the Tallulah Ranger District of Chattahoochee National Forest in Georgia to form 27.5 miles of trails for horseback riding in the hills and valleys of the southern Blue Ridge Mountains and along the Chattooga River.

5. Sumter National Forest
   Enoree Ranger District
   Rt. 1, Box 179
   Whitmire, SC 29178
   (864) 276-4810

The 28-mile Buncombe Trail traverses the hilly terrain of the piedmont area of South Carolina. It is open year round free of charge, and no permits are required for use of the trail or facilities. Primitive camping is available at Brick House Campground on FR-358 off SC-66. Facilities include 23 campsites, toilets, water, tables, fire rings, spaces for tents or trailers, corrals and a loading ramp.

6. Sumter National Forest
   Long Cane Ranger District
   Room 201, Federal Building
   P.O. Box 3168
   Greenwood, SC 29648
   (864) 229-2406

The Long Cane Trail consists of 26 miles that pass through the scenic piedmont area of South Carolina. It is open to horseback riders, hikers and non-motorized mountain bikers. A parking area and primitive campground is available at Fell Hunt Camp near the trailhead off SC-47. Toilets, water, trash bins and horse hitching areas are available free of charge.

STATE PARKS AND FORESTS

The South Carolina Forestry Commission has a new fee schedule for horseback riding on state forest land. The fees are as follows: $3.00/day for an individual State Forest Passport/Daily use permit or $15.00 per year for an annual individual permit passport. Groups or clubs of over 50 people will be charged either $150 per ride or five percent of gross receipts from the events that utilize the forests. Proceeds from these fees will go toward constructing and maintaining the trails and facilities.

1. South Carolina State Parks
   1205 Pendleton St.
   Columbia, SC 29201
   (803) 734-0156

2. Baker Creek State Park
   Rt. 3, Box 50
   McCormick, SC 29835
   (864) 443-2457

Offers 2 miles of trails, primitive camping (trailer tie)

3. Croft State Park
   450 Croft State Park Rd.
   Spartanburg, SC 29302
   (864) 585-1283

Located 5 miles southeast of Spartanburg, SC near the foothills of the Blue Ridge Mountains. Offers 40-45 miles of trails, stable and show ring. Fifty campsites are available with water and electrical hookups; groups may reserve ten sites for use. Hot showers and restrooms are also available.

- Rocky Ridge Trail: strenuous, 3.5 miles
- Foster's Mill Loop Trail: strenuous, 6.5 miles
- Lake Johnson Loop Trail: moderate, 2.4 miles
- Fairforest Creek Loop Trail: moderate, 3.5 miles

Proof of a negative Coggins test within the past 12 months is required before entering the equestrian facilities.

4. Kings Mountain State Park
   1277 Park Rd.
   Blacksburg, SC 29702
   (864) 222-3209

(King Mountain State Park continued)
In conjunction with Kings Mountain National Military Park, offers 20 miles of
bridle trails. Group camping, stables, bathhouse and laundry facilities are available within the state park.

5. Lee State Park
   Rt. 2, Box 1212
   Bishopville, SC 29010
   (803) 428-3833

Offers 10 miles of bridle trails, camping, water and electrical hookups, hot
showers and restrooms. Equestrian facilities include stables, rental stalls and show
ring.

6. Manchester State Forest
   6740 Headquarters Rd
   Wedgefield, SC 29168
   (803) 494-8196

Several miles of trails are designated for horseback riding in this state forest on
over 17,000 acres of ridges, sandhills, bays, and swamplands. The High Hills of
Santee Passage of the Palmetto Trail passes through here and connects equestrian
campgrounds at Mill Creek Park and Poinsett State Park.

7. Poinsett State Park
   6660 Poinsett Park Rd
   Wedgefield, SC 29168
   (803) 494-8177
   Hours: 11:00-noon, 4-5 p.m.

Offers an equestrian campground (by reservation only) that serves as an access
for the High Hills of Santee Passage of the Palmetto Trail.

8. Sand Hills State Forest
   P.O. Box 128
   Patrick, SC 29584
   (803) 498-6478

Equestrian group camping and a day use parking area are available within this
46,000-acre wildlife management area in Chesterfield and Darlington counties.

(Sand Hills State Forest continued)
All dirt roads within the state forest can be used as riding trails and are designated by TT (truck trails) and a number. Horses must stay on existing roads and designated horse trails. Do not tie horses to trees; use hitching posts, high picket line, or trailer tie. When riding the Mountain Road, horses must be kept on the road except when obtaining water at the spillway's designated site. Horses may also be watered at the Mountain Pond near Area 9.

REGIONAL TRAILS, PRIVATE STABLES AND OUTFITTERS

1. Anne Springs Close Greenway
   P.O. Box 1209
   Fort Mill, SC 29716
   Greenway Headquarters: (803) 548 7252
   Nature Center: (803) 547-0234
   Leroy Springs & Company: (803) 547-1000

Offers 14 miles of easy bridle trails over hills and through woods, past lakes and historical areas on 2,300-acre preserve; open year round for day use or primitive overnight horse camping; has restrooms and public drinking water; other activities include hiking, bicycling, primitive camping, fishing, boating, picnicking.

2. Bell-View Stables
   owner: Ralph Bell
   manager: Benny Tidwell
   5177 Tennis Lane
   Summerton, SC 29148
   for reservations: (803) 478-8998 or (803) 478-8999

Features a traditional old western cattle drive with camping, dances, campfire sessions, and chuck wagon. Scenic horseback riding along the shores of Lake Marion.

3. Clemson Experimental Forest
   Department of Forest Resources
   College of Agriculture, Forestry, and Life Sciences
   School of Natural Sciences
   261 Lehotsky Hall
   Box 341003
   Clemson, SC 29634-1003
   (864) 656-3302 or (864) 656-4847

(Clemson Experimental Forest continued)
Offers approximately 40 miles of trails on over 18,000 acres for day use only, no overnight facilities are available. Includes the Fants Grove Area Equestrian Trails and the Lake Issaqueena Recreation Area. Organized group activities require permission from the office and a fee is charged, depending on the type of activity. In the future some additional user fees my be adopted and an improved trail map will be available.

4. High Hills of Santee Passage of Palmetto Trail
   Palmetto Trails
   1314 Lincoln St., Suite 213
   Columbia, SC 29201-3154
   (803) 771-0870

This 14-mile section of the Palmetto Trail traverses sandy terrain through the beautiful Manchester State Forest, joining Mill Creek Park to Poinsett State Park. Equestrian camping and day use parking areas are available at both parks. The Palmetto Trail is a proposed "mountains to the sea" path over 320 miles long in South Carolina. Founded in 1994, the first passages are open with the High Hills of Santee Passage providing one of the trail's few areas open to horseback riding. A detailed description of flora, fauna, and facilities is available in the *Palmetto Trail Guidebook.* Contact the above address for a copy.

5. Hound Hollow Farm
   Becky Tolson
   123 Old Sanders Rd
   Pendleton, SC 29670
   (864) 224-8205

Offers stable as a vacation or layover spot. Has indoor stalls, 2 holding pens with turnout pen, pasture, feed, 100'x200' riding ring and 60' round pen. Located near several miles of public trails on hundred of acres. Several bed and breakfasts in the area. A negative Coggins test and all updated vaccinations are required.

6. Mill Creek Park
   P.O. Box 206
   Pinewood, SC 29125
   (803) 452-5501

Offers equestrian facilities with stables, camping, showers, picnic areas, hiking, mountain biking, fishing, and lake access with pier. Located near several miles

(Mill Creek Park continued)
of trails within Manchester State Forest and is an access point for the High Hills of Santee Passage portion of the Palmetto Trail. Camping reservations for Mill Creek Park are handled through the Sumter County Recreation Department. Contact at 155 Haynsworth St., Sumter, SC 29150 or call (803) 436-2248.

7. Myrtle Beach Trail

Horseback riding is allowed on the beach from November to February. Call the Pee Dee Regional Office at (843) 626-3939 to find out exact times and current regulations, or write to: P.O. Box 2533, Myrtle Beach, SC 29578-2533. Stabling is available at Sea Winds Stable, 4486 Dick Pond Road, Myrtle Beach, SC 29578; Ray Elvis, owner. Call (843) 293-7320 to make reservations. Proof of a current negative Coggins test within the past twelve months is required. A local campground (no horse camping) is Ocean Lakes Family Campground, Hwy 17 South, Myrtle Beach, SC 29577. For reservations, call (843) 238-1451.

ADDITIONAL CONTACTS

1. South Carolina Department of Agriculture
   Mary Ellen Tobias, Equine Marketing Specialist
   (803) 734-2200
   for more information on the South Carolina horse industry

2. South Carolina Department of Parks, Recreation and Tourism
   Division of Travel and Tourism
   P.O. Box 71
   Columbia, South Carolina 29202
   (803) 734-0235

3. South Carolina Horsemen's Council (SCHC)
   P.O. Box 11280
   Columbia, SC 29211
   (803) 734-2187
   Offers a new 36-page guidebook, "Favorite Horse Trails of South Carolina." Cost is $4.95. Contact the above address for a copy.

4. SCHC State Trails Committee
   chairman: Verida Marchette
   2945 Old Muldrows Mill Road
   Florence, SC 29601
   (843) 662-6568

TENNESSEE

The state of Tennessee requires proof of a negative Coggins test within the past twelve months for all horses before entering public parks and facilities.

NATIONAL PARKS AND FORESTS

1. Big South Fork National River and Recreation Area
   Visitor's Center
   Rt. 3, Box 401
   Oneida, TN 37841
   (423) 879-3625

This is a 113,000-acre national recreation area with 200+ miles of trails and 180 miles of backcountry roads. Offers four stable facilities for horses: Bandy Creek Stables (423) 879-4013, Charit Creek Lodge (see "Regional Trails, Private Stables and Outfitters" below), Station Camp Equestrian Camp (423) 569-3321, and Bear Creek Equestrian Camp. Reservations are suggested for each area.

2. Cherokee National Forest
   2800 North Ocoee Street NW
   P.O. Box 2010
   Cleveland, TN 37320
   (423) 476-9700

3. Cherokee National Forest (Southern District)
   Hiwassee Ranger District
   Drawer D
   Etowah, TN 37331
   (423) 263-5486

Offers public trails and dispersed primitive horse camping.
Chestnut Mountain Trail: 5.7 miles; Unicoi Mountain Trail: 9.9 mile loop; Starr Mountain Trail: 17 miles

4. Cherokee National Forest (Northern District)
   Nolichucky Ranger District
   504 Justis Drive
   Greeneville, TN 37743
   (423) 638-4109

(Cherokee National Forest, Nolichucky Ranger District continued)
Seven horse trails combine to provide over 25 miles. Riding is also permitted on
several open and closed roads within the district. Tent camping (9 campsites)
and one horse hitching area is available at the Old Forge Recreation Area.

5. Cherokee National Forest (Southern District)
   Tellico Ranger District
   Rt. 3, Tellico River Road
   Tellico Plains, TN 37385
   (423) 253-2520

21 miles of bridle trails

6. Great Smoky Mountains National Park
   Superintendent
   107 Park Headquarters Rd.
   Gatlinburg, TN 37738
   (423) 436-1200

See the chapter on "Great Smoky Mountains National Park" for detailed information

7. Natchez Trace National Scenic Trail
   National Park Service
   5335 Old 96 Highway
   Franklin, TN 37064
   (615) 790-9323

Offers 27 miles of trails for day use with your own horses; no camping. On the
weekends, Kinderhook Livery Stables offers rental horses for guided trail rides.
Contact at (615) 682-3969.

U.S. ARMY CORPS OF ENGINEERS

1. Cordell Hull Lake
   Resource Manager
   U.S. Army Corps of Engineers
   71 Corps Lane
   Carthage, TN 37030
   (931) 735-1034

(Cordell Hull Lake continued)
10 and 12 mile trails, primitive camping

2. Red Oak Ridge Trail
   Resource Managers Office
   U.S. Army Corps of Engineers
   Dale Hollow Lake
   5050 Dale Hollow Dam Road
   Celina, TN 38551
   (931) 243-3136

18 miles of trails, primitive camping, tie-ups and stalls available

3. Twin Forks Trail
   Resource Manager's Office
   J. Percy Priest Lake
   3737 Bell Road
   Nashville, TN 37214
   (615) 889-1975

17 miles of trails, picnic and parking area, restrooms

STATE PARKS, STATE FORESTS AND CITY PARKS

1. Cedars of Lebanon State Park
   Superintendent's Office
   328 Cedar Forrest Road
   Lebanon, TN 37087
   (615) 443-2769

12 miles of trails. Stalls are available for overnight boarding. Other facilities include cabins, campgrounds, bathhouses, dumpsites and laundromat.

2. Chickasaw State Park
   Rt. 2, Box 32
   Henderson, TN 38340
   (901) 989-5141

5 miles of trails, rental horses available, cabins, campground and stalls

3. Fairview Nature Park
   P.O. Box 69
   Fairview, TN 37062
   (615) 799-2484 or (615) 799-0422

15 miles of trails, parking and picnic areas, restrooms

4. Fall Creek Falls State Park
   Park Headquarters
   Rt. 3
   Pikeville, TN 37367
   (423) 881-3297

2 miles of trails open only to rental horses. Facilities include cabins, camp-grounds, water, electric hookups.

5. Franklin State Forest
   P.O. Box 68
   Winchester, TN 37398
   (931) 967-0757

10-12 miles of logging roads, primitive camping

6. Frozen Head State Park and Natural Area
   964 Flat Fork Rd
   Wartburg, TN 37887
   (423) 346-3318

15 miles of trails, no overnight horse camp or horse facilities are available

7. Lone Mountain State Forest
   Tennessee Division of Forestry
   302 Clayton Howard Rd
   Wartburg, TN 37887
   (423) 346-6655

13.5 miles of trails, primitive camping

8. Meeman-Shelby State Park
   Rt. 3
   Millington, TN 38053
   (901) 876-5201
   Shelby Forest Stables (901) 876-5756

2 miles of trails open only to rental horses

9. Natchez Trace State Resort Park
   Rt. 1, Box 265
   Wildersville, TN 38388
   (901) 968-3742

200 miles of trails. Facilities include camping, cabins, bathhouses, dumpsites,
electric and water hookups.

10. Norris Dam Watershed
    City of Norris
    20 Chestnut Dr.
    P.O. Box G
    Norris, TN 37828
    (423) 494-7645

Several miles of public use trails for day use only. Stalls available at Carousel
Stables (423) 494-9535.

11. Percy Warner Park
    Headquarters
    50 Vaughn Rd
    Nashville, TN 37221
    (615) 370-8051

10 miles of trails. Park at the equestrian center on 2500 Old Hickory Blvd.

12. Standing Stone State Forest
    Division of Forestry
    District Office
    380 S. Lowe, Suite 7
    Cookeville, TN 38501
    (931) 823-6538 or (931) 526-9502 (District Office)

(Standing Stone State Forest continued)
25-30 miles of trails. Standing Stone State Park offers camping facilities.

13. Warriors Path State Forest
    P.O. Box 5026
    Kingsport, TN 37663
    (423) 239-8531 or (423) 323-8543 (stables)

2 miles of trails open only for guided rides on rental horses

REGIONAL TRAILS, PRIVATE STABLES AND OUTFITTERS

1. Big Sandy Trail Ride
   4797 Eastlawn Dr.
   Rockford, IL 61108
   (615) 941-1083 or 1-800-941-1083 PIN:BSTR (2787)

Located in Big Sandy, TN near Kentucky Lake. Six-day guided rides in June and October. Private parties can make reservations. Offers camping with electric hookups, bathhouses, entertainment, meals. Stalls and feed are available.

2. Birdsong Trail Ride
   Rt. 2, Box 132
   Camden, TN 38320
   (901) 584-4280

Six-day guided trail rides in April, May, June, September, and October. Private group rides can be reserved for weekends. Offers camping, electric hookups, bathhouses, entertainment, hay rides, meals, stalls, feed available.

3. Bucksnort Trail Ride, Inc.
   920 Clearview Rd
   Cottontown, TN 37048
   (615) 325-2827

Six-day guided trail rides in April, June, and October. Offers camping, electric hookups, bathhouses, entertainment, meals. Stalls and feed available. Private group rides can be reserved.

4. Buffalo River Trail Ride, Inc.
   P.O. Box 591
   Waynesboro, TN 38485
   (931) 722-9170

Week-long rides in June, August, and October. Private week-long or 3-day-week-end rides can be reserved for groups. Offers camping, hookups, bathhouses, meals, entertainment. Stalls and feed available.

5. Callalantee Resort Stables
   Roan Valley
   George Barrett, office manager
   P.O. Box 48
   Mountain City, TN 37683-0048
   (800) 444-6615 or (423) 727-5756

Located on over 6,000 acres near Roan Valley Golf Estates in Johnson County, adjacent to the Cherokee National Forest. Offers guided and nonguided trail rides on your own personal horses through 120 miles of old logging trails, highland meadows and trips into Cherokee National Forest. Offers 50 primitive lighted campsites, 40-5'x 10' tie stalls, restrooms and showers (modern bath-house). A limited number of rental horses, pack and riding mules are also available for use. Open daily year round for individuals or groups. Reservations are requested.

6. Charit Creek Lodge
   P.O. Box 350
   Gatlinburg, TN 37738
   (423) 430-3333 or (423) 429-5704

Offers horseback riding, hiking trails and lodging; located in Big South Fork National River and Recreation Area

7. Davy Crockett Riding Stables and Bed & Breakfast Horse Barn
   owner: J.C. Morgan
   Hwy 73
   Townsend, TN 37882
   (423) 448-6411

Offers guided trail rides, camping and overnight boarding of your horse; located near GSMNP, open year round

8. English Mountain Scenic Trail Rides
   Smokey Mountain Woodlands, Inc.
   1091 Alpine Drive
   P.O. Box 4580
   Sevierville, TN 37864
   (423) 428-8652

Offers horseback vacations with your own horses or they provide rental horses; several miles of scenic trails on English Mountain; offers cabins, chalets and condo suites, pool, tennis courts, mini golf, gift shop and grill

9. Gilbertson's Lazy Horse Retreat
   938 School House Gap Rd.
   Townsend,TN 37882
   (423) 448-6810

Offers cabins, stalls for overnight boarding; open year round, located near GSMNP

10. Lyric Springs Bed and Breakfast
    7306 S. Harpeth Road
    Franklin, TN 37064
    (615) 329-3385

Offers overnight boarding of your own horse, bed and breakfast; located near Natchez Trace National Scenic Trail

11. Mountain View Riding Stable
    Rt. 1, Box 351 AA
    Benton, TN 37307
    (423) 338-6394

30 miles of trails open only for guided rides on rental horses. Licensed outfitter with Cherokee National Forest. Also offers whitewater rafting in the nearby Ocoee River, hay rides and a trout pond.

12. Namaste Acres Barn, Bed and Breakfast
    5436 Leipers Creek Rd
    Franklin, TN 37064
    (615) 791-0333

(Namaste Acres Barn, Bed and Breakfast continued)
AAA-approved equestrian bed and breakfast; access trail connects to the Natchez Trace National Scenic Trail (27 miles); located 20 miles southwest of Nashville, numerous attractions and vacation spots nearby

13. Next to Heaven Stables
    1239 Wears Valley Road
    Townsend, TN 37882
    (800) 339-6226 or (423) 448-9150

Offers guided and nonguided trail rides on rental horses or your own personal horses; stalls available

14. Twin Valley Bed & Breakfast Horse Ranch
    2848 Old Chilhowee Road
    Walland, TN 37886
    (423) 984-0980

Offers guided trail rides, stabling, riding instruction, primitive cabins, bed and breakfast in authentic log home, fishing and hiking; by reservation only; located in the Great Smoky Mountain foothills with access to trails in Chilhowee Mountain

15. Willowbridge Farm
    2920 Jones Cove Rd.
    Sevierville, TN 37862
    stables: (423) 453-2257; inn: (423) 453-6068

Offers guided trail rides on rental horses or bring your own mount; overnight boarding and pasture available, bed and breakfast; located near GSMNP

16. Wonderland Stables and Hotel
    3889 Wonderland Way
    Sevierville, TN 37862
    (423) 436-5490

Offers guided trail rides on rental horses or trail ride on your own horse, stalls for overnight boarding, hotel and rental cabins

ADDITIONAL CONTACTS

1. Tennessee Department of Agriculture
   Division of Marketing
   Box 40627
   Nashville, TN 37204
   (615) 360-0160

A free brochure entitled "Tennessee Equine Trail Guide" is offered by the Tennessee Department of Agriculture. It lists public horse trails, private stables, and outfitters within the state. Contacts are also listed so you can find out more detailed information on the trails.

2. Tennessee Department of Tourist Development
   P.O. Box 23170
   Nashville, TN 37202-3170
   (615) 741-2158

VIRGINIA

Virginia currently requires proof of a negative Coggins test within the past twelve months for each horse before entering public parks and facilities.

NATIONAL PARKS AND FORESTS

1. George Washington National Forest
   101 North Main St.
   P.O. Box 233
   Harrison Plaza
   Harrisonburg, VA 22801
   (540) 433-2491

   Deerfield Ranger District
   2314 W. Beverley
   Staunton, VA 24401
   (540) 885-8028

   Dry River Ranger District - 200 miles of trails
   112 N. River Rd.
   Bridgewater, VA 22812
   (540) 828-2591

   James River Ranger District
   313 S. Monroe St.
   Covington, VA 24426
   (540) 962-2214

   Lee Ranger District - 200 miles of trails
   Rt. 1, Box 31-A
   Edinburg, VA 22824
   (540) 984-4101

   Shenandoah County National Forest - 100 miles of trails
   Rt. 1, Box 156
   Woodstock, VA 24664
   (540) 459-5619

Pedlar Ranger District
2424 Magnolia Ave.
Buena Vista, VA 24416
(540) 261-6105

Warm Springs Ranger District - 50 miles of trails
Rt. 2, Box 30
Hot Springs, VA 24445
(540) 839-2521

2. Jefferson National Forest
P.O. Box 241
210 Franklin Road
Roanoke, VA 24001
(540) 982-6270

Blacksburg Ranger District - 250 miles of trails, camping at White Pine
Horse Camp
110 S. Park Dr.
Blacksburg, VA 24060
(540) 552-4641

Clinch Ranger District - 23 miles of trails, camping
Rt. 3, Box 820
Wise, VA 24293
(540) 328-2931

Glennwood Ranger District - 65 miles of trails
P.O. Box 10
Natural Bridge Station, VA 24579
(540) 291-2188

Mount Rogers National Recreation Area
Rt. 1, Box 303
Marion, VA 24354
(540) 783-5196

200+ miles of trails, camping; see detailed listing at the end of this chapter

Wythe Ranger District - 17 miles of trails
1625 W. Lee Hwy.
Wytheville, VA 24382
(540) 228-5551

New Castle Ranger District - 31 miles of trails
Box 246
New Castle, VA 24127
(540) 864-5195

3. Shenandoah National Park
P.O. Box 727
Luray, VA 22835
(540) 999-2266

STATE PARKS

1. Virginia Division of State Parks
203 Governor St., Suite 306
Richmond, VA 23219
(804) 786-2132

2. Claytor Lake State Park
Rt. 1, Box 267
Dublin, VA 24084
(540) 674-5492

2 miles of trails open only to rental horses

3. Grayson Highlands State Park
Rt. 2, Box 141
Mouth of Wilson, VA 24363
(540) 579-7092

5 miles of trails within the state park connect to 200+ miles of trails in the Mount
Rogers National Recreation Area; facilities include camping, stalls, bathhouse,
restrooms; see detailed listing at the end of this chapter

4. Hungry Mother State Park
Rt. 5, Box 109
Marion, VA 24354
(540) 783-3422

1+ mile of trail open only to rental horses

5. New River Trail State Park
   Rt. 1, Box 81X
   Austinville, VA 24312
   (540) 699-6778

This linear state park follows an old railbed and parallels the scenic New River for much of its route. Currently 55 miles of the trail are open to the public. Once completed, the trail will stretch 57 miles through southwest Virginia from Galax to Pulaski. Other popular park activities include hiking, bicycling, picnicking, and fishing. Horse trailer parking is available at the Cliffview, Shot Tower, and Draper entrances. Horse rental and riding stable is located on Cliffview Road near the Cliffview entrance. Horseshoe Campground is near the state park and Claytor Lake. Contact at Rt. 1, Box 223, Draper, VA 24324; (540) 980-0278.

6. Pocahontas State Park
   10300 Park Rd.
   Chesterfield, VA 23832
   (804) 796-4255

5 miles of trails

7. Sky Meadows State Park
   Rt. 1, Box 540
   Delaplane, VA 22025
   (703) 592-3556

5 miles of trails

8. York River State Park
   5526 Riverview Rd.
   Williamsburg, VA 23188
   (757) 566-3036

5 miles of trails

REGIONAL TRAILS

1. Battlefield Equestrian Society
   P.O. Box 150
   Catharpin, VA 22018
   (703) 754-4181

(Battlefield Equestrian Society continued)
20 miles of trails

2. Clarks Crossing Park
   9850 Clarks Crossing Rd.
   Vienna, VA 22180
   (703) 352-5900

3 miles of trails that connect to 30+ miles of trails in the W & O.D. Railroad Regional Park

3. Fairy Stone Farms
   Rt. 2, Box 185
   Bassett, VA 24055
   (540) 629-5902

15 miles of trails

4. Fountainhead Park
   10875 Hampton Rd
   Fairfax Station, VA 22039
   (703) 250-9124

20 miles of trails

5. Hungry Horse Farm
   Mountain Trail Excursions
   Rt. 1, Box 316
   Ivanhoe, VA 24350
   (540) 744-3210

Offers trail riding vacations in the Blue Ridge Mountains of southwest Virginia; camping, home-cooked meals, personalized service for small groups; stabling and cabins available

6. Manassas National Battlefield Park Horse Mounted Operation
   6511 Sudley Rd.
   Manassas, VA 22110
   (703) 754-8694

(Manassas National Battlefield Park Horse Mounted Operation continued)
20 miles of trails

7. Rails to River Trail
   18108 Michael Faraday Ct.
   Reston, VA 22090
   (703) 471-5415

Offers 6 miles of trails that connect to 30+ miles of trails in the W & O.D. Railroad Regional Park; camping and restrooms available

8. Tamarack Park
   10400 Hunter Station Rd.
   Herndon, VA 22070

2 miles of trails that connect to 30+ miles of trails in the W & O.D. Railroad Regional Park

9. Virginia Creeper Trail
   Abingdon Convention and Visitor's Bureau
   335 Cummings St.
   Abingdon, VA 24210
   (540) 676-2282 or 1-800-435-3440

Designated as a National Recreation Trail, this 34.3-mile multiple-use trail was once an old railbed. It connects Abingdon, VA with the Virginia-North Carolina state line, 1.1 miles east of Whitetop Station, VA. Between the Iron Bridge and the state line, almost 16 miles of this trail are part of the Mt. Rogers National Recreation Area in Jefferson National Forest. Originally a footpath used by the Indians and later by pioneers such as Daniel Boone, it became the railbed for the Virginia-Carolina Railroad. This railroad was nicknamed the Virginia Creeper because of the train's slow pace climbing the mountain's steep hills. For more information (trail map, local lodging, food, etc.) contact the Abingdon Convention and Visitor's Bureau. Also the Virginia Creeper Trail Club can be contacted at P.O. Box 2382, Abingdon, VA 24212 for additional information.

10. Virginia Mountain Outfitters
    Deborah J. Sensabaugh
    Rt. 1, Box 244
    Buena Vista, VA 24416
    (540) 261-1910 or (540) 261-3841

(Virginia Mountain Outfitters continued)
Offers riding vacation packages in the Blue Ridge Mountains that can include lodging and meals at Lavender Hill Farm Bed and Breakfast. Also has overnight trail rides, mountain pack trips, and educational rides for Scouts or youth groups.

11. W & O.D. Railroad Regional Park
    21293 Smiths Switch Rd
    Ashburn, VA 22011
    (703) 689-1437

33 miles of trails; connects to the Rails to River Trail where camping facilities are available

ADDITIONAL CONTACTS

1. Department of Conservation & Recreation
   203 Governor St., Suite 302
   Richmond, VA 23219
   (804) 786-1712

For free informational brochures, in-state residents call 1-800-866-9222.

2. Virginia Division of Tourism
   1021 E. Cary St., Dept. VT
   Richmond, VA 23219
   (804) 786-4484 or 1-800-VISIT VA

3. Virginia Horse Council
   P.O. Box 72
   Riner, VA 24149
   (540) 382-3071

The Virginia Horse Council offers a free brochure entitled "Virginia Horse Riding Trail Guide" that contains information on public bridle trails in the state. Contacts are listed so you can obtain more detailed information on the trails and facilities.

MOUNT ROGERS NATIONAL
RECREATION AREA

Address: Rt. 1, Box 303 Marion, Virginia 24354
Telephone: (540) 783-5196

Grayson Highlands State Park
Rt. 2, Box 141 Mouth of Wilson, Virginia 24363
(540) 579-7092

LOCATION: Go north on US-21 to Sparta, then take US-221 South. Turn right onto RT-93 towards Mouth of Wilson. Turn right at Laurel Springs, still following RT-93. Cross the New River and turn left on US-58, towards Marion, VA. Turn left on US-58 West beyond Mouth of Wilson. Go 8 miles and turn right on Hwy 362 North (park entrance).

SEASON: Park: open year round (day use)
Horse camp: open April or May to November
DAILY HOURS: Dawn to 10:00 p.m.

FACILITY REVIEW
TYPE: day use and/or overnight horse camping
HORSE CAMPING FACILITIES: 23 primitive campsites (tent or horse trailer with sleeper; no water or electrical hookups)
CAMPING FEE: $8.50/day Check out time is 4:00 p.m.
HOT SHOWERS: yes (bathhouse with electricity)
RESTROOMS: flush toilets
OTHER FACILITIES: fire grill and picnic table at each campsite, laundry sinks, dump station
STABLE FACILITIES: 58 tie stalls (38 covered/20 uncovered)
STABLING FEE: $5.50/covered $3.50/uncovered
DAY RIDERS FEE: none
PARK ENTRANCE FEE: $1.00

TRAIL REVIEW
TYPE: marked; connects to Virginia Highlands and Little Wilson Creek Wilderness Area
TERRAIN: mountainous/rocky-rugged
DIFFICULTY: moderate-difficult
LENGTH: 200+ miles
WATER: yes

TRAIL MAP: Mount Rogers National Recreation Area. Grayson Highlands State Park.

TRAIL NOTES: Several trails consist of wide and rocky roads that pass through open bald mountains, wilderness areas and forests. Some trails are dry, rocky creek beds with large boulders. Areas of some trails are very muddy due to the large amount of rainfall in the higher elevations.

A bridle trail (1.3 miles long) begins at the stable area. The trail forks at Massie Gap. The northwest fork leads to the Virginia Highlands Horse Trail and the northeast fork goes to the Little Wilson Creek Wilderness Area. These trails are recommended for experienced riders and well-shod horses due to the extremely rocky terrain. Be prepared for extreme weather changes in this area due to the high elevation. A clear sky can quickly turn to cloudy or foggy conditions of low visibility.

RULES/REQUIREMENTS: Proof of a current negative Coggins test within the past twelve months is required. All trails close at dusk. All horses must be kept overnight in stable areas. Horses are only allowed on designated trails and not in the campgrounds or any other areas of the park. Maximum stay is 14 days.

HIGHLIGHTS: The rocky mountain ridges have a similar appearance to the mountains in the western United States. Open mountain balds provide spectacular views of other ridges and valleys. Backcountry and wilderness areas, wildlife, wild ponies.

GENERAL/HISTORICAL NOTES: Mount Rogers is the highest point in Virginia at an elevation of 5,729 feet. It is named for William Barton Rogers, a geologist. The bald mountain areas in the Mount Rogers National Recreation Area are called the Crest Zone and were caused many years ago by burning and grazing practices. Free roaming ponies are privately managed and live within the park's boundaries. They are frequently seen grazing in the Crest Zone. The Appalachian Trail (for hikers) can be accessed from the Massie Gap area in the park.

OTHER ACTIVITIES: hiking, backpacking, camping. Pony auction is held every September. Hunting and fishing are allowed in the wilderness areas.

NEAREST CITIES/FACILITIES: Lansing, Marion, Galax

ADDITIONAL HORSE CAMPS AND OUTFITTERS IN THE MOUNT ROGERS NATIONAL RECREATION AREA:

1. High Country Horse Camp
located on State Rd 600, 0.7 mile from Weavers General Store in Konnarock, VA
Cathy Moore and Joe Stephenson, owners; contact at (540) 388-3992 or Rt. 1, Box 202-A1, Troutdale, VA 24378
open year round; offers campground with electric and water hookups, hitching posts, showers, ice, tack, groceries, breakfast and supper buffets, occasional entertainment on Saturday nights, social hall; call for reservations

2. Fox Creek Horse Camp
located on Route 603
primitive campsites, group camping, pit toilets, no showers; open year round; campers can shower at nearby Grindstone Campground for a fee of $2.00 per vehicle

3. Scales on Pine Mountain
primitive campsites, no toilet or shower facilities; accessible only by a primitive, substandard road; open year round

4. Raven Cliff Horse Camp
located near Wytheville
primitive horse camping, pit toilets; open year round

5. Hussy Mountain Horse Camp
located off US-21 near Speedwell
primitive campsites, sanitary facilities; open year round

6. Mount Rogers High Country Outdoor Center
Gary L. Honeycutt; Box 151, Troutdale, VA 24378-0151; (540) 677-3900; offers pack trips and wagon trains

Fairwood Livery is near Troutdale on Route 603 and offers rental horses during the summertime.

"The good Lord did his part in creating the beautiful mountains, the pure water, the tall grass, the serene spots we treasure. He provided the setting for the memories we treasure long after the trip is over. Let us do our part to keep it beautiful, clean and unabused by our visits and activities."

Back Country Horsemen

PART III - FIRST AID

INTRODUCTION TO FIRST AID

Every horseman needs to know basic first aid principles and carry a first aid kit, not only for themselves but also for their horses. Accidents can and do happen on the trail. This chapter is a basic introduction to first aid and is not intended to replace certification or education in First Aid. Serious injuries and conditions should be treated by a qualified person with medical training. Always seek proper medical or veterinary attention.

First aid is just what its name implies—the aid first given to a victim immediately following an injury or illness. Enrolling in a first aid course taught by a local college, school or hospital is beneficial for everyone. It cannot be emphasized enough to enroll in an approved CPR course that includes accurate instruction, practice, and certification of the CPR techniques. Wilderness survival classes are also a good idea for riders who spend any time in the backcountry.

Preassembled first aid kits are available at many sporting goods, outfitting and camping stores, or choose to compose your own. Your local veterinarian can provide you with first aid tips regarding your horse. Veterinarians often sell prepackaged equine first aid kits, and can assist with specific items you may want to include. Remember to evaluate your own needs when preparing a kit.

A small first aid kit for the trail should contain only essential supplies and should be easily carried with you while riding. A larger kit containing more items can be stored in your truck or horse trailer. A large fishing tackle box with drawers makes a sturdy first aid kit. The various compartments are nice for keeping your supplies separate and organized.

The following lists suggest items for large and small first aid kits. Most items are inexpensive and can be found at your local drugstore. Be sure to ask a person knowledgeable in medical or veterinary care if in doubt of the kit's application or use.

SMALL TRAIL FIRST AID KIT:
- Band-Aids®
- Steri-strip®
- adhesive tape
- 4 x 4-inch sterile gauze sponges
- Kling® (roller gauze bandage material)
- elastic gauze (Vetrap® or Conform®)
- Betadine solution
- insect bite/sting medication
- insect repellent
- snakebite kit
- aspirin or aspirin substitute (ibuprofen, acetaminophen)
- Benadryl® (for bee stings and allergies in humans)

- antibiotic ointment
- hoofpick

LARGE FIRST AID KIT:
- stopwatch or wrist watch with second-hand
- twitch
- stethoscope
- thermometer
- tweezers
- small bandage scissors
- various sizes of sterile syringes and sterile hypodermic needles (3, 12 and 20 cc syringes; 18 and 20 gauge needles)
- Penicillin (injectable antibiotic)
- Dipyrone® or Banamine® (injectable colic medication)
- Epsom salt
- Saline solution
- mineral oil
- Vaseline® or KY Jelly®
- Corona® ointment
- DMSO®
- eye medications (for humans and horses)
- Absorbine® liniment
- Hydrogen peroxide
- Pepto Bismol®, Kaopectate® or Imodium® (for diarrhea or upset stomach in humans)
- absorbent cotton (sheet or roll)
- ace bandage
- additional bandage material (4 x 4-inch sterile gauze sponges, elastic gauze, adhesive tape)
- cotton-tipped swabs
- electrolyte solution (for dehydration in horses; see below for recipe)

ELECTROLYTE SUPPLEMENT:
2 parts table salt (NaCl)
2 parts Lite salt (KCl)
1 part feed grade limestone

Combine 2 ounces of this mixture with water and squirt it into the horse's mouth by syringe. The ingredients of this supplement (not including water) may instead be added to the grain. Offer plenty of water.

CHAPTER 13

FIRST AID FOR HUMANS

If an accident or injury should occur on the trail, stop and treat as soon as possible. The victim should be kept warm and comfortable but not too hot. If available, cover the victim with a blanket, sleeping bag or jacket.

If you suspect fractures of the spine or a head injury, do not move the victim unless danger is imminent. If a spine injury is suspected the entire spine including the neck needs to be immobilized before moving to safety. Emergency Medical Service needs to be contacted immediately. In cases of extreme emergency, including suspected spine or head injury, send or signal for help as soon as possible. Keep the victim comfortable and monitor the vital signs.

HUMAN NORMAL VITAL SIGNS

Temperature: 98.6 degrees Fahrenheit
Pulse (for adults): 70-82 beats per minute
Respiration (for adults): 15-20 breaths per minute

AILMENTS

ASPHYXIATION (Suffocation)

The victim should be moved to fresh air. Begin CPR life support and send for medical assistance. If the victim has fallen and a head, neck or back injury is suspected, be *extremely* careful. It is best not to move a victim with this type of injury. Try to maintain an open airway.

BITES AND STINGS

ANIMAL BITES: Wash the wound well with soap and water. Afterwards flush the wound under running water for several minutes to clean out any debris. If the wound continues to bleed, apply a pressure dressing then apply a clean bandage to keep the wound protected. These wounds are painful and can become swollen quickly. The major problems associated with animal bites are the risks of infection and Rabies. Seek medical help as soon as possible.

BEE STINGS: Remove the stinger if still in place. Apply ice or a sting swab to the area to relieve pain and swelling. After the initial symptoms are gone, wash the area with soap and water. People known to have allergic reactions to bee stings should always carry medication prescribed by their doctor. An allergic reaction is a dangerous condition characterized by hives, edema (swelling), shortness of breath, and shock.

SNAKEBITE: It is important to try and differentiate between a poisonous and nonpoisonous snake. Snakebites can cause a variety of symptoms including pain, swelling, nausea, vomiting, shortness of breath and shock. A major problem caused by the poison venom is tissue damage around the bite area.

Nonpoisonous: Clean the area with soap and water. Flush the puncture wounds for several minutes with running water. Apply a bandage and seek medical help.

Poisonous: Stay calm and move slowly. Keep the victim quiet and comfortable until medical care can be obtained. Follow the instructions in your snakebite kit. Cold compresses and cool running water can be applied to the wound to help reduce swelling. Get medical care as soon as possible.

TICK BITE: Remove the tick carefully from the skin with a pair of tweezers. Be sure to remove the entire tick, including the head. A small drop of mineral oil applied to the tick will sometimes aid in loosening its grip. Clean the area with soap and water. Ticks are carriers of bacteria responsible for Rocky Mountain Spotted Fever and Lyme Disease. Beware of any flu-like symptoms, high fever, nausea or rash within the next several days to weeks following a tick bite.

BLEEDING

MINOR: Clean the wound with soap and water. Flush with running water. Apply a clean compress.

MAJOR: Direct pressure and elevation are the two main keys to help stop bleeding. Apply direct pressure to the wound with gauze sponges, handkerchief, bandanna, etc. Elevate the site above the level of the heart if possible (such as in the case of an injured extremity). If more dressings are needed to help stop the bleeding, add them to the old ones. Do not remove the old dressings or you may disrupt the clotting process. Try to keep the victim calm.

Once the bleeding has stopped, gently wash it with soap and water. Apply a clean bandage. Deep wounds should have medical attention as soon as possible to reduce the possibility of infection. Tetanus immunization should be updated if the victim is unsure of vaccination history.

Use elevation and direct pressure to stop bleeding. A clean
bandanna can serve as a pressure bandage.

NOSEBLEED: The victim should sit down and lean forward. Pinch the nostrils
shut and have the victim breathe through their mouth. Cold compresses may
also be applied around the nose to help slow bleeding. Keep the victim calm
until bleeding stops or until medical help can be obtained.

BURNS

MINOR (first degree): If a small area of the body is burned, like a finger or hand,
run cold water over the burn for several minutes. You may apply an antibiotic
ointment and wrap the burned area with a clean dressing. If a large area has a
minor burn, you may consider applying sunburn cream to the affected area to
help relieve the pain. Aspirin or an analgesic may be taken if needed to relieve
pain.

MAJOR (blistered or burned through the skin, third degree): Wrap the victim
in a clean, dry sheet. Do not attempt to clean the burns or remove any clothing
next to the burned areas. Make the victim lie down and try to keep them calm
while you get help. The victim needs to have medical help as soon as possible.

CHEMICAL BURNS: Wash the burned area with cool, running water. A cool
shower would be ideal if available. Get medical help as soon as possible.

CHOKING: Choking victims usually clutch at their throat. The rescuer should ask the victim if he/she can speak (this differentiates between a partial and total obstruction).

PARTIAL OBSTRUCTION: If the victim can make any kind of noise, air is able to pass by the obstruction. Do not interfere at this point with the victim's attempts to dislodge the object.

TOTAL OBSTRUCTION: The victim cannot speak or make any kind of noise. Stand behind the victim and make a fist. Place your fist (thumb side) in the pit of the victim's stomach. Grasp the fist with your other hand. Press your fist upward and into the stomach five times. Repeat the series of five abdominal thrusts until successful.

NOTE: It is best to take a CPR course to learn and practice the proper techniques of first aid for a choking victim.

ELECTRIC SHOCK

Do *not* touch the victim unless you are absolutely certain the electricity is off. Shut off the power source first! Use a dry wooden stick, cloth or rubber hose (nonconductive) to move the victim away from the electric source. Administer CPR if the victim has no pulse or respiration. Keep the victim warm and get medical help quickly.

EYE INJURIES

FOREIGN BODY: Pull the lower eyelid down to see if the object is lodged there. Use a moistened cotton swab or corner of a handkerchief to gently lift off the foreign body. If the object is lodged on the upper lid, the victim should look down as the upper lid is pulled up and away. Lift the foreign body off the eyelid or flush the eye with sterile saline solution.

BRUISES (Black eye): Cold compresses should be applied to the area for twenty minutes. Repeat every 20 minutes for the first twenty-four hours to help reduce the pain and swelling. After the first twenty-four hours, heat should then be applied to help in the absorption of the hematoma. Seek medical attention as soon as possible.

CHEMICAL BURNS: Flush the eyes generously with water or saline. Get medical assistance immediately.

FAINTING

Place the victim on his or her back and ensure an open airway. If smelling salts are available, place them briefly under the victim's nose to be inhaled. Check the victim's pulse. Rescue breathing should be given if the victim is not breathing. Get medical help if the fainting episode lasts longer than one to two minutes or if the victim does not have a pulse. Begin CPR in cases where the victim does not have a pulse.

FRACTURES

After any type of injury or fall, do not immediately move the victim. First ask the person if anything feels broken. If a neck or back fracture is suspected, do not move the victim at all. The sharp bone fragments could cause even more serious damage to the surrounding tissue. Broken arms or legs should first be properly splinted for support before attempting transport. Heavy magazines, pieces of wood or a bed pillow can be used for makeshift splints. Get medical assistance as soon as possible.

A pillow can serve as a temporary splint for a fractured limb.

FROSTBITE

Symptoms of frostbite are usually seen on the hands, feet, face and ears. The skin color changes from red to gray or white. Blisters may form on the skin during the thawing process. Apply warming compresses gently to the affected areas. Do not rub the skin or you may cause further damage to the tissue. Place gauze pads or clean, dry pieces of cloth between the toes or fingers to keep them separated.

Keep the areas as clean as possible. Do not break open the blisters. Seek medical help as soon as possible.

HEAD INJURY/CONCUSSION

Head injuries should be carefully evaluated over time because symptoms of a concussion may not be visible soon after an accident. Anyone who has injured his head, neck or back should not be moved immediately. The victim should go to an emergency room if there is any question as to the seriousness of the injury. Observe for the following symptoms:
- loss of consciousness
- inability to arouse the victim from sleep (check often and arouse a person that falls asleep after a head injury)
- vomiting
- discharge of blood or fluid from the ears
- continual headache
- dizziness
- pupils of eyes are unequal in size
- confusion
- lack of coordination

HEART ATTACK

Symptoms include:
- discomfort, pressure or pain in the chest
- pain radiating into the left arm, neck or jaw
- sweating
- weakness
- shortness of breath

Call for medical help immediately. Make the victim lie down and stay calm. Perform CPR if the victim stops breathing and has no pulse.

HEAT EXHAUSTION

Symptoms include:
- muscle pains or cramps
- nausea
- dizziness
- thirsty
- sweating
- weakness

Get the victim in a cool, breezy or shady place quickly and loosen clothing. Have the victim lie down and elevate their lower legs slightly. Give small sips of water or Gatorade®. You may add one teaspoon of salt to one quart of water for the victim to drink. Place cool, damp compresses around the head, neck and other areas to cool the skin.

HYPOTHERMIA

Symptoms include:
- uncontrollable shivering
- slurred speech
- memory loss
- loss of coordination
- weakness
- drowsiness

Hypothermia is a condition where the victim cannot maintain his/her heat and the body temperature drops to a dangerous level. This is a real emergency as it can often cause death. Hypothermia is most common when a person is cold, wet and exhausted. It can happen at any time of the year, even in summer at high elevations.

It is imperative that the victim gets warm. Remove all wet clothes and replace with dry clothing. Cover the patient with a blanket or sleeping bag. Building a fire and giving warm drinks (no alcohol) can also help. Erect a tent or some form of shelter to block off the wind. Get medical assistance as soon as possible. Hypothermia can kill so take the necessary precautions to prevent it from occurring.

INTESTINAL UPSET

Vomiting and diarrhea are symptoms of a variety of disorders. Possible causes include food poisoning and viral infection. The victim should avoid eating solid foods. Taking Pepto-Bismol®, Kaopectate® or Imodium® can help to control the symptoms. Monitor the victim's temperature and administer aspirin or an aspirin substitute for fever. If symptoms persist, seek medical help.

POISONING

Contact Poison Control or the Emergency Medical Service (EMS) quickly. Milk or water should be given to the victim to dilute the poison in nearly all cases. Do not give fluids or cause vomiting if the victim is unconscious or having convulsions.

Do not make the victim vomit if the poison is a petroleum product (gasoline, lighter fluid, etc.) or a strong acid or alkali (bleach, cleaners, etc.). Vomiting causes more problems when these harsh substances have been ingested.

In cases where vomiting is indicated (poisonous foods), warm salt water can be given to the victim to drink. Mix one tablespoon of salt to one glass of warm water to induce vomiting.

SHOCK

Symptoms include:
- weak and rapid pulse
- sweating
- cold and clammy skin
- irregular breathing
- dilated pupils
- nausea
- decreased blood pressure
- unconsciousness

Shock is a serious condition that can be fatal. It occurs when the circulatory system collapses after an injury. The victim should lie down. Elevate the feet and legs unless injuries warrant otherwise. Keep the victim warm by covering with a blanket or sleeping bag. Check pulse and respiratory rate regularly. Seek medical help quickly.

STRAINS/SPRAINS

Keep the injured part elevated if feasible to reduce swelling. Apply ice packs or cold compresses as soon as possible for approximately twenty minutes. Repeat every twenty minutes. After the first twenty-four hours, warm compresses may be applied. The affected area may be wrapped for support with an ace bandage between the cold/warm applications.

UNCONSCIOUSNESS

Lay the victim flat on his/her back and attempt to arouse. Be sure the victim's airway is open and check for a pulse. Administer CPR if there is no respiration or pulse. Keep the victim warm. Do not give food or water to an unconscious person. If the victim begins to vomit, turn the head to the side to prevent choking. Get medical help as soon as possible.

CHAPTER 14

FIRST AID FOR HORSES

This section should be used as a guide for the horseman until proper veterinary care can be obtained. In all major cases of injuries or ailments, be sure to seek veterinary assistance. Out on the trail you may have to improvise when you treat a medical problem, and whether in humans or horses, common sense is the best medication. Read and study books on horse health management to be better prepared for emergency situations, but your best source for first aid tips and advice is your local veterinarian.

Most importantly, keep your cool and do not panic.

When a horse suffers an injury, you should first choose a proper restraint method before attempting examination and treatment. An injured or sick animal will often have unpredictable behavior. Be careful when working around and trying to control an injured horse, even a normally gentle horse. A twitch may need to be applied to the horse's upper lip for adequate restraint. A thorough examination should always include checking the horse's vital signs.

EQUINE NORMAL VITAL SIGNS

Temperature: 99-101 degrees Fahrenheit
Pulse: 28-48 beats per minute
Respiration: 8-16 breaths per minute
Capillary Refill: 1-2 seconds

Temperature:

1. Properly restrain the horse.
2. Shake the thermometer down several times so the mercury level is below 95 degrees Fahrenheit.
3. Lubricate the bulb end of the thermometer with Vaseline® or K-Y Jelly®. Insert this end gently into the horse's rectum about half of the thermometer's length.
4. A string attached to a clothespin should be tied to the other end of the thermometer. The clothespin can be clipped onto the horse's tail or you may choose to just hold onto the thermometer to prevent it from sliding forward and becoming "lost" inside the horse's rectum.
5. Leave the thermometer in the rectum for about two to three minutes before removing. Pull it out very gently and wipe it off. Rotate it until you can see the

mercury well enough to read the temperature. Digital thermometers are also available that do an excellent job of monitoring body temperature.

Pulse:

The pulse can be felt by placing your fingertips on the following areas of the horse: under the jaw, behind the left elbow, or under the dock of the tail. Another method is by listening directly to the heart rate with a stethoscope. Place the stethoscope at the area just behind the horse's left elbow. You should hear the "lub-dup" sound of the horse's heart.

Use a watch with a secondhand and count the beats you feel or hear for fifteen seconds. This number can be multiplied by four to give you the correct pulse rate for one minute. It is not uncommon for the heart rate to be 80-100 beats per minute immediately following strenuous exercise. However, a healthy horse's pulse should return to the normal range within a short period of time after exercise has stopped. A consistently high pulse above 60 beats per minute could indicate a problem such as exhaustion or colic.

Respiration:

Count the number of breaths by observing the horse's flank. The ribcage will expand and relax with each breath. You can count for fifteen seconds and multiply by four to find out the number of breaths per minute.

It is normal for a horse to pause occasionally, much like a sigh, between breaths. Abnormal respiration is exhibited by a faster, more regular rate with none of the slight delays in breathing.

Capillary Refill:

The gums, tongue and insides of the nostrils compose the mucous membranes. They should have a healthy, pink color which indicates the circulatory system is functioning properly. In cases of shock, exhaustion, dehydration and severe colic, the gums are often a different color and warn of a serious condition.

Capillary refill can be defined as the time it takes the mucous membranes to return to a normal pink color after pressure is exerted to blanch out (turn white) the small blood vessels, or capillaries, within the tissue.

A simple method to test the capillary refill time is to lift the horse's upper lip so the gums are visible. Observe the color of the gums and tongue. Press your fingertip against an area of the gum until it blanches. Release your fingertip pressure and count, "one thousand, two thousand,..." until the pink color returns. Healthy horses should have an almost immediate refill time of one to two seconds. A slow capillary refill time of three seconds or more is an indication of a major problem. Other danger signs are gums that are dark red, blue, brown, yellowish or pale in color.

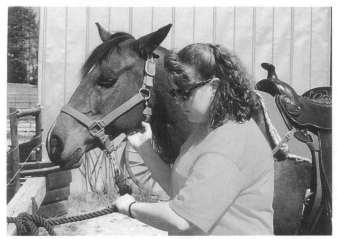

Above: Taking the pulse under the jaw.
Below: Checking capillary refill and gum color.
Courtesy of Scott Holden

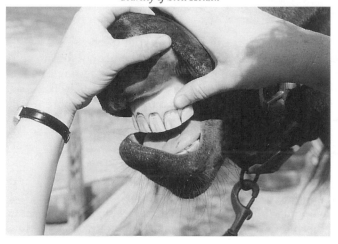

AILMENTS

AZOTURIA and TYING UP

Azoturia is caused by excess lactic acid production in the muscles due to overfeeding and sudden physical overexertion of the horse. The muscles contract and stiffen. Symptoms usually appear soon after exercise has begun and consist of stiffness in gait, reluctance to move, profuse sweating, anxiety, muscular spasms and dark colored urine.

Immediate treatment is necessary and should include complete rest, covering with a blanket to conserve body heat and keeping the horse on its feet. Do *not* move or feed the horse. You may offer water. Call a veterinarian as soon as possible.

Horses afflicted with this condition often suffer repeat episodes. Simple preventative measures are to reduce the amount of grain fed to the horse on off days when it is not worked, avoid stall confinement and always warm up gradually when exercising.

Tying up is a syndrome appearing similar to azoturia. Signs are milder and usually occur after long periods of exercise. The muscles are depleted of energy and appear to "tie up" or spasm. Treatment is often the same except water and electrolytes should be given to replenish lost body fluids and salts. Preventative measures include gradual conditioning, frequent rest periods, and administering electrolytes during and after strenuous exercise. See "Exhaustion" in this chapter.

COLIC

Colic is a condition where the horse has pain or discomfort in the abdomen. There are several types and causes of colic. The major cause of colic is intestinal parasites, or "worms." Another common cause is poor feeding practices. Providing poor quality feed, irregular feeding habits or too much change in the diet can all contribute to colic cases.

Types of colic are displacement (twist), flatulent (gas), obstructive (similar to impaction), and thrombo-embolic. A displaced, or twisted, intestine is a very grave situation; surgery is often the only way to save a horse in this condition. Gas in the bowels can cause a mild case of colic. Obstructive is more serious and occurs when a bowel is blocked by a foreign body or impacted with food. Intestinal parasites are responsible for thrombo-embolic colic when they migrate into the blood vessels near the intestines. They cause tissue damage and blockages, or thrombi.

It is best to contact a veterinarian in all cases of colic. Distinguishing between a minor and major case can be difficult, and a horse's health can take a downhill course very quickly.

Symptoms include restlessness, repeatedly lying down and getting up, rolling on the ground, looking or kicking at the abdomen, sweating, pawing the ground, and lack of appetite.

Check the pulse since it is a good indicator of severe pain in the horse. A consistent pulse rate of sixty or above can suggest a serious problem. Also check the capillary refill time and the gum color. Place your ear next to the horse's flank and listen for any gut sounds. Gurgling noises should normally be heard in the abdomen. A sign of colic is when no sounds are heard. Take note of the frequency, consistency and presence or absence of the horse's manure.

First aid should consist of removing all feed and water and getting or keeping the horse on its feet. Do not allow the horse to roll on the ground since this can result in a twisted intestine. If possible, walk the horse quietly and try to keep it calm. Walking helps to stimulate the bowels to relieve gas pockets or pass the blockage or manure. However, do not force the horse to walk.

Some injectable medications such as Banamine® and Dipyrone® help to stimulate gut action and reduce the pain. They are only available through prescription by a qualified veterinarian. Your vet can assist you with the proper dosage and administration techniques.

As with other diseases and ailments, prevention is the best medicine. Regular deworming every six weeks is a very important key to colic prevention. Always provide good quality hay and grain free of dust and mold. Plenty of fresh, clean water should be available at all times.

Try to stay on a regular feeding schedule. Divide feedings into smaller portions two or three times daily instead of one large feeding. Horses are grazers by nature and are designed with a small stomach that prefers small amounts of feed at a time. Always properly cool out your horse after exercise. An overheated horse should be walked and offered only small amounts of water every few minutes until it is completely cooled down.

EYE INFECTIONS AND INJURIES

Minor eye problems are often due to an irritant such as flies or a foreign object. Symptoms are squinting or frequent blinking, discharge or weepiness from the eye, and a swollen eyelid.

If external pests such as flies are the cause, apply antibiotic drops or ointment prescribed by your veterinarian to the affected eye or eyes. Fly repellent should also be applied around the eyes to prevent continued irritation. Roll-on fly repellents are excellent for this use and are available at most tack and feed stores.

If a small foreign object is suspected, flush the eye well with saline in an effort to rinse out the irritant. This is best accomplished with a syringe. Apply an antibiotic medication to the affected eye. Contact a veterinarian if symptoms persist.

Major injuries to the eye such as punctures or bruises require veterinary attention. Remove a foreign object only if it will not cause additional injury to the eye. In most cases, leave the eye alone until veterinary examination. Protect the eye from further injury and bright light by applying a simple bandage or blindfold over the eye. This will also aid in reducing pain.

EXHAUSTION

Symptoms of exhaustion include unwillingness to move, depression, disori-entation, lack of interest in surroundings, lack of appetite or thirst, and muscular trembling. Overexertion, warm temperatures and high humidity can lead to exhaustion, especially in horses that are not in good condition.

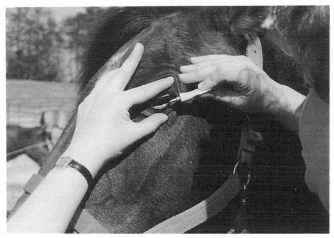
Applying eye ointment.
Courtesy of Scott Holden

Treatment should consist of keeping the horse quiet and on its feet. Walk the horse slowly but do not force it to move. The best way to cool down a horse quickly is to apply cool water with a sponge or towel to the head, neck and jugular area, and legs. These areas have numerous superficial blood vessels that aid in the cooling process. If a stream is nearby, you may also stand the horse up to its fetlocks in the water to help cool it out.

The large muscles of the back or hindquarters should not be cooled with water because this can result in muscle cramps or "tying up." See "Azoturia and Tying Up" in this chapter. Also, the body temperature of a horse often continues to climb higher by pouring cool water over these muscles. Blood vessels in these large muscles may constrict in response to the cool water. Heat will then be retained instead of dissipating near the skin surface.

Offer small amounts of water and administer electrolytes if available. Electrolytes are mineral salts that are lost through sweating and need to be replaced. Allow the horse to graze on grass or hay to stimulate gut motility, but do not feed any grain. Consult a veterinarian as soon as possible. As always, the best medicine is prevention. Know the warning signs and most of all, know your horse and its limitations. Experienced horsemen that frequently trail ride gain valuable insight and a sixth sense into their mount and its individual habits. Pay close attention to the horse's attitude and way of going.

FOUNDER (Laminitis)

Founder is a condition where the sensitive tissues inside the hoof, called laminae, become inflamed. The tissues swell but the hard walls of the hoof cannot expand to accommodate them. Extreme pain and tissue damage results from the pressure. There are numerous causes of this chronic ailment such as overeating, improper feeding and watering practices, obesity, poor shoeing techniques, retained placentas, and too much work on hard surfaces, especially in unfit horses. Certain infectious diseases such as pneumonia could also trigger founder.

Symptoms are lameness, unwillingness to move, fever, sweating, and warmth around the coronary band. Horses afflicted with founder often have an unusual body stance where the forefeet and forelegs are stretched out in front of them in an attempt to relieve the pressure and pain. The rear feet and legs are often tucked up underneath them. Signs do not always appear until several hours after the causative incident.

If you know or suspect a possible founder situation, don't wait until symptoms occur. Immediate treatment can help reduce the disease's long term effects. Consult a veterinarian at once. The feet can be soaked in warm water for twenty minutes several times a day to aid circulation in the tissues of the hooves.

Stalls or hitching areas should have deep bedding material such as sawdust or sand to support the tissues of the hooves. Avoid standing the horse on hard surfaces for very long periods of time. In cases of grain overload, remove access to all feed and water. The vet will usually prescribe medications that are appropriate for the particular type of founder.

Preventative measures are simple. Employ proper feeding and watering practices, keep feed supplies inaccessible to horses, obtain veterinary attention for mares after foaling, practice good farrier techniques, avoid too much concussion on hard ground, and always properly condition your horse.

FRACTURES

A horse with a broken leg is a serious situation requiring immediate treatment. The first priority is to keep the animal calm and eliminate excessive movement. The fractured limb must be temporarily splinted before any further movement or transport of the animal.

Bed pillows often make excellent temporary splints. Wrap the pillow securely around the leg and use elastic-type bandage material to hold it in place. Two stout wooden sticks on either side of the leg should be wrapped within the bandage to provide more support. The joints above and below the fracture should be immobilized.

Transport of the horse should be attempted with extreme care. Proper treatment and quick repair by a qualified veterinarian will increase the chances of a successful outcome. Unfortunately, due to the horse's size, fractures are not easy injuries to deal with and euthanasia is often the result.

GALLS AND SADDLE SORES

Improperly-fitted or dirty tack can cause surface wounds of the skin. Galls can be found anywhere on the horse, while saddle sores are usually seen only on the withers. It is most important to eliminate the cause of the sores. Keep tack, saddle pads and girths as clean as possible. Equipment should be properly adjusted to fit the horse.

First aid for galls and saddle sores is the same as for other wounds. Clean well with an antiseptic such as Betadine and apply an antibiotic ointment. Cold packs will sometimes help to reduce swelling. Use fly spray to keep flies and other insects away from the site. Rest is often the only way to completely heal the wound.

Temporary measures to relieve some of the pressure on the sores, reduce the amount of friction and rubbing, and to keep riding the horse are:

- Galls: cut a small, round piece of foam and place at the wound area between the piece of tack and sore
- Saddle sores: cut a small hole in the saddle pad at the area of the wound

LAMENESS

Lameness is a condition where the horse's foot or leg experiences pain due to an injury or ailment. There are many causes of lameness and the condition itself can be acute or chronic. Basic symptoms are limping, holding the foot up, unwillingness to move, and bobbing the head up and down at the trot. Other possible signs include swelling, tenderness and painful to the touch, and heat in the limb.

It is essential that the cause of the lameness be diagnosed in order to properly treat it. Check for the obvious causes such as a loose shoe, foreign object or rock stuck in the foot, and bruises on the sole of the hoof. Clean out the feet with a hoofpick. Work your way up the legs carefully, feeling with your hands and taking note of any abnormalities such as cuts, lumps or bumps. As with other ailments, contact a veterinarian for advice and treatment of persistent or unexplained lameness.

Sometimes simply allowing rest and applying cold water therapy will alleviate the problem. Use a hose to run cold water or apply ice packs or cold water bandages to the affected leg for twenty minutes at least three or four times daily. This can reduce the pain and swelling associated with certain types of lameness such as sprains or strains.

These stress injuries usually heal better if a firm bandage is applied for support. First, wrap the affected leg with plenty of cotton padding. A track bandage, ace bandage or Vetrap® should then be evenly and securely applied around the leg. Be extremely careful that you do not apply Vetwrap® too tightly.

A puncture wound to the bottom of the foot is often caused by a nail, metal debris, or sharp piece of glass. It should be treated like other types of puncture wounds to the body. The wound should be opened with a hoof knife. Clean it as much as possible by flushing with a disinfectant like as Betadine solution. Soak the foot daily in warm water with Epsom salts.

Try to keep dirt and debris out of the wound by bandaging it. A good way to keep a foot bandage clean and dry is to slide a small, plastic garbage bag over the hoof and apply duct tape around the fetlock, but avoid wrapping the tape too tightly. Always promptly change any bandage that gets wet. Be sure the horse's tetanus immunization is up-to-date. Injectable antibiotics are usually recommended by a veterinarian.

Preventative measures consist of taking proper care of your horse's feet and legs. The old adage "no hoof, no horse" could also say "no leg, no horse." Correct shoeing and proper farrier care are a must. Pick out the feet regularly, especially before and after riding. A good way to cause a stone bruise is by forgetting to clean out the hooves prior to a long, hard ride.

As you ride, watch carefully where your horse is stepping and travel slower when riding over rugged terrain. Be sure to gradually limber up the horse by walking for several minutes at the beginning of a workout. Include a long walk at the end of a ride to properly cool out.

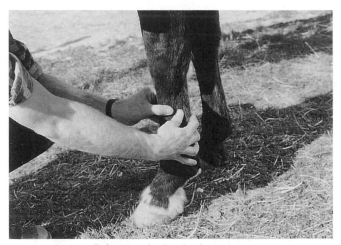

Palpating the leg for lameness.

RESPIRATORY INFECTIONS

A host of diseases can cause signs of a respiratory infection. Although symptoms of a disorder can vary, generally watch for coughing, nasal discharge, fever, listlessness and lack of appetite.

Monitor the horse's vital signs and observe for labored or quick, shallow breathing. Treatment must include rest, access to fresh, clean air, and keeping the horse warm and free from chilling and drafts. Isolate the infected horse from other horses to prevent the possible spread of disease. A veterinarian should be contacted for advice on medications. Antibiotics and a cough suppressant may be prescribed. Keeping horses current on vaccinations for the most common respiratory diseases is the best preventative measure.

SNAKEBITES

Snakebites usually occur on the horse's nose when it stretches its head down to investigate the snake, or on the lower legs when the horse accidentally steps near the snake. The two identical puncture wounds caused by the fangs are unmistakable. Extreme swelling and pain are also signs. Differentiate between a poisonous and nonpoisonous snake if possible, although snakebites are not usually fatal in horses. The major problem with poisonous venom is the possibility of serious tissue damage and sloughing.

Bite wounds should be carefully cleaned and flushed like any other puncture wound. Apply an antibiotic ointment. Swelling in the limb should be treated according to the skin temperature. If the leg feels warm, cold water therapy is best. This is accomplished easiest by using a water hose to run cold water on the affected area. Coolness of the limb calls for warm Epsom salt soaks. Soak towels or track bandages in a warm Epsom salt solution and wrap them around the swollen tissue. In either case, therapy should be administered for twenty minutes three or four times daily.

Bites about the face and nose are dangerous due to the possibility of the swelling causing suffocation. You must act quickly. If the horse begins to have difficulty breathing, carefully insert your fingers into the nostrils and hold them open. Another temporary remedy is to insert a piece of garden hose, approximately four to six inches long, into each nostril. Ice packs should be applied around the bite wounds to help reduce the swelling.

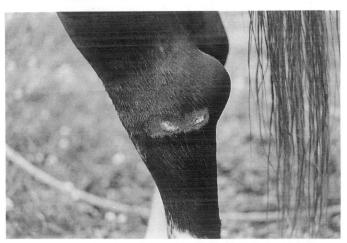

The two small, identical fang marks of a snakebite are usually accompanied by extreme swelling.

Be sure to continually monitor the horse's vital signs, appetite and attitude for any drastic changes. Injectable antibiotics are usually recommended to reduce the possibility of infection. Get veterinary assistance for advice and/or treatment. A small snakebite kit should always be carried with you on the trail.

WOUNDS

ABRASIONS: These types of wounds occur when the skin surface is injured or "scraped." No suturing is required. Scar tissue must have time to fill in the wound area. Proper cleaning of the wound is important. Flush the area well with an antiseptic and warm water. You may use small pieces of roll cotton to wipe out the wound site with Betadine solution. Apply an antibiotic ointment and try to keep the wound clean. Repel flies and other external parasites away from the site with fly spray.

BRUISES: Bruises often result from kicks by other horses. Ice packs applied to the bruised area several times a day help to reduce the soft tissue swelling. DMSO® can also help. Monitor closely to prevent complications.

LACERATIONS: First aid for cuts should include, first and foremost, controlling the bleeding. Apply direct pressure by way of gauze sponges or a clean towel. A bleeding laceration on the lower limb may be controlled by applying a pressure bandage. You may have to use your imagination out on the trail for bandage material if none is available. A clean T-shirt or bandanna could serve the purpose in a pinch.

Once the wound has clotted, it needs to be cleaned. Flushing the site with saline is best if available. A physiological saline solution can be prepared by mixing one teaspoonful of noniodized table salt to one pint of warm water. Flush the wound well and inspect. You should further clean the wound by using some small pieces of sheet absorbent cotton that have been soaked in warm water and an antiseptic like Betadine solution.

Horses are susceptible to proud flesh, an excess growth of granulation tissue. Proud flesh usually occurs on the horse's lower legs so always be especially careful when treating injuries in these areas. Do not apply oil-based or nonveterinary type products on lower limb wounds.

Depending on the type and location of laceration, the wound may need suturing. Deep wounds should have veterinary attention as soon as possible. Suturing should occur within four to six hours after the injury for the least scarring and the best chance of proper healing. Until veterinary help can arrive, a laceration on the horse's limb should be bandaged to keep it from becoming further contaminated. Do *not* put medication into wounds requiring sutures.

BANDAGING TECHNIQUES: Thoroughly clean the wound and then apply a few 4 x 4-inch sterile gauze sponges over the wound site. All bandages should be well-padded to help apply even pressure as well as to prevent it from slipping. Sheet or roll absorbent cotton can be used for this padding and should be applied evenly above and below the gauze sponges. A disposable diaper is a simple substitution if sheet cotton is unavailable or if the wound area is extremely large. If desired, you may cover the padding with a roller gauze such as Kling®. Next, apply an elastic gauze such as Conform® or Vetrap® to hold the bandage in place. A track or ace bandage may be substituted if nothing else is available.

Be sure to apply the elastic gauze as evenly and snugly as possible without pulling too tight. Leave a small amount of padding extending above and below the wrap. Adhesive tape may be applied around the bandage to ensure the end of the wrap does not unfasten.

Wounds that veterinarians do not recommend suturing but do require bandaging are handled differently. Bandaging techniques are often the same, except an antibiotic ointment is usually prescribed for the wound and should be applied to the sterile gauze sponges. Follow the veterinarian's advice for bandaging instructions and the recommended antibiotic ointment. As a rule, bandages should be changed every 24-48 hours unless it becomes wet or the wound has an extreme amount of drainage. In these cases, bandage changes should be more often.

PUNCTURE: Puncture wounds are especially dangerous because they tend to seal off. Without good drainage, infection becomes a problem and abscesses are possible. It is important that these types of wounds are flushed well and have special attention. Punctures often occur when a horse steps on a nail or another sharp object. For first aid of puncture wounds in the foot, see "Lameness."

ROPE BURNS: Minor rope burns can be treated like abrasions. Clean the wound and apply antibiotic ointment to keep the area soft while it heals. Deep rope burns need veterinary care. Cold water or ice packs can be used to reduce inflammation.

NOTE: It is *extremely* important for horses to have a yearly tetanus booster. If in doubt of your horse's immunization history, a tetanus vaccine should be given following an injury. Open wounds provide an entry site for the organisms responsible for the deadly tetanus disease. Also, most major wounds should be treated with injectable antibiotics, such as Penicillin, to reduce the risk of infection. As always, consult a veterinarian's advice concerning treatments and dosages.

Hittin' the Trail Tonight
by
Bruce Kiskaddon

The moon rides high in the cloudless sky
And the stars are shinin' bright
The dark pines show on the hills below
The mountains capped with white.

My spurs they ring and the song that I sing
Is set to my horse's stride
We gallop along to an old-time song
As out on the trail we ride.

You can hear the sound as he strikes the ground
On the frozen trail below
His hoof beats hit and he fights the bit
He's slingin' his head to go.

We'll ride the trail till the stars turn pale
And camp at the break of dawn,
Nobody will know which way I go,
They'll only know I'm gone.

I did not try to say goodbye,
Let somebody else do that,
I'll ride alone and I'll find a home
Wherever I hang my hat.

Let people that set and talk explain
Jest whether I'm wrong or right
My horse is pullin' the bridle reins
I'm hittin' the trail tonite.

The moon shines down on the rollin' plains
And the tops of the mountains white
My horse is pullin' the bridle reins
I'm hittin' the trail tonite.

PART IV - CAMP RECIPES

CAMP COOKING

Cooking delicious and nutritious meals in camp can be quite a challenge sometimes. A long day on the trail usually brings on a hearty appetite, but most horsemen do not want to spend several hours cooking a good meal. The recipes included in this chapter are basically quick and easy. They provide some ideas as you attempt to cook along the trail.

Plan your main menus ahead of time, preferably before leaving on your trip. Being prepared will make cooking in camp much easier and more fun. The trail snacks are healthy foods that can be prepared at home, and then conveniently carried on the trail with you.

Use of a small gas stove or portable grill is ideal. Meals can be prepared quicker than with a campfire and it eliminates the need for finding firewood. Sporting goods and outfitters stores usually carry several handy items useful for camp cooking. Cookbooks with camping recipes can often be found in these specialty stores or in bookstores. Discount department stores such as Wal-Mart and K-Mart also stock camp cookware at bargain prices.

BEVERAGES

HOT CHOCOLATE DRY MIX

8 quart pkg. dry milk	1 box XXXX sugar
2 lb. box Nestle Quik®	Miniature marshmallows
6 ounce jar Cremora®	(optional)

Mix all ingredients together thoroughly. Store in airtight container. When preparing drink, mix one-half cup dry mix to one-half cup boiling water.

LEMONADE

6 lemons	1 gallon pitcher
1 gallon water	sweetener (sugar)

Squeeze lemons and remove seeds from juice. Add juice and desired amount of sweetener to water. Mix well and chill.

SUN TEA

3 family-size tea bags	1 gallon glass jar with lid
1 gallon water	sweetener (sugar)
lemon juice	

Place water and tea bags in jar and cover loosely with lid. Place in sunshine and let it steep for 3-4 hours. Remove tea bags; add sweetener and lemon juice if desired. Chill.

ADDITIONAL SUGGESTIONS: Dry mix packages of Kool-Aid® are easy to prepare in camp. Boxed fruit juices provide a nutritious drink on the trail. They can be placed in the freezer or on ice the night before you plan to ride. The next day put them in your saddlebag while still frozen and in a few hours after they have thawed, you will have a nice, cool drink. Coffee-drinkers, don't forget your coffeepot!

BREADS

DROP BISCUITS

1 cup flour	1/4 teaspoon cream of tartar
2 teaspoons baking powder	1 teaspoon sugar
1/4 cup shortening	dash of salt
1/3 cup nonfat milk	honey or maple syrup

NOTE: Nonfat milk can be made by adding 1/3 cup of water to 3 tablespoons of powdered milk.

Mix all dry ingredients together in a plastic bag. Add 1/3 cup of water (the part in the nonfat milk) to the dry ingredients. Squeeze the bag until the mixture is completely moistened; do not knead. Place an iron skillet on the grill and heat a small amount of corn oil to coat the sides of the skillet. Drop biscuit dough by the spoonfuls into the skillet and cover with a lid. Cook for 15 minutes or until done.

FRIED CORN FRITTERS

2 cups self-rising corn meal	2 tablespoons corn oil
1/2 cup flour	1 chopped onion
1 1/2 cups buttermilk	

Mix corn meal and flour. Add oil, buttermilk and onion. Fry in skillet until golden brown.

QUICK BISCUITS

1 cup Bisquick Baking Mix®	1/3 cup water
3 tablespoons powdered milk	1 teaspoon sugar

Mix Bisquick, powdered milk and sugar and place in a plastic bag. Add water to bag. Squeeze ingredients well until moistened and soft. Drop spoonfuls of dough into a Teflon coated pan and cover with a lid. Place pan on grill and cook for 10-15 minutes. Makes 8 biscuits.

DESSERTS

COWBOY COOKIES

1 cup brown sugar	3 eggs
1 cup sugar	1/4 cup milk
1/2 cup margarine	1 teaspoon vanilla
2 cups flour	1/2 teaspoon salt
1 1/2 teaspoons baking powder	2 cups oats
1 bag chocolate chips	1 cup nuts

This recipe can be prepared at home and makes a good dessert for either on the trail or in camp. Mix all ingredients well. Place on a cookie sheet and bake at 350 degrees for 15 minutes. Cut into squares and serve.

FRIED APPLES

2 apples	2 tablespoons margarine
2 tablespoons honey	cinnamon

Peel and slice apples into wedges. Melt margarine in skillet then add apple wedges. Cook apples until done. Sprinkle cinnamon over apples and add honey to skillet. Stir and heat mixture completely.

GRAHAM CRACKER SURPRISE

Place whole graham crackers in the bottom of a 9 x 13-inch pan.

Mix and boil the following ingredients:

2 sticks margarine	1 beaten egg
1 cup sugar	1 cup evaporated milk

Add:

1 cup chopped nuts	1 teaspoon vanilla
1 cup graham cracker crumbs	

Pour the mixture over the graham crackers that line the pan. Place a layer of whole graham crackers on the top of mixture. Frost with confectioners sugar frosting and top with a few chopped nuts.

HUMDINGERS

1/2 cup margarine
3/4 cup sugar
1 1/2 cups crisp rice cereal
2 tablespoons toasted sesame
  seeds

1 cup chopped pecans
1 cup chopped dates
1 teaspoon vanilla
confectioners sugar

Combine margarine, sugar and dates in a saucepan and cook over medium heat for 5 minutes. Remove pan from heat and stir in cereal, pecans, vanilla and sesame seed. Shape into 1-inch balls and roll in confectioners sugar.

OATMEAL FUDGE

2 cups sugar
1/2 cup milk
3 cups oatmeal
2 teaspoons vanilla

1/4 stick margarine
1/4 cup cocoa
1/2 cup peanut butter

Mix together sugar, milk, margarine and cocoa in a saucepan. Boil for one minute on high heat. Add oatmeal, vanilla and peanut butter. Stir together thoroughly and spoon out on a cookie sheet or wax paper quickly.

ADDITIONAL SUGGESTIONS: Prepackaged pudding cups, fruit cups, sweet rolls and Jell-O®. Any kind of brownies, cookies or cakes may be prepared easier at home and taken with you.

MAIN DISHES

BEANS AND BEEF

1 lb. hamburger	1/4 cup brown sugar
1 32-oz can pork and beans	1/2 teaspoon salt
1/2 cup catsup	1 small chopped onion
1/2 cup BBQ sauce	1 chopped green pepper

Brown hamburger, onions and green pepper; drain. Mix catsup, BBQ sauce, brown sugar and salt with pork and beans. Add bean mixture to hamburger. Simmer 15 minutes or until heated throughout, stirring often. Serves six-eight.

CHICKEN FRIED STEAK

beef cutlets	1 egg
3/4 cup milk	cooking oil
1 cup flour	salt and pepper

Heat cooking oil in large skillet (1/4-inch deep). Mix egg and milk in small bowl. Coat each piece of steak in flour and then in egg/milk mixture. Repeat the flour coating and place each piece of meat in the cooking oil. Fry until golden brown on each side. Add salt and pepper. Drain on a paper towel.

CHILI CHEESE DOGS

1 can cheddar cheese soup	buns
1 can chili	water
8 hot dogs	

Empty soup and chili into a saucepan. Add one-half can of water. Cut hot dogs into small chunks and add to saucepan; stir. Heat until warm throughout. Pour over buns. Serves four.

CHUCK WAGON SURPRISE

1 lb. ground beef
1 chopped onion
1 chopped green pepper
8 oz elbow macaroni, cooked
    and drained

1 32-oz jar chunky
    spaghetti sauce
2 cups shredded sharp
    Cheddar cheese

Brown ground beef with onion and green pepper, stirring until crumbly; drain. Add macaroni, spaghetti sauce and cheese; mix well. Simmer until heated through. Serves six-eight.

CRAZY BEANS

1 lb. sausage
1 chopped green pepper
1 chopped onion
2 stalks chopped celery
1 can tomato soup

1 6-oz can tomato paste
1 1-lb. can butter beans
1 1-lb. can baked beans
1 1-lb. can kidney beans
1/2 cup brown sugar

Brown sausage, onion, green pepper and celery in skillet. Place browned sausage and vegetables in a large pot and add the remaining ingredients. Heat until warm throughout, stirring often. Serves six to eight.

EASY PATTIES

1 lb. ground beef
2 eggs
20 crushed crackers

1 chopped onion
1/2 cup catsup

Combine all ingredients in a bowl and mix well. Shape into patties. Cook in a skillet or over the grill until done. Serves five to six.

GRILLED MEATS
(chicken, steak, fish)

Cut meat into bite-sized portions and marinate in desired sauce. Grill and stir in preferred vegetables such as onions, peppers, mushrooms or tomatoes. Turn and baste often; cook until done.

GRILLED CHICKEN VARIATIONS: coat chicken fillets in one of these marinades before grilling for a different taste

- melted margarine and seasoning salt
- Italian dressing

OTHER POSSIBLE MARINADES FOR MEATS:

- soy sauce
- mixture of one crushed garlic clove, 1/2 teaspoon Dijon mustard, 2 teaspoons lemon juice, 1 teaspoon red wine vinegar, 1/4 cup olive oil, salt and pepper to taste
- BBQ sauce: mix 1/2 cup catsup, 1/2 cup Kraft BBQ sauce, 1/2 teaspoon salt, 1/4 cup brown sugar

SKILLET MACARONI AND GROUND BEEF

1 lb. ground beef	2 8-ounce cans tomato sauce
2 cups uncooked elbow macaroni	1 1/2 tbl. Worcestershire sauce
1/2 cup minced onion	1 teaspoon salt
1/2 cup chopped green pepper	1/4 teaspoon pepper
1 cup water	

Brown ground beef, onions and green pepper in large skillet, stirring until crumbly. Add remaining ingredients. Simmer covered for 20-25 minutes or until macaroni is tender. Serves four-five.

STIR-FRY CHICKEN AND VEGETABLES

1 7-ounce can chicken	1 tablespoon cornstarch
1 1-lb. can oriental vegetables	1 tablespoon soy sauce
1 7-ounce can sliced and drained	Garlic salt
water chestnuts	2 tablespoons cooking oil

Heat oil in skillet. Add vegetables and water chestnuts. Stir-fry until tender. Add soy sauce, garlic salt and a mixture of cornstarch and water to cover the vegetables. Cook until thickened. Stir in chicken and heat until mixture is warm. Serves four.

TEXAS CHILI

1 lb. ground beef
1 lb. 12 oz. can whole tomatoes
1/2 cup sweet pickle relish
1/2 teaspoon oregano

1 15-oz. can kidney beans
3/4 cup chopped onions
1/4 teaspoon garlic powder
2 tablespoons chili powder

Brown ground beef. Add all other ingredients and simmer in a large pot or cook in a crock pot until done. Make 6-7 recipes for 30-35 people.

TEXAS HASH

1 lb. ground beef
1 cup uncooked minute rice
1 medium onion, sliced

1 16-ounce can tomatoes
1 medium green pepper
salt and pepper

optional ingredients: 1 can red kidney beans, 1/2 teaspoon chili pepper

Brown ground beef with onion. Stir well until beef is crumbly; drain. Add tomatoes, salt and pepper. Bring to a boil and then add rice. Reduce the heat and let it simmer covered for 15 minutes or until done. One can of tomato soup and one can of water may be substituted for tomatoes. Serves four.

VEGETABLES

BAKED POTATOES

baking potatoes   salt and pepper
margarine

Scrub potatoes well and wrap in aluminum foil. Cook on covered grill for 40 minutes or until done. Add margarine, salt and pepper to taste. Extra, cooked potatoes can be used at breakfast as hashed browns or in potato salad recipe.

CORN ON THE COB

ears of corn   salt
margarine   water

Shuck, silk and clean ears of corn. Rub lightly with margarine and sprinkle with a teaspoon of water. Wrap in aluminum foil and grill for 20 minutes, turning often. Add salt to taste.

VARIATION: This is an old Indian way to roast corn. Partially shuck ear, just enough to inspect and remove any bad places and silks. Soak whole ear of corn (shuck and all) in water for one hour. Wrap whole ear in aluminum foil and place on grill, turning every 5 minutes. Roast for about 15-20 minutes. Add margarine and salt to taste.

GRILLED CAULIFLOWER

1 head cauliflower   salt and pepper
margarine

Rinse cauliflower head with water. Wrap entire head, including leaves and stem, in aluminum foil and place on grill. Bake for about 20 minutes. Unwrap from foil and remove stem and leaves. Add margarine, salt and pepper to taste.

251

GRILLED SQUASH

2-3 large squash   salt and pepper
margarine

Scrub squash well. Wrap each whole squash in aluminum foil and cook on
covered grill for 20 minutes. Slice and add margarine, salt and pepper to taste.

POTATO CHIPS

4 large potatoes   margarine
garlic salt   cooking oil
salt and pepper

Scrub potatoes well; do not peel. Cut into thin slices. Heat oil in skillet. Mix
potato slices with melted margarine. Add garlic salt, salt and pepper to taste and
mix well. Add small portions of potatoes to preheated oil, cooking for 3-5 minutes
or until done. Drain on a paper towel. Serves 3-4.

POTATO SALAD

3-4 baked potatoes   1/4 cup chopped celery
3/4 cup mayonnaise   2 hard-boiled eggs
1/4 cup chopped onion   salt and pepper

Potatoes can be baked the night before over the grill. Remove the potato skins
and chop cool potatoes. Add onion, celery, mayonnaise, salt and pepper. Chop
egg yolks and add to potato mixture. Mix all ingredients well.

STIR-FRY VEGETABLES

small slices of vegetables (squash, zucchini, onions, peppers, cauliflower, and
broccoli)
olive oil

Cut small slices of desired vegetables and brush lightly with olive oil. Grill,
covered, for about 5 minutes on each side, turning and basting often.

TEXAS COLE SLAW

1 1/2 lb. cabbage
1 teaspoon salt
1/2 onion
1/2 green pepper
1/4 cup and 2 tablespoons sugar

1/2 teaspoon dry mustard
1/2 teaspoon celery seed
1/4 cup vinegar
1/3 cup corn oil

Shred cabbage, green pepper and onion. Add 1/4 cup sugar. Toss well then set aside. Combine remaining ingredients and 2 tablespoons sugar. Bring to a boil and pour over cabbage mixture. Place in covered bowl and chill for 3-4 hours. Serve.

TRAIL SNACKS

BEEF STICK

2 lbs. ground beef (chuck)
1/2 teaspoon garlic salt
2 tablespoons Morton's
    Tender Quick®

1/2 teaspoon black pepper
1 teaspoon liquid smoke
1 cup water

Mix all ingredients well and form into 2 rolls. Chill overnight. Bake at 350 degrees for one hour.

LUMBERJACK LOGS

1 cup peanut butter
1 cup graham cracker crumbs
1 cup instant nonfat dry milk

1 cup raisins
1 cup honey

Mix peanut butter, honey and dry milk together. Chop raisins and mix into peanut butter mixture. Blend in graham cracker crumbs. Form logs by rolling teaspoonfuls of mixture on wax paper. Place on a cookie sheet and chill 1 hour. Makes about 70 bars.

NUT LOG

1 box vanilla wafers
2/3 box raisins
1 can sweetened condensed milk

2 cups chopped nuts
powdered sugar

Crush the wafers and add raisins, nuts and milk. Roll into a log shape. Roll in powdered sugar and chill. Slice and serve.

TRAIL MIX

3 cups Crispex® cereal
1 1/2-cups cheese tidbits
1 1/2-cups thin pretzels
1 1/2-cups sunflower seeds
3 tablespoons Worcestershire sauce

1 1/2-cups peanuts
1/2 cup margarine
1 teaspoon garlic salt
1 teaspoon seasoning salt
1 teaspoon lemon juice

Preheat oven to 250 degrees. Melt margarine in 13x9x2-inch pan in oven until melted. Remove pan from oven and stir in garlic salt, seasoning salt, lemon juice and Worcestershire sauce. Add all other ingredients and mix well until all tidbits are coated. Heat in oven for one hour, stirring every 15 minutes. Spread on a paper towel to cool. Store in sealed plastic bags.

APPENDIX I

ADDITIONAL SOURCES OF INFORMATION
(maps, books and clubs)

For information on membership, guidebooks or maps concerning the Appalachian Trail:

    Appalachian Trail Conference
    P.O. Box 807
    Harpers Ferry, WV 25425-0807
    (304) 535-6331

For information on membership, guidebooks or forming a Back Country Club in your area, contact:

    Back Country Horsemen
       of America
    P.O. Box 597
    Columbia Falls, MT 59912

For information on the North Carolina Horse Council, legislative activities, membership, etc.:

    North Carolina Horse Council
    P.O. Box 12999
    Raleigh, NC 27605
    Phone: (919) 821-1030
    Fax: (919) 828-9322

For information on the national Horse Council organization:

    American Horse Council
    1700 K St. N.W., Suite 300
    Washington, DC 20006
    (202) 296-4031

For North Carolina State University equine short courses, clinics or general horse information:

    Extension Horse Husbandry
    North Carolina State University
    Box 7621
    Raleigh, NC 27695-7621
    (919) 515-5784

For books, maps and information about the Great Smoky Mountains National Park:

    Great Smoky Mountains
    National History Association
    Gatlinburg, TN 37738
    (423) 436-7318

For maps of the national forests, wilderness areas, Appalachian Trail, Blue Ridge Parkway, and other areas of interest:

    Cradle Of Forestry In America
       Interpretive Association
    1001 Pisgah Hwy
    Pisgah Forest, NC 28768

For maps on the national parks or a free catalog:

    Trails Illustrated
    P.O. Box 3610
    Evergreen, CO 80439
    1-800-962-1643

For information on endurance trail riding:

American Endurance Ride
    Conference
701 High Street, Suite 203
Auburn, CA 95603
(530) 823-2260

For information on competitive trail riding:

NATRC (North American Trail
    Ride Conference)
Box 338
Sedalia, CO 80135
(303) 688-2292

For an excellent equine magazine that contains advertisements for trail and camping equipment and publishes numerous articles on trail riding and horseback vacations:

Western Horseman
P.O. Box 7980
Colorado Springs, CO
    80933-7980
1-800-877-5278 or (719) 633-5524

APPENDIX II

ADDITIONAL GOVERNMENT AND DEPARTMENTAL AGENCIES

National Park Service
Office of Public Inquiries
Box 37127
Washington, DC 20013-7127
(202) 208-4747

National Park Service
Southeast Region
75 Spring St. SW
Atlanta, GA 30303
(404) 331-4998

North Carolina Department of
Environment, Health
and Natural Resources
Division of Parks and Recreation
P.O. Box 27687
Raleigh, NC 27611-7687
(919) 733-PARK

North Carolina Division of
Travel and Tourism
430 N. Salisbury St.
Raleigh, NC 27603
(919) 733-4171 or 1-800-VISIT NC

North Carolina Wildlife
Resources Commission
512 Salisbury St.
Raleigh, NC 27611
(919) 733-7191

USDA Forest Service
Pacific Northwest Region
Box 3623
Portland, OR 97208
(503) 221-2877
Contact to receive the free publication "Horse Sense on National Forest Packtrips"

USDA Forest Service
Southern Region
1720 Peachtree Rd NW
Atlanta, GA 30367
(404) 347-2384

USDA Forest Service
Washington Office
Auditor's Office
201 14th St. SW
P.O. Box 96090
Washingon, DC 20090-6090
(202) 205-1760

U.S. Army Corps of Engineers
South Atlantic Division
Attn: CESAD-CO-R
77 Forsyth St. SW, Room 313
Atlanta, GA 30335-6801

U.S. Fish and Wildlife Service
Southeast Regional Office
75 Spring St. SW.
Atlanta, GA 30303
(404) 331-3594

APPENDIX III

SOURCES OF TRAIL AND CAMPING SUPPLIES

Camping supplies:
(call for free catalog)

Bass Pro Shops
1935 S. Campbell
Springfield, MO 65898-0400
1-800-BASS PRO

Cabela's
812-13th Ave.
Sidney, NE 69160
1-800-237-4444

Campmor
810 Rt. 17 North
P.O. Box 997-K
Paramus, NJ 07653-0997
1-800-526-4784

Gander Mountain
Box 248, Hwy W
Wilmont, WI 53192
1-800-558-9410

Sims Stoves
P.O. Box 21405
Billings, MT 59104
(406) 259-5644

The Sportsman's Guide
411 Farwell Ave.
So. St. Paul, MN 55075-0239
1-800-888-.30-06
Customer Serv.: 1-800-888-5222

Campstoves:

Pyromid Inc.
3292 S. Hwy 97
Redmond, OR 97756
1-800-824-4288
Pyromid Outdoor Cooking
    System (portable grill, stove,
    oven, roaster and smoker
    combination)

Sims Stoves
P.O. Box 21405
Billings, MT 59104
(406) 259-5644

Cellular Phone Holster:

Modern Farm
Box 60413
Cody, WY 82414
1-800-443-4934

Chuck Wagon (attaches to horse
    trailers):

Horse Trailer "Chuck Wagon"
Strong Enterprises
18530 Mack Ave., Box 259A
Grosse Pointe Farms, MI 48236
(313) 885-0241

Easyboot®:

Easyboot®
P.O. Box AAA Pojoaque Station
Santa Fe, NM 87501
1-800-447-8836 or (505) 455-7817

Farrier Tool Pouch:

Wagon Mound Ranch Supply
P.O. Box 218
Wagon Mound, NM 87752
1-800-526-0482

First-Aid Kits:

Equi-Aid Trail Kit
Chadds Ford Trading Co.
#4 Hadco Road
Wilmington, DE 19804
(302) 444-7156

VSI Vet Kit
905 S. Kent
Liberty, MO 64068
1-800-831-7245

Picket Line Kit:

Rollin Beauchane
29600 S. Dryland Road
Canby, OR 97013
1-800-772-6282 or (503) 651-3690

Portable corrals and stalls:

"J" Stall, Inc.
7572 Vantage Drive
Huntington Beach, CA 92647
1-800-426-3555

Porta Paddock
Black Rock, Inc.
10425 N. 60th Ave.
Merrill, WI 54452
1-800-560-4515 or (715) 675-4515

Port-A-Stall
Division of Steel Systems, Inc.
213 S. Alma School Road
P.O. Box 4126
Mesa, AZ 85211
(602) 649-3997

Portable Trailer Panels
Dick and Debbie Hanson
Salinas, CA 93907
1-800-847-7037 or (831) 663-5415

Portable electric corrals:

Jim Anderson
2000 Well St.
Baker City, OR 97814
(541) 523-7617

Gallagher Power Fence Systems
P.O. Box 708900
San Antonio, TX 78270-8900
1-800-531-5908

Safe-Fence Electric System
J.L. Williams Co.
P.O. Box 209
Meridian, ID 83680
1-800-843-3702 or (208) 888-9115
also available through
     local dealer:
Smokey J. Mountain
P.O. Box 516
Matthews, NC 28106
(704) 753-4341

Portable or permanent hot shower models:

Out Pack Shower Co.
P.O. Box 110
Mountain Ranch, CA 95246
1-800-242-3922

Portable refrigerator and food warmer:

Koolatron Cooler/Warmer
    Comtrad Industries
    2820 Waterford Lake Dr.
    Suite 106
    Midlothian, VA 23113
    1-800-992-2966

Trail riding supplies, equipment and clothing (call for free catalog):

Bargain Corral
P.O. Box 415
Wylie, TX 75098
1-800-955-5616

Chick's
P.O. Drawer 59
Harrington, DE 19952
1-800-444-2441

Colorado Tent Company
2228 Blake St.
Denver, CO 80205-2097
1-800-354-TENT

Country Supply
P.O. Box 400
Ottumwa, IA 52501-0400
1-800-637-6721

Libertyville Saddle Shop
P.O. Box M
Libertyville, IL 60048
1-800-872-3353

Saddle Software Systems
1760 Broadway
Grand Junction, CO 81503
(970) 858-3607

Sims Stoves
P.O. Box 21405
Billings, MT 59104
(406) 259-5644

Soda Creek Western Outfitters
P.O. Box 4343, Dept. WH
335 Lincoln Ave.
Steamboat Springs, CO 80477
1-800-824-8426

State Line Tack, Inc.
Rt. 121, P.O. Box 1217
Plaistow, NH 03865-1217
1-800-228-9208

Texas Outfitters Supply, Inc.
Rt. 6, Box 25-Dept. W
Sulphur Springs, TX 75482
1-800-551-3534

Valley Vet Supply
East Hwy. 36, P.O. Box 504
Marysville, KS 66508
1-800-468-0059

Walker's Pack Saddlery
68633 Allen Canyon Loop (WH)
Wallowa, OR 97885
(541) 569-2226

Western ASTM Helmet:

The Horsemen's General Store
P.O. Box 429, U.S. Route 36
Lena/Conover, OH 45317
(513) 368-2386 or 1-800-343-0167

Instructional 2-hour video "Summer
Pack Trip" that covers packing,
camping, trail techniques and the
booklet "A Packing Guide for Mules
and Horses" by Vern Smith:

Vern Smith Productions
P.O. Box 117
Ucon, ID 83454
(208) 523-2033

APPENDIX IV

RIDING VACATIONS AND STABLING
INFORMATION NATIONALLY

(brochures, guidebooks, etc.)

Adventure Guides Inc.
7550 E. McDonald Dr., Suite M
Scottsdale, AZ 85250
1-800-252-7899 or (602) 596-0226

American Wilderness Experience
Box 1486
Boulder, CO 80306
1-800-444-3833

Destination U.S.A.
9330B State Ave.
Suite 213
Marysville, WA 98270
(360) 659-2255

Equitour
"Riding Holidays"
Bitterroot Ranch
Dubois, WY 82513
1-800-545-0019

FITS Equestrian
685 Lateen Road
Solvang, CA 93463
1-800-666-3487 or (805) 688-9494

Horse Lovers Vacation Guide
"Riding Vacations"
P.O. Box 502-A
Richfield, OH 44286
(216) 659-6007

*Nationwide Overnight Stabling
    Directory and Equestrian
    Vacation Guide*
Equine Travelers of America, Inc.
Box NR-322
Arkansas City, KS 67005-0322
(316) 442-8131

North American Horse Travel Guide
Roundup Press
Box 109
Boulder, CO 80301-0109
1-800-460-9166 or (303) 444-9484

*Saddle Up! A Guide to Planning the
    Perfect Horseback Vacation*
Equus USA
Rt. 7, Box 124-MU
Sante Fe, NM 87505
1-800-982-6861 or (505) 982-6861

U.S. Stabling Guide
Balzotti Publications
5 Barker St.
Pembroke, MA 02359
1-800-829-0715

BIBLIOGRAPHY

American Heart Association. *Student Manual for Basic Life Support.* [n.p.], 1981.

Bailey, Nevajac. *The Save Your Horse Handbook.* Omaha, Nebraska: Farnam Companies, Inc., 1979.

Battaglia, Richard A. and Vernon B. Mayrose. *Handbook of Livestock Management Techniques.* Minneapolis, Minnesota: Burgess Publishing Co., 1981.

Beeman, G. Marvin, DVM. *Know First-Aid For Your Horse* (Third edition). Omaha, Nebraska: Farnam Companies, Inc., 1975.

Biggs, Walter C. and James F. Parnell. *State Parks Of North Carolina.* Winston-Salem, NC: John F. Blair, Publisher, 1989.

BYW, Flat Rock Baptist Church. *Heirloom Cookbook.* Waverly, Iowa: G & R Publishing Co., 1985.

De Hart, Allen. *North Carolina Hiking Trails* (2nd edition).Boston, Massachusetts: Appalachian Mountain Club Books, 1988.

Education and Safety Committee of the Back Country Horsemen. *Back Country Horsemen's Guidebook* (Second edition). Columbia Falls, Montana: Hungry Horse News, 1991.

Georgia Department of Natural Resources. *Georgia State Parks and Historic Sites.* [n.p.], October 1993.

Hoffland, Rusty. *A Guidebook to Mountain Getaways in Georgia, North Carolina and Tennessee.* Atlanta, Georgia: On the Road Publishing, 1990.

Kadash, Kathy. "Western Preview." *Western Horseman,* Aug., 1993, pp.86-89.

Ladies Circle of Victory Baptist Church. *Treasured Recipes.* [n.p.],, [n.d.].

Manning, Russ and Sondra Jamieson. *The Best of the Great Smoky Mountains National Park.* Norris, Tennessee: Mountain Laurel Place, 1991.

Mayer, Barbara J. "Why Get Into The Riding Habit?" *Arabian Horse Times.* May, 1988, pp. 150-151.

National Park Foundation. *The Complete Guide to America's National Parks.* New York, New York: The Viking Press, 1986.

North Carolina Department of Environment, Health, and Natural Resources. *Yours to Discover, North Carolina Parks and Recreation.* [n.p.],[n.d.].

North Carolina Horse Council. "Support Your Horse Industry, Join N.C.H.C." vol. 1, no. 1, Fall Quarter 1991.

North Carolina Horse Council. "Wildlife Commission Closes Trails." Special Edition, 1992.

North Carolina Telephone Pioneers of America. *Carolina Cooking.* Nashville, Tennessee: Favorite Recipes Press, 1990.

North Carolina Wildlife Resources Commission. *Hunting and Fishing Maps for North Carolina Game Lands.* Raleigh, NC: North Carolina Wildlife Resources Commission, June 1993.

North Carolina Wildlife Resources Commission. *North Carolina Inland Fishing, Hunting and Trapping Regulations Digest.* [n.p.], 1993.

Parham, Jim. *Off the Beaten Track,* vol.II: Pisgah National Forest. Almond, NC: WMC Publishing, 1992.

Paulo, Karen. *America's Long Distance Challenge.* Dutton, New York: Trafalgar Square Publishing, 1990.

Smith, Fran Devereux. "Vacation Opportunities." *Western Horseman.* Feb., 1994, pp. 90-95.

Smith, Fran Devereux. "Vacation Reading." *Western Horseman.* Feb., 1997, p. 155.

South Carolina Department of Parks, Recreation and Tourism. *South Carolina State Parks, Cabins/Camping and Other Facilities.* [n.p.], 1993.

Spence, Annette. *Get Fit for Summer.* Michael Friedman Publishing Group, Inc., 1990, pp.22-25.

Tennessee Department of Agriculture. *Tennessee Equine Trail Guide.* [n.p.], June 1993.

The Campground Directory. Lake Forest, Illinois: Woodall Publishing Co., 1993.

The Roads of North Carolina. Fredericksburg, Texas: Shearer Publishing, 1989.

United States Department of Agriculture, Forest Service. *A Guide to Your National Forests.* [n.p.], 1991.

United States Department of Agriculture, Forest Service. *Horse Trails - National Forests in North Carolina.* [n.p.], Dec. 1995.

United States Department of Agriculture, Forest Service. *Mount Rogers High Country and Wildernesses.* Washington, D.C.: U.S. Government Printing Office, 1991.

United States Department of Agriculture, Forest Service. *National Forests in North Carolina.* [n.p.], 1991.

United States Department of Agriculture, Forest Service Southern Region. *Francis Marion and Sumter National Forests.* [N.p.], June 1989.

United States Department of Agriculture, Forest Service Southern Region. *Trail Guide to the Chatthoochee-Oconee National Forests Georgia.* [n.p.], 1993.

United States Department of the Interior, Forest Service. *South Toe River Trail Map.* [n.p.], 1990.

United States Department of the Interior, National Park Service. *Great Smoky Mountains Trail Map and Guide.* Evergreen, Colorado: Trails Illustrated, 1991.

Virginia Horse Council. *Public Horse Trails in Virginia.* [n.p.],[n.d.].

Wheatley, George. *Stable Management for the Owner-Groom.* North Hollywood, California: Wilshire Book Company, 1977.

INDEX